Categorial Grammar

To Lena and Joan

Categorial Grammar

Logical Syntax, Semantics,
and Processing

GLYN V. MORRILL

OXFORD
UNIVERSITY PRESS

OXFORD

UNIVERSITY PRESS

Great Clarendon Street, Oxford OX2 6DP

Oxford University Press is a department of the University of Oxford.
It furthers the University's objective of excellence in research, scholarship,
and education by publishing worldwide in

Oxford New York

Auckland Cape Town Dar es Salaam Hong Kong Karachi
Kuala Lumpur Madrid Melbourne Mexico City Nairobi
New Delhi Shanghai Taipei Toronto

With offices in

Argentina Austria Brazil Chile Czech Republic France Greece
Guatemala Hungary Italy Japan Poland Portugal Singapore
South Korea Switzerland Thailand Turkey Ukraine Vietnam

Oxford is a registered trade mark of Oxford University Press
in the UK and in certain other countries

Published in the United States
by Oxford University Press Inc., New York

British Library Cataloguing in Publication Data

Data available

Library of Congress Cataloging in Publication Data

Library of Congress Control Number: 2010927168

Typeset by SPI Publisher Services, Pondicherry, India
Printed in Great Britain
on acid-free paper by
MPG Books Group, Bodmin and King's Lynn

ISBN 978–0–19–958985–2 (Hbk)
      978–0–19–958986–9 (Pbk)

1 3 5 7 9 10 8 6 4 2

Contents

Preface

Since its revival in the 1980s a variety of theories of categorial grammar have come into being such as combinatory categorial grammar (Steedman 1987, 2000), type logical grammar (Morrill 1994, Moortgat 1997), pregroup grammar (Lambek 1999, 2008), abstract categorial grammar (de Groote 2001, Muskens 2001), and symmetric categorial grammar (Bernardi and Moortgat 2007). This book represents an appraisal of type logical categorial grammar fifteen years after the publication of my first book. It aims to develop categorial grammar in the spirit of the Lambek calculus of the 1950s but renewing it in the light of linear logic and, especially, proof nets.

Alternative theories of categorial grammar have various merits but that propounded here is, I believe, both the closest to categorial grammar as originally conceived and the closest to the modern paradigm of logic. The book is a report on the efforts of many over several decades to provide logical syntax, semantics, and processing. It presents research but provides exercises to facilitate its use as an advanced textbook. The raison d'être is to explain linguistic theory which is articulated mathematically. The reader needs to be ready to take on board this mathematical linguistics. Appendix A provides an overview of the mathematical background assumed. A more complete preparation may be obtained from Partee *et al.* (1990).

The reader should probably scan Appendix A first to get familiarized with notations and so forth; the main chapters of the book are designed to be read in sequence, although the first three chapters of Part III do not depend on Part II. The exercises are intended to enhance the understanding of those who are new to the field.

Acknowledgements

Love and thanks to Anna for encouraging me to take a sabbatical and to write this book, and for looking after Lena and Joan (hola!) so well, especially while I have been away.

Thanks to the Association for Computational Linguistics and to CSLI Publications for kindly providing copyright permissions on the material of Chapters 4 and 10 respectively.

This work was partially supported by DGICYT project SESAAME-BAR (TIN2008–06582–C03–01).

Thanks to my university, the Universitat Politècnica de Catalunya, for sabbatical leave to write this book during the first six months of 2009. Thanks to the Department of Philosophy, King's College London, for hosting my sabbatical, especially to Ruth Kempson, for every kindness, to Shalom Lappin, for use of his office and computer, and to Wilfried Meyer-Viol for valuable chapter by chapter comments on the first draft. Thanks also to OUP reviewers for most helpful comments on the book proposal and on the first draft.

The form this book has taken has been influenced by, and has benefitted from, many people over a period of twenty-five years. I thank Michele Abrusci, Houda Anoun, Daniela Bargelli, Chris Barker, Guy Barry, Johan van Benthem, Raffaella Bernardi, Pierre Bourreau, Wojciech Buszkowski, Bob Carpenter, Claudia Casadio, Annabel Cormack, Alexander Dikovsky, David Dowty, Mario Fadda, Sean Fulop, Anna Gavarró, Eleni Gregoromichelaki, Philippe de Groote, Herman Hendriks, Mark Hepple, Pauline Jacobson, Gerhard Jäger, Mark Johnson, Ruth Kempson, Ewan Klein, Geert-Jan Kruijff, Natasha Kurtonina, Alain Lecomte, François Lamarche, Jim Lambek, Shalom Lappin, Neil Leslie, Xavier Lloré, Josep Maria Merenciano, Wilfried Meyer-Viol, Richard Moot, Michael Moortgat, Reinhard Muskens, Dick Oehrle, Sylvain Pogodalla, Carl Pollard, Mike Reape, Christian Retoré, Dirk Roorda, Sylvain Salvati, Teresa Solias, Mark Steedman, Hiroyuki Uchida, Oriol Valentín, Koen Versmissen, and others. It has been a pleasure and a privilege to be your interlocutor.

Barcelona   G.V.M.
November 2009

List of figures

List of tables

Abbreviations and symbols

A, B, C, D	syntactic types, propositional formulas
P	atomic syntactic type
$\tau, \tau', \tau_1, \tau_2$	semantic types
$s, s', s'', s_1, s_2, s_3$	syntactical objects
boldface	syntactic constants
a, b	syntactic variables
$\alpha, \beta, \gamma, \delta$	syntactic forms
m, m'	semantical objects
italics	semantic constants
$x, y, z, w, \ldots$	semantic variables
ϕ, ψ, χ, ω	semantic forms
Γ, Δ	configurations
AB	Ajdukiewicz/Bar-Hillel calculus
L	Lambek calculus
Lb	Lambek calculus with brackets
DL	discontinuous Lambek calculus
n-DL	n-discontinuous Lambek calculus
BDLC	basic discontinuous Lambek calculus
CYK	Cocke-Younger-Kasami
PPS	partial proof structure

Part I
Lambek Categorial Grammar

At the heart of what we call logical categorial grammar is the Lambek calculus. The seminal paper is Lambek (1958). In the 1950s J. Lambek and N. Chomsky were acquainted with each other and with each others' work and both knew about both mathematics and linguistics. Lambek went into the former and Chomsky the latter. The Lambek paper was virtually lost for decades. The term 'Lambek calculus' appears to have been coined by J. van Benthem when the paper was rediscovered in the 1980s.

1

Introduction

> 'The search for rigorous formulation in linguistics has a much more serious
> motivation than mere concern for logical niceties or the desire to purify well-
> established methods of linguistic analysis.'

Chomsky, 1957: 5

Some things are more than words can say, but astonishingly natural language seems sufficient and efficient for expressing most of our experience and serving most of our communicative purposes. This book develops a way of analysing natural language syntax, semantics, and processing called categorial grammar. Although we can only touch on a few of the better-known landmarks in the immense scope and richness of language, insofar as we do go we attempt to proceed with as much regard as possible for mathematical desiderata. We try to broach a difficult problem by an exacting methodology.

1.1 Formal grammar

Up until the nineteenth century the most comprehensive grammatical work was the *Ashtadhyayi* ('Eight Chapters') of Panini (6th century BC) (Katre, 1987), which is also the oldest extant grammar in the world. It is an analysis of Sanskrit as then spoken in the north-west region of India (now Pakistan). It comprises just under 4,000 commented algebraic statements (context-sensitive rewrite rules).

The founders of modern logic and linguistics were Gottlob Frege (1848–1925) and Ferdinand de Saussure (1857–1913) respectively.

In his *Begriffsschrift* ('idea/concept writing' or 'ideagraphy') Frege (1879) introduced quantificational predicate logic as if from nowhere, the greatest step forward in logic since Aristotle. He used a graphical notation,[1] not the textual notation that has since become standard. Frege was concerned to try to provide a formal foundation to arithmetic and to this end he philosophized carefully on semantics. In addition to introducing predicate logic, contributions of his that are important to us here are the functorial analysis of language (the origin of categorial grammar), compositionality or 'Frege's Principle' (the cornerstone of formal semantics; it was implicit, but not explicit, in Frege's writing), and the theory of sense and reference (*Sinn* and *Bedeutung*).

Saussure (1915) cited the canonical use of language as the cycle of a speech-circuit. A speaker expresses a psychological idea by means of a physiological articulation. The signal is transmitted through the medium by a physical process incident on a hearer who, from the consequent physiological impression, recovers the psychological idea. The hearer then replies, becoming the speaker, and so the roles of speaker and hearer keep swapping, and the circuit cycles. For the communication to be successful, speakers and hearers must have shared associations between forms and meanings. De Saussure called these *signifiers* and *signifieds* respectively and he called the pairing of a signifier with a signified a *sign*. This relation in a language is both one-to-many (ambiguity) and many-to-one (paraphrase). We take it as a goal of formal grammar to define (models of parts of) languages seen as such relations.

1.2 Categorial syntax

It appears that the first use of the term 'categorial grammar' is in the title of Bar-Hillel *et al.* (1960), but categorial grammar began with Ajdukiewicz (1935), two decades before *Syntactic Structures*. Ajdukiewicz (1935) classified expressions by recursively defined non-directional fractional types, with basic types name and sentence. A type $\frac{B}{A}$ signified an expression which forms an expression of type B when combined with an expression of type A. Thus there is a cancellation schema:

(1) $\frac{B}{A} A \Rightarrow B$

Ajdukiewicz defined a string of words as satisfying 'syntactic connection' if and only if some ordering of its word types reduces to the distinguished type by successive cancellations.

Let us assume basic types as shown in Table 1.1. The particular choice of basic types in categorial grammar is something that the formalism leaves open. For typographical ease, let us write a fractional type $\frac{B}{A}$ as $B|A$. We may assign

---

[1] Cf. the proof nets we shall see here.

TABLE 1.1. Basic categorial types

CN	common noun
CP	complementized sentence
N	(referring) nominal; name
PP	prepositional phrase
S	(declarative) sentence; statement

TABLE 1.2. Non-directional lexical type assignments

bow	:	*CN*
cloud	:	*CN*
have	:	$(S\|N)\|(S\|N)$
I	:	*N*
in	:	$PP\|N$
my	:	$N\|CN$
set	:	$((S\|N)\|PP)\|N$
the	:	$N\|CN$

FIGURE 1.1. Non-directional reduction of *I have set my bow in the cloud*

some non-directional lexical types as shown in Table 1.2. Then the words in the sentence *I have set my bow in the cloud* (from Gen 9:13) reduce as shown in Fig. 1.1. Ajdukiewicz intended such syntactic connectivity to be a necessary condition for well-formedness, but obviously not a sufficient one, since it took no account of word order.

Bar-Hillel (1950) and Bar-Hillel (1953) introduced a directional version of the system of Ajdukiewicz (1935), known as the system **AB** after the initials of its progenitors. We shall write $A\backslash B$ for the type of an expression which concatenates with an expression of type A on its left to form an expression of type B, and we shall write B/A for the type of an expression which concatenates with an expression of type A on its right to form an expression of type B. Thus there are the cancellation schemata:

(2) a. $A, A \backslash B \Rightarrow B$
   b. $B/A, A \Rightarrow B$

Then in **AB** we may assign directional lexical types as shown in Table 1.3. The directional derivation of our expression is now represented in Fig. 1.2. It is this system **AB** that Bar-Hillel *et al.* (1960) called categorial grammar and proved to be equivalent in generative power to context-free grammar.

   Lambek (1958) was an independent reinvention of categorial grammar. Bar-Hillel (1953) saw categorial cancellation as analogous to the arithmetical law:

(3) $\frac{B}{A} \times A = B$

But in Lambek (1958) cancellation is analogous to the logical law of modus ponens:

(4) $A \rightarrow B, A \Rightarrow B$

TABLE 1.3. Directional lexical type assignments

bow	:	CN
cloud	:	CN
have	:	$(N \backslash S)/(N \backslash S)$
I	:	N
in	:	PP/N
my	:	N/CN
set	:	$((N \backslash S)/PP)/N$
the	:	N/CN

FIGURE 1.2. Directional derivation of *I have set my bow in the cloud*

In what is the quintessence of logical categorial grammar, the Lambek calculus has, just as much as the rules of use (modus ponens), the rules of proof (conditionalization):

(5) $\dfrac{A, \Gamma \Rightarrow B}{\Gamma \Rightarrow A \backslash B}$ $\dfrac{\Gamma, A \Rightarrow B}{\Gamma \Rightarrow B / A}$

Note that these are recursive rules. If the reader tries to think of categorial grammar just in terms of phrase structure schemata the whole point of this book will be missed. We work from the conception of categorial grammar of Lambek (1958). Versions of categorial grammar like Head-Driven Phrase Structure Grammar (Pollard and Sag 1987, 1994) and Combinatory Categorial Grammar (Steedman, 2000) extend **AB** minimally on a needs-driven basis. But Type Logical (Categorial) Grammar (Morrill, 1994; Moortgat, 1997; Oehrle, 1999) as here aspires that its formalism be a pure logic in the technical sense of logic that has emerged in the course of the twentieth century.

1.3 Categorial semantics

The inspiration for Ajdukiewicz (1935) can be traced back to the semantic categories of his colleague Leśniewski and earlier work of Husserl, Russell's theory of types and ultimately Frege's functorial analysis of language. Ajdukiewicz called a $\frac{B}{A}$ a 'functor' (and A the 'argument') and so from the beginning there was the suggestion that a categorial functor is a function semantically, which applies to its argument's semantics. Hence, where $\tau_1 \rightarrow \tau_2$ is the type of functions mapping from the domain of τ_1 to the domain of τ_2, it is natural to assume a *type map* T relating syntactic types to semantic types such that:

(6) $T(A \backslash B) = T(B / A) = T(A) \rightarrow T(B)$

Such a type map appears in Montague (1973) who used a categorial notation for syntactic categories in compositional formal semantics using typed lambda calculus and higher-order logic. But Montague made no real use of categorial syntax. And Ajdukiewicz, Bar-Hillel, and Lambek had no categorial semantics, even though typed lambda calculus and higher-order logic had been introduced in Church (1940).

The lambda semantics (combinators) for individual categorial schemata are self-evident, but van Benthem (1983) and Moortgat (1988) established the systematic association of typed lambda calculus logical semantics with the Lambek calculus (logical syntax) in its entirety. We shall see this categorial semantics throughout the book.

1.4 Categorial processing

We can address two kinds of processing: human language processing (comprehension and production) and algorithmic language processing (parsing and generation); the latter may be interpreted as a model of the former, under the construal of mental activity as computation (the *computational metaphor*).

When we consider how the speech cycle proceeds it is seen that human language processing is incremental. Introspection indicates that we process utterances in the course of their perception. Sometimes we (correctly or incorrectly) anticipate or finish utterances. Likewise, we develop our thoughts in the course of production, usually beginning to speak without yet knowing how we will finish. The incrementality of human language processing is confirmed and analysed in detail in psycholinguistic experimentation.

A linguistic theory can gain psychological credibility if it can account for incrementality and other performance phenomena. This can be done by describing an algorithmic processing model of the theory and explaining how properties of human language performance are shared or predicted by the computational model. Combinatory Categorial Grammar (Steedman, 1987) can support left-branching and therefore compositionally incrementally interpretable derivations, but manifests spurious ambiguity, whereby multiple derivations assign the same semantics.

The Dependency Locality Theory of Gibson (1998) accounts for a range of performance phenomena in terms of the incremental resolution of dependencies, but dependency grammar does not assign logical semantics.

Morrill (2000) gives an account of incremental processing complexity and acceptability in terms of logical categorial grammar proof nets which assign semantics canonically (there is no spurious ambiguity).

The logical syntax, semantics, and processing of categorial grammar is the topic of this book.

1.5 Outline of the book

After this chapter, the first part of the book studies Lambek categorial grammar in detail: syntax (Chapter 2), semantics (Chapter 3), and processing (Chapter 4). The logical theory and linguistic applications of Lambek calculus are quite well-understood, and Part I aims to gather together and instate this kernel of logical categorial grammar.

Part II deals with the extension of Lambek categorial grammar to logical categorial grammar in general. Lambek categorial grammar is principled and concise, but we need to extend its expressivity to expand the range of linguistic coverage. Trying to preserve its spirit and good logical properties while widening its empirical scope, we survey four extensions with type-constructors that observe the paradigms of logical connectives. In Chapter 5 we consider bracket operators for structural inhibition and structural facilitation (for islands and extraction); in Chapter 6, discontinuity operators for syntax/semantics mismatch (for quantification and many other phenomena); in Chapter 7, lattice operators (for polymorphism and coordination of unlike categories); and in Chapter 8, (normal) modal operators (for intensionality).

Part III collates some further empirical and technical possibilities and issues in Lambek categorial grammar processing. Chapter 9 considers the incremental processing complexity metric in relation to aphasic comprehension. Chapter 10 examines how representation of lexical semantics by proof nets can enable preevaluation of the interaction of lexical and derivational semantics. And Chapter 11 addresses chart parsing. We conclude in Chapter 12.

2

Syntax

In categorial grammar expressions are classified by types built out of basic types by recursively applying type-constructors. In the system **AB** the type-constructors are the binary (infix) operators '\' which we shall call 'under' and '/' which we shall call 'over'. The system **L** of the (associative) Lambek calculus adds a third type-constructor '•' called 'times' or 'product'. Where **P** is a set of basic (or primitive or atomic) types, we may define the set **F** of types of **L** in Backus-Naur Form as follows:

(1) F ::= P | F•F | F\F | F/F

We have already remarked that the slash operators of categorial grammar can be compared to logical implications, but there is a difference from standard logic. Standard logic deals with reasoning over propositions which are not like material resources with multiplicity, weight, location, or size, etc., but which are immaterial, weightless, locationless, or eternal.

In grammar, occurrences of words and positions of words matter. We cannot in general delete, duplicate, or permute words or expressions and expect properties like grammaticality and meaning to be preserved. We do not have a freely applying law of idempotency $(x + x = x)$ nor a freely applying law of commutativity $(x + y = y + x)$. Instead we have occurrence-sensitivity and order-sensitivity.[1]

Hence, in the Lambek calculus the types of words and expressions over which we reason are structured as lists (sequences). The slash operators

---

[1] Technically, the Lambek calculus **L** is the multiplicative fragment of non-commutative intuition-istic linear logic without empty antecedents.

of functors are *directional* implications which indicate concatenation *to the immediate left* or *to the immediate right*. And the resources are consumed in the inference process so that neither the functor nor the argument remain available after the inference, but are transformed, just as the reactants do not remain after a chemical reaction, but are transformed.

In the same way that under and over are directional and resource-sensitive implications, so the product operator of the Lambek calculus is an ordered and resource-sensitive conjunction. A type $A \bullet B$ represents an expression of type A (on the left) concatenated with an expression of type B (on the right). For example, one of the types of the expression *my bow in the cloud* would be $N \bullet PP$ since it can be analysed as the concatenation of the N *my bow* (on the left) with the PP *in the cloud* (on the right). So the verb *set* from Chapter 1 could now be alternatively typed $(N \backslash S)/(N \bullet PP)$.

2.1 Categorial logic

We have described $A \backslash B$ and B/A as the types of expressions which concatenate with an A on the left and right respectively to form a B. But if this is what we mean then there are shortcomings in the calculus of **AB**. For example, since an A concatenates with an $A \backslash B$ on the right to form a B, an expression of type A is also of type $B/(A \backslash B)$, so we ought to have the law of type shift (the Montague rule, type raising, or type lifting):

(2) $A \Rightarrow B/(A \backslash B)$

And likewise by symmetry:

(3) $A \Rightarrow (B/A) \backslash B$

Similarly, since an $A \backslash B$ concatenates with an A on the left to form a B, a $B \backslash C$ concatenates with an $A \backslash B$ on the left to form an expression which concatenates with an A further on the left to form a C. So the following type shift ought to be licensed (the Geach rule, or division):

(4) $B \backslash C \Rightarrow (A \backslash B) \backslash (A \backslash C)$

And by symmetry:

(5) $C/B \Rightarrow (C/A)/(B/A)$

The calculus **AB** lacks these type shifts, and any number of others since type lifting and division should be taken into account not just at the outermost level but also recursively within subtypes. So we want to augment **AB**. But how could we know for sure when we have a calculus that captures exactly what we think we mean by the type-constructors?

Logic as it has come to be established in the twentieth century provides a particular paradigm for saying just what we mean. On the one hand (model theory) it defines a formal interpretation of connectives which determines the true laws or *validities* of a system. On the other hand (proof theory) it defines a calculus which is a formal system determining the derivable *theorems* of the system. Ideally, the semantically defined validities of the model theory and the syntactically defined theorems of the proof theory should coincide.

The property that every theorem is valid is called *soundness*. The property that every validity is a theorem is called *completeness*. To have both soundness and completeness is to have a perfect match: everything that is said is true, and everything that is true is said. But to achieve the ideal of logically proven soundness and completeness we need in the first place to have given mathematicized model theory and proof theory.

There is a tension between model theory and proof theory. On the one hand we seek proof theory which is mathematically and computationally natural and elegant. On the other hand we seek model theory which is simple and concrete. But to find a semantics for which a natural proof theory is complete it may be easier or necessary to adopt an abstract model theory. And to find a calculus which is complete for a simple model theory it may seem or be necessary to adopt a less elegant proof theory.

This tension comes up in categorial logic. In the past the author has favoured semantic simplicity on the grounds that simpler models make claims about reality which are stronger ontologically, that is, which are more refutable and therefore stronger scientifically. However, the more complex proof theories that these require, which may not always be forthcoming, correspondingly constitute weaker scientific claims when interpreted as theories of mental/psychological structure/processes. In this book we opt for proof-theoretic simplicity. We adopt model theory which is as concrete as seems possible, but accept it at least provisionally as a theory of ontological reality which is partially abstract.

2.2 Proof theory of categorial connectives

Let a *sequent* $A_1, \ldots, A_n \Rightarrow A, n \geq 1$, comprise an *(antecedent) configuration* $A_1, \ldots, A_n$ which is a (finite, non-empty) list of types, together with a *succedent* type A. Lambek (1958) defined the system for deriving sequents shown in Fig. 2.1 for the connectives under, over, and product. This is called a Gentzen sequent calculus. Γ and Δ range over configurations, and $\Delta(\Gamma)$ signifies a configuration Δ with a distinguished subconfiguration Γ. Each rule has the form $\frac{\Sigma_1 \cdots \Sigma_n}{\Sigma_0}, n \geq 0$ where the Σ_i are sequent schemata, and asserts that if the *(premises)* $\Sigma_1, \ldots, \Sigma_n$ are derivable then the *conclusion* Σ_0 is derivable. The

$$\frac{}{A \Rightarrow A}\,id \qquad \frac{\Gamma \Rightarrow A \qquad \Delta(A) \Rightarrow B}{\Delta(\Gamma) \Rightarrow B}\,Cut$$

$$\frac{\Gamma \Rightarrow A \qquad \Delta(C) \Rightarrow D}{\Delta(\Gamma, A\backslash C) \Rightarrow D}\,\backslash L \qquad \frac{A, \Gamma \Rightarrow C}{\Gamma \Rightarrow A\backslash C}\,\backslash R$$

$$\frac{\Gamma \Rightarrow B \qquad \Delta(C) \Rightarrow D}{\Delta(C/B, \Gamma) \Rightarrow D}\,/L \qquad \frac{\Gamma, B \Rightarrow C}{\Gamma \Rightarrow C/B}\,/R$$

$$\frac{\Delta(A, B) \Rightarrow D}{\Delta(A\bullet B) \Rightarrow D}\,\bullet L \qquad \frac{\Gamma \Rightarrow A \qquad \Delta \Rightarrow B}{\Gamma, \Delta \Rightarrow A\bullet B}\,\bullet R$$

FIGURE 2.1. The Lambek sequent calculus

rules feed one another so that in a derivation the conclusion of one rule may be a premise of the next. The rule id has no premises and simply asserts that its conclusion is derivable. An example of a derivation is as follows:

$$(6)\quad \frac{\dfrac{P \Rightarrow P \qquad Q \Rightarrow Q}{P, P\backslash Q \Rightarrow Q}\,\backslash L \qquad \dfrac{Q \Rightarrow Q \qquad R \Rightarrow R}{Q, Q\backslash R \Rightarrow R}\,\backslash L}{\dfrac{\dfrac{P, P\backslash Q, Q\backslash R \Rightarrow R}{P\backslash Q, Q\backslash R \Rightarrow P\backslash R}\,\backslash R}{}}\,\backslash L$$

Observe how in this format a derivation is a tree each local tree of which is an instantiation of a rule. The leaves are instances of the conclusion of id; the root or *endsequent* is the overall conclusion derived.

Given a sequent $\Gamma \Rightarrow A$, we write $\vdash_L \Gamma \Rightarrow A$ (it is a theorem of the Lambek calculus) if and only if it is derivable in this calculus, that is, it is the endsequent of some derivation; otherwise we write $\nvdash_L \Gamma \Rightarrow A$ (it is not a theorem of the Lambek calculus), that is it is not the endsequent of any derivation. We say that the *derivability relation* $\Rightarrow$ holds between Γ and A if and only if $\vdash_L \Gamma \Rightarrow A$. We give the schemata of some characteristic theorems of the Lambek calculus in Fig. 2.2.

The rules divide into the *identity* rules id and Cut and the *logical* rules \L, \R, /L, /R, •L, and •R.

Regarding the identity rules, the identity axiom id and the Cut rule establish the reflexivity and transitivity respectively of the derivability relation, that is, that it is a preorder.

The logical rules comprise a L(eft) and a R(ight) rule for each connective. Each rule introduces the connective reading from premise(s) to conclusion: in

$B/A, A \Rightarrow B$	forward application
$A, A\backslash B \Rightarrow B$	backward application
$A \Rightarrow (A{\bullet}B)/B$	forward coapplication
$B \Rightarrow A\backslash(A{\bullet}B)$	backward coapplication
$A{\bullet}(B{\bullet}C) \iff (A{\bullet}B){\bullet}C$	associativity
$(A\backslash B)/C \iff A\backslash(B/C)$	switching
$A/(B{\bullet}C) \iff (A/C)/B$	currying and uncurrying
$(A{\bullet}B)\backslash C \iff B\backslash(A\backslash C)$	currying and uncurrying
$A \Rightarrow B/(A\backslash B)$	forward type lifting
$A \Rightarrow (B/A)\backslash B$	backward type lifting
$A/B \Rightarrow (A/C)/(B/C)$	forward division
$B\backslash C \Rightarrow (A\backslash B)\backslash(A\backslash C)$	backward division
$C/B, B/A \Rightarrow C/A$	forward composition
$A\backslash B, B\backslash C \Rightarrow A\backslash C$	backward composition

FIGURE 2.2. Some laws of the Lambek calculus

the antecedent in the case of a L(eft) rule and in the succedent in the case of a R(ight) rule. This is a characteristic property of Gentzen sequent calculus: the rules deal with a single occurrence of a single connective, fully modularizing the inferential properties of the connective with respect to the *use* of a single connective (left rules) or the *proof* of a single connective (right rules). This is to be contrasted with calculi in which rules are given involving multiple interacting connectives or connective occurrences. The Lambek sequent calculus is more pure, indeed perfectly pure, in this respect.

2.3 Model theory of categorial connectives

Došen (1985) provided partially ordered semigroup models for the Lambek calculus and proved completeness for them. This notion of model is as follows. A partially ordered (p.o.) semigroup $(L, +; \leq)$ is a structure comprising a set L, a binary associative operation $+$ on L, and a partial order $\leq$ on L which is compatible with $+$ (see Appendix A). We say that $C \subseteq L$ is *downward closed* if and only if for all $s, s' \in L$, if $s \in C$ and $s' \leq s$ then $s' \in C$. An *interpretation* for the Lambek calculus with primitive types **P** comprises a p.o. semigroup $(L, +; \leq)$ and a *valuation* $[\![\cdot]\!]$ which maps **P** into *denotations* which are downward closed subsets of L. Then the valuation is extended to complex types as follows:[2]

(7) $[\![A \backslash C]\!] =_{df} \{ s \in L \,|\, \text{for all } s' \in [\![A]\!], s' + s \in [\![C]\!] \}$

(8) $[\![C / B]\!] =_{df} \{ s \in L \,|\, \text{for all } s' \in [\![B]\!], s + s' \in [\![C]\!] \}$

(9) $[\![A \bullet B]\!] =_{df} \{ s \in L \,|\, \text{there exist } s_1 \in [\![A]\!] \ \& \ s_2 \in [\![B]\!] \text{ such that } s \leq s_1 + s_2 \}$

We can now define a notion of validity. We define the denotation $[\![A_1, \ldots, A_n]\!] =_{df} [\![A_1 \bullet \cdots \bullet A_n]\!]$. We read a sequent as asserting that in all interpretations, the denotation of its antecedent is a subset of the denotation of its succedent. Depending on the sequent this may or may not be true. We call a sequent *valid* if and only if it is true:

(10)   DEFINITION (*validity of a sequent*).
We call a sequent $A_1, \ldots, A_n \Rightarrow A$ *valid* if and only if in every interpretation, $[\![A_1, \ldots, A_n]\!] \subseteq [\![A]\!]$; otherwise we call the sequent *invalid*.

The sequent calculus of Fig. 2.1 is sound with respect to these models. Consider for example the rule of \L. The first premise tells us that by hypothesis $[\![\Gamma]\!] \subseteq [\![A]\!]$. Therefore by the interpretation of under, $[\![\Gamma, A \backslash C]\!] \subseteq C$. But the second premise tells us that by hypothesis $[\![\Delta(C)]\!] \subseteq [\![D]\!]$. Therefore, $[\![\Delta(\Gamma, A \backslash C)]\!] \subseteq [\![D]\!]$.

(11)   PROPOSITION (*Soundness of* **L**).
The Lambek calculus is sound with respect to p.o. semigroups.

Došen (1985) proves that the Lambek calculus is also complete with respect to these p.o. semigroup models.

Buszkowski (1986) showed a stronger result, proving completeness with respect to semigroups. In this notion of model an interpretation comprises a semigroup $(L, +)$ and a valuation $[\![\cdot]\!]$ of types as subsets of L such that:[3]

(12) $[\![A \backslash C]\!] =_{df} \{ s \in L \,|\, \text{for all } s' \in [\![A]\!], s' + s \in [\![C]\!] \}$

(13) $[\![C / B]\!] =_{df} \{ s \in L \,|\, \text{for all } s' \in [\![B]\!], s + s' \in [\![C]\!] \}$

(14) $[\![A \bullet B]\!] =_{df} \{ s_1 + s_2 \in L \,|\, s_1 \in [\![A]\!] \ \& \ s_2 \in [\![B]\!] \}$

---

[2]   As a consequence the denotations of all types are downward closed subsets of L.

[3]   These models are a special case of the p.o. semigroup models in which the partial order is the identity relation.

A real-world speech stream can be seen as a sequence over some vocabulary: as the succession in time of, for example, phonemes, syllables, morphemes, or words, that is as (finite) strings over a (finite) vocabulary. The set of all such strings over an alphabet forms a semigroup under the associative operation of concatenation (see Appendix A). When we restrict the Buszkowski interpretation to these special cases we call them string-models or L(anguage)-models. Algebraically they are (finitely generated) *free* semigroups, that is they satisfy the simplification laws:

(15)   if $s+s' = s+s''$ then $s' = s''$
        if $s'+s = s''+s$ then $s' = s''$

Since language in time appears to satisfy the cancellation laws (15), the free semigroup models seem to be the most ontologically committed and therefore scientifically incisive models. Furthermore, Pentus (1995) proved completeness for them. However, we do not see a way to maintain in extended Lambek calculus only free algebraic models.

2.4 Lambek categorial grammar

Let us define a lexicon as a finite relation between non-empty expressions and types. Thus complex expressions may receive lexical types, but not the empty string, and expressions may receive multiple lexical types, but only a finite number, and there are only a finite number of lexical expressions.

Given a Lambek categorial lexicon Lex and a distinguished type S, we define the language $L(Lex, S)$ generated as follows:

(16) $L(Lex, S) =_{df} \{s_1 + \cdots + s_n | \exists A_1, \ldots, A_n, n \geq 1, (s_1, A_1), \ldots, (s_n, A_n) \in Lex \ \& \vdash_L A_1, \ldots, A_n \Rightarrow S\}$

Pentus (1992) proved that the class of languages generated by Lambek categorial grammars is the class of context-free languages (without the empty string).

Consider the sentence *John loves Mary*. Let the type of the proper names be N, and that of the transitive verb, $(N\backslash S)/N$. Then the sequent corresponding to the sentence is:

(17) $N, (N\backslash S)/N, N \Rightarrow S$

This has the following proof in the sequent calculus:

(18)
$$\frac{N \Rightarrow N \quad \dfrac{N \Rightarrow N \quad S \Rightarrow S}{N, N\backslash S \Rightarrow S}\backslash L}{N, (N\backslash S)/N, N \Rightarrow S}/L$$

Next consider the sentence *Today it rained amazingly*. Let us treat *it rained* as S and the modifiers as S/S and $S\backslash S$, so that the sequent corresponding to the sentence is:

(19) $S/S, S, S\backslash S \Rightarrow S$

The sentence is ambiguous. It can be read as asserting that it rained today and it is amazing that it did, or as asserting that it rained today and the manner of raining was amazing. Accordingly, here are two derivations of (19):

(20)
$$\cfrac{\cfrac{S \Rightarrow S \quad S \Rightarrow S}{S \Rightarrow S \quad S, S\backslash S \Rightarrow S}\backslash L}{S/S, S, S\backslash S \Rightarrow S}/L \qquad \cfrac{\cfrac{S \Rightarrow S \quad S \Rightarrow S}{S \Rightarrow S \quad S/S, S \Rightarrow S}/L}{S/S, S, S\backslash S \Rightarrow S}\backslash L$$

But now consider the sentence *The cat slept*. With the obvious types, the sequent corresponding to the sentence is:

(21) $N/CN, CN, N\backslash S \Rightarrow S$

This also has two derivations in the sequent calculus:

(22)
$$\cfrac{\cfrac{N \Rightarrow N \quad S \Rightarrow S}{CN \Rightarrow CN \quad N, N\backslash S \Rightarrow S}\backslash L}{N/CN, CN, N\backslash S \Rightarrow S}/L \qquad \cfrac{\cfrac{CN \Rightarrow CN \quad N \Rightarrow N}{N/CN, CN \Rightarrow N}/L \quad S \Rightarrow S}{N/CN, CN, N\backslash S \Rightarrow S}\backslash L$$

However the sentence is not ambiguous. This derivational ambiguity is *spurious*: the two derivations do not correspond to different readings. Various forms of categorial grammar suffer from spurious ambiguity, but in Chapter 4 we shall see proof nets, the canonical derivations/syntactic structures of logical categorial grammar, and these have no spurious ambiguity.

Exercise 2.1. Can you find more derivations of (19)?

Let us recall the lexical assignments of Chapter 1, with a modification of the type for the prepositional ditransitive verb:

(23) **bow**   : CN
      cloud : CN
      have   : $(N\backslash S)/(N\backslash S)$
      I   : N
      in   : PP/N
      my   : N/CN
      set   : $(N\backslash S)/(N\bullet PP)$
      the   : N/CN

The sequent corresponding to the sentence *I have set my bow in the cloud* is then:

(24) $N, (N\backslash S)/(N\backslash S), (N\backslash S)/(N\bullet PP), N/CN, CN, PP/N, N/CN, CN \Rightarrow S$

This has the proof given in Fig. 2.3.

2.5 Cut-elimination

Every logical rule in the Lambek sequent calculus has the property that every type in the premise(s) is a (sub)type of the conclusion: either the types are the same in premise(s) and conclusion (these are called the *side formulas/types*) or else the types in the premise(s) are the immediate subtypes of the type in the conclusion with the main connective that is inferred (this is called the *active formula/type*).

The Cut rule does not have this subformula property. The cut formula *A* does not occur in the conclusion and can be any type.

Consider the following procedure to enquire whether a sequent is a theorem: try each way of matching the sequent against the conclusion of a rule and the possible corresponding premise(s) from which it could have been derived by that rule; then explore whether these in turn are derivable, and so on up to axiom links. We call this *backward chaining* proof search. The unary logical rules only ever give rise to one premise subgoal. The binary logical rules can give rise to multiple pairs of premise subgoals, but only a finite number because there are only a finite number of ways of partitioning finite configurations into subconfigurations. But the Cut rule confounds the backward chaining procedure because the cut formula in the premises could be any one of the infinite number of types—we cannot try them all. It is the only rule that causes the problem.

When Gentzen (1934) introduced sequent calculus for standard logic, he proved *Cut-elimination*: that every theorem can be proved without the use of Cut. He called this his 'Haupsatz' (main clause/theorem) and Cut-elimination is paramount in the philosophy and analytical techniques of proof theory and their application to computation.[4]

Lambek (1958) proved that the Lambek sequent calculus enjoys Cut-elimination:[5]

(25)   THEOREM (*Cut-elimination for* L).
       In L, every theorem has a Cut-free proof.

---

[4] We make an application of Cut-elimination to categorial processing in Chapter 11.
[5] The proof is much easier than that for standard logic because of the absence of the structural rule of contraction.

$$
\cfrac{
  \cfrac{
    \cfrac{CN \Rightarrow CN \quad N \Rightarrow N}{N/CN, CN \Rightarrow N}\;/L
    \qquad
    CN \Rightarrow CN
    \qquad
    \cfrac{N \Rightarrow N \quad PP \Rightarrow PP}{PP/N, N \Rightarrow PP}\;/L
  }{
    \cfrac{PP/N, N/CN, CN \Rightarrow PP}{N/CN, CN, PP/N, N/CN, CN \Rightarrow N\bullet PP}\;\bullet R
  }
  \qquad
  \cfrac{
    \cfrac{
      \cfrac{N \Rightarrow N \quad S \Rightarrow S}{N, N\backslash S \Rightarrow S}\;\backslash L
    }{N\backslash S \Rightarrow N\backslash S}\;\backslash R
    \qquad
    \cfrac{N \Rightarrow N \quad S \Rightarrow S}{N, N\backslash S \Rightarrow S}\;\backslash L
  }{
    N, (N\backslash S)/(N\backslash S), N\backslash S \Rightarrow S
  }\;/L
}{
  N, (N\backslash S)/(N\backslash S), (N\backslash S)/(N\bullet PP), N/CN, CN, PP/N, N/CN, CN \Rightarrow S
}\;/L
$$

FIGURE 2.3. Sequent derivation for *I have set my bow in the cloud*

In view of the observations made above, there then follow the subformula property and decidability:

(26)   COROLLARY (*subformula property for* L).
     In L, every theorem has a proof containing only its subformulas.

Proof. By Cut-elimination every theorem has a Cut-free proof and all rules other than Cut have the subformula property.   □

(27)   COROLLARY (*decidability of* L).
     In L, it is decidable whether a sequent is a theorem.

Proof. Theoremhood is decided by backward-chaining in the finite Cut-free sequent search-space.   □

It follows furthermore that the problem of deciding whether a string s is of type A according to a Lambek categorial grammar is also decidable. We consider choices of lexical types $s_1 : A_1, \ldots, s_n : A_n$ such that $s = s_1 + \cdots + s_n$. Since the lexicon is finite and we do not have the empty string, there are only a finite number of such choices. For each we test whether the sequent $A_1, \ldots, A_n \Rightarrow A$ is a theorem using the decision procedure above.

Given a grammar formalism, we define the time-complexity (see Appendix A) of the *fixed language recognition* (FLR) problem as the time required, as a function of string-length, to determine whether a given string belongs to the language defined by a fixed grammar. By the context-freeness result of Pentus (1992) the FLR complexity of Lambek categorial grammar is the same as that of context-free grammar, namely n^3.

Given a grammar formalism, we define the time-complexity of the *universal language recognition* (ULR) problem as the time required, as a function of both string-length and grammar size, to determine whether a given string belongs to the language defined by a given grammar. Pentus (2006) proved that the problem of deciding L-theoremhood is NP-complete; therefore the ULR problem for Lambek categorial grammar is NP-complete. We consider this in Chapter 12.

3

Semantics

Semantics is concerned with meaning. The eventual meaning (significance) of an utterance in context may be indefinitely far-reaching; in grammar we try to give characterizations of semantic properties abstracted over use and context.

The initial step is the attribution of *readings* to expressions. A reading of an expression is a way in which it can be construed. An expression can have more than one reading, and this is called *ambiguity*. For example, *The boy saw the girl with the telescope* can be construed as readings in which the boy had the telescope or the girl had the telescope. This ambiguity would usually be analysed as a *structural ambiguity* between two syntactic structures in which the prepositional phrase *with a telescope* is either an adverbial modifier attached to *saw* or an adnominal modifier attached to *girl*. Another kind of ambiguity is exhibited in the example *I went to the bank*, which can either mean that I went to the place where they keep money, or that I went to the place where the ground slopes markedly, perhaps beside a river. This ambiguity would usually be analysed as a *lexical ambiguity* between two homonymous nouns *bank*.

Different expressions can sometimes share a common reading, and this is called *paraphrase*. For example, most people would agree that there is a level at which *John loves Mary* and *Mary is loved by John* are paraphrases.

In semantic judgements of readings, as in the data of any science, there may be inconsistencies and uncertainties within and across sources, but we can try to proceed on the basis of what is clearest: addressing first and primarily the observations on which there is most consensus, and the data which are most robust.

We have said that a reading is a construal of an expression, but how can we substantiate construal? In the case of a declarative sentence, a construal would seem to include a taking hold of how things would have to be in order for the sentence to hold true. This involves considering how a reading of an expression reaches out to, or is interpreted in, the world. In particular, we need to connect a reading with entities in the world (*reference*) and with states of affairs holding in the world (*truth*).

In *truth-conditional semantics* we attempt to characterize the readings of declarative sentences in terms of their *truth-conditions*: in terms of how the world would have to be in order for a reading to be true. This involves theorizing on how the world is, or is considered to be by language, across any number of situations: the ontology and structure of the world, at least as seen by language, and this makes truth-conditional natural language semantics a far-reaching and highly ambitious discipline. But semantics does not undertake to answer whether a reading is actually true in the real world, only how the world would have to be, in terms of mathematical entities and structure, in order for it to be true.

We think that positing mathematical entities and structures as models of reality does not identify reality with those mathematical entities, in semantics or any science, however successful: that is that of its nature, science, no matter how mathematicized or comprehensive, never begins to substitute the being of reality.

Readings of declarative sentences are related by *entailment*. We say that one reading entails another if the truth of the first necessitates the truth of the second. Again, we do not undertake to determine whether the readings are true, but seek properties at a level of hypothetical abstraction: there is entailment when if the first were true, then the second would have to be true. For example, the meaning of *John came in* entails that of *Someone came in*. Observe that entailment is reflexive and transitive.

Truth-conditional semantics characterizes entailment directly: one reading entails another if the truth conditions of the first include those of the second, where inclusion is formalized as set-theoretic containment of the class of (satisfying) models. Such entailment inherits the properties of reflexivity and transitivity from the set-containment relation.

In our architecture, a syntactic derivation together with a choice of items for lexical insertion determines the truth-conditions of a reading of the sentence derived. We consider derivations in different formats: sequent calculus, natural deduction, and proof nets. And we express the truth-conditional semantics via translation of derivations into terms ('semantic forms') of higher-order logic for which a recursive (compositional) interpretation is defined.

If we wish, such machinery may be regarded as merely the technical means of definition of a semantically interpreted natural language-like fragment: as logical information engineering. However, it is tempting to interpret the formalism psychologically: as cognitive science. Different formats of derivation and/or of the semantic forms can be presented as candidate mental structures: the structures of psychological processes and/or representations. Chapter 4 campaigns for the candidature of proof nets as processing structures on the basis of incrementality and acceptability and preferred readings in performance phenomena. The terms of the higher-order logic may be posited as a language of thoughts or ideas, but in Chapter 10 we consider how proof nets may be proffered as candidates for this semantic structure also.

3.1 Intuitionistic implication and conjunction

Fregean semantics analyses meanings into functions, and the lambda calculus is a notation for functions. The development of Fregean semantics in typed lambda calculus is well-established, see for example Cann *et al.* (2009). The connection of this with categorial logic comes via the so-called Curry–Howard correspondence, the relation between typed lambda calculus and intuitionistic logic, which we review here and in the next section.

Assuming a set $\mathbf{P}$ of atomic formulas, let us define the set X of formulas thus:

(1) $X ::= \mathbf{P} \mid X \wedge X \mid X \rightarrow X$

We call $\wedge$ 'conjunction' and it is to have a meaning like 'and'. We call $\rightarrow$ 'implication' and it is to have a meaning like 'if ... then ...'. Gentzen (1934), as well as introducing sequent calculus, introduced a format of reasoning called 'natural deduction'. In natural deduction proofs are essentially trees (of formulas), but there is in addition some coindexing of leaves with dominating nodes, to deal with hypothetical reasoning. The rules of natural deduction for intuitionistic conjunction and implication are as shown in Fig. 3.1.

$$\frac{A \quad A \to B}{B} E \to \qquad \frac{\overset{A^i}{\vdots}\; B}{A \to B} I \to^i$$

$$\frac{A \wedge B}{A} E \wedge_1 \qquad \frac{A \wedge B}{B} E \wedge_2 \qquad \frac{A \quad B}{A \wedge B} I\wedge$$

FIGURE 3.1. Natural deduction rules for $\{\to, \wedge\}$-intuitionistic logic

Starting from single formulas as leaves, proofs are built up by extending and joining smaller proofs at their roots according to the rules. For example:

(2)
$$\frac{\dfrac{A \quad B^i}{A \wedge B} I\wedge \quad (A \wedge B) \to C}{\dfrac{C}{B \to C} I \to^i} E \to$$

There are two kinds of rule for each connective: the E(limination) rules which eliminate the connective reading from premise(s) to conclusion, and the I(ntroduction) rules which introduce the connective reading from premise(s) to conclusion. The rule of implication introduction involves coindexing and is called a rule of hypothetical reasoning. At the time the $I\to^i$ inference is made at the root, leaves dominated by the inference which are labelled with A may be *closed* by marking them with a coindex i. Any number of such As may be so closed: some, none, or all. The leaves which are not coindexed are called *open*. A natural deduction proof asserts that its root formula is derivable from its open leaf formulas; for example, (2) asserts that $B \to C$ is derivable from $\{A, (A \wedge B) \to C\}$, which we write as the sequent:

(3) $A, (A \wedge B) \to C \vdash B \to C$

Fig. 3.2 shows another example of a proof, of $A \to (A \to (B \to C)) \vdash B \to (A \to C)$.

Exercise 3.1. Give natural deduction proofs of the following sequents.

  a. $A \wedge B, A \to C \vdash C$
  b. $A \wedge B, B \to C \vdash C$
  c. $A \vdash (A \to B) \to B$

$$
\dfrac{\dfrac{\dfrac{\dfrac{\dfrac{A^i \qquad A \to (A \to (B \to C))}{A \to (B \to C)} \; E \to \quad A^i}{B \to C} \; E \to \quad B^j}{C} \; E \to}{A \to C} \; I \to i}{B \to (A \to C)} \; I \to j
$$

FIGURE 3.2. A natural deduction proof

d. $A \to B, B \to C \vdash A \to C$

e. $B \to C \vdash (A \to B) \to (A \to C)$

f. $A \to (B \to C), C \to D \vdash A \to (B \to D)$

g. $A \to (A \to B) \vdash A \to B$

h. $A \to B, A \to (B \to C) \vdash A \to C$

i. $B \vdash A \to B$

j. $A \to (B \to C) \vdash B \to (A \to C)$

k. $(A \wedge B) \to C \vdash A \to (B \to C)$

l. $A \to (B \to C) \vdash (A \wedge B) \to C$

3.2 Typed lambda calculus and the Curry–Howard correspondence

The untyped lambda calculus was introduced as a model of computation by Alonzo Church. It uses a variable binding operator (the λ) to name functions, and forms the basis of functional programming languages such as LISP. It was proved equivalent to Turing machines, hence the name Church–Turing Thesis for the hypothesis that Turing machines (and untyped lambda calculus) capture the notion of algorithm. Untyped lambda calculus has the Church–Rosser or diamond property (that normal forms are unique) but is not strongly normalizing, that is, some terms do not have a normal form, corresponding to the computation of partial functions.

Church (1940) defined the simply, that is just functionally, typed lambda calculus, and by including logical constants, higher-order logic. Here we also add Cartesian product types.

(4)   DEFINITION (*types*). The set T of *types* is defined on the basis of a set δ of *basic types* as follows:

$$
\text{T} ::= \delta \mid \text{T} \to \text{T} \mid \text{T\&T}
$$

(5) DEFINITION (*type domains*). The *type domain* D_τ of each type τ is defined on the basis of an assignment d of non-empty sets (*basic type domains*) to δ as follows:

$$D_\tau = d(\tau) \qquad \text{for } \tau \in \delta$$
$$D_{\tau_1 \to \tau_2} = D_{\tau_2}^{D_{\tau_1}} \qquad \text{functional exponentiation}$$
$$\text{i.e. the set of all functions from } D_{\tau_1} \text{ to } D_{\tau_2}$$
$$D_{\tau_1 \& \tau_2} = D_{\tau_1} \times D_{\tau_2} \quad \text{Cartesian product}$$
$$\text{i.e. } \{\langle m_1, m_2\rangle \mid m_1 \in D_{\tau_1} \ \& \ m_2 \in D_{\tau_2}\}$$

(6) DEFINITION (*terms*). The sets Φ_τ of *terms* of type τ for each type τ are defined on the basis of a set C_τ of constants of type τ and a denumerably infinite set V_τ of variables of type τ for each type τ as follows:

$$\Phi_\tau ::= C_\tau \mid V_\tau \mid (\Phi_{\tau' \to \tau}\, \Phi_{\tau'}) \mid \pi_1 \Phi_{\tau \& \tau'} \mid \pi_2 \Phi_{\tau' \& \tau}$$
$$\Phi_{\tau \to \tau'} ::= \lambda V_\tau \Phi_{\tau'}$$
$$\Phi_{\tau \& \tau'} ::= (\Phi_\tau, \Phi_{\tau'})$$

A term which does not contain constants is called *pure*.

Each term $\phi \in \Phi_\tau$ receives a semantic value $[\phi]^g \in D_\tau$ with respect to a valuation f which is a mapping sending each constant in C_τ to an element in D_τ, and an assignment g which is a mapping sending each variable in V_τ to an element in D_τ, as shown in Fig. 3.3.

An occurrence of a variable x in a term is called *free* if and only if it does not fall within any part of the term of the form $\lambda x\cdot$; otherwise it is *bound* (by the closest λx within the scope of which it falls). A *closed term* is one which contains no free variables. The result $\phi\{\psi_1/x_1, \ldots, \psi_n/x_n\}$ of substituting terms $\psi_1, \ldots, \psi_n$ (of types $\tau_1, \ldots, \tau_n$) for variables $x_1, \ldots, x_n$ (of types $\tau_1, \ldots, \tau_n$) in a term ϕ is the result of simultaneously replacing by ψ_i every free occurrence of x_i in ϕ, $1 \le i \le n$. We say that ψ is *free for x in ϕ* if and only if no free variable in ψ becomes bound in $\phi\{\psi/x\}$. Renaming of variables (α-conversion) may be required to ensure that substitutions are free in this sense. The laws of lambda conversion in Fig. 3.4 obtain.

$$[c]^g = f(c) \qquad\qquad\qquad\qquad \text{for } c \in C_\tau$$
$$[x]^g = g(x) \qquad\qquad\qquad\qquad \text{for } x \in V_\tau$$
$$[(\phi\,\psi)]^g = [\phi]^g([\psi]^g) \qquad\qquad\quad \text{functional application}$$
$$[\pi_1\phi]^g = \mathbf{fst}([\phi]^g) \qquad\qquad\quad\ \text{first projection}$$
$$[\pi_2\phi]^g = \mathbf{snd}([\phi]^g) \qquad\qquad\quad \text{second projection}$$
$$[\lambda x_\tau \phi]^g = D_\tau \ni d \mapsto [\phi]^{(g - \{(x, g(x))\}) \cup \{(x, d)\}} \quad \text{functional abstraction}$$
$$[(\phi, \psi)]^g = \langle [\phi]^g, [\psi]^g\rangle \qquad\qquad\quad \text{ordered pair formation}$$

FIGURE 3.3. Semantics of typed lambda calculus

$$\lambda y \phi = \lambda x(\phi\{x/y\})$$
if x is not free in ϕ and x is free for y in ϕ
α-conversion

$$(\lambda x \phi\ \psi) = \phi\{\psi/x\}$$
if ψ is free for x in ϕ
$$\pi_1(\phi, \psi) = \phi$$
$$\pi_2(\phi, \psi) = \psi$$
β-conversion

$$\lambda x(\phi\ x) = \phi$$
if x is not free in ϕ
$$(\pi_1\phi, \pi_2\phi) = \phi$$
η-conversion

FIGURE 3.4. Laws of lambda-conversion

When we apply the laws of lambda-conversion from left to right we speak of lambda-reduction, evaluation, or normalization. A term is in normal form when (no part of) it can undergo β- or η-reduction. In contrast to the untyped lambda calculus, the normalization of terms (evaluation of 'programs') in the typed lambda calculus is not only Church–Rosser, that is to say that normal forms are unique (up to α-conversion), but *terminating*: every term reduces to a normal form in a finite number of steps.

Exercise 3.2. Normalize the following lambda terms (Carpenter, 1996).

a. $(\lambda x(walk\ x)\ a)$
b. $\lambda x((love\ x)\ y)$
c. $\lambda x((love\ y)\ x)$
d. $(\lambda x((love\ y)\ x)\ a)$
e. $(\lambda x(love\ (sister\ x))\ x)$
f. $(\lambda x((love\ x)\ y)\ y)$
g. $(\lambda x((love\ x)\ x)\ y)$
h. $(\lambda x\lambda y((love\ x)\ y)\ y)$
i. $((\lambda x\lambda y((love\ x)\ y)\ a)\ b)$
j. $((\lambda x\lambda x(walk\ x)\ a)\ b)$
k. $(\lambda x(x\ b)\ walk)$
l. $(\lambda x(x\ b)\ (love\ a))$
m. $\lambda x(walk\ x)$
n. $(\lambda x walk\ x)$
o. $(\lambda y\lambda x((love\ y)\ x)\ a)$
p. $(\lambda y(y\ walk)\ \lambda x(x\ a))$

Exercise 3.3. Normalize the following lambda terms (Carpenter, 1996).

    a. $(\lambda x (walk\ \pi_1(x, y))\ a)$
    b. $(\lambda x (walk\ \pi_2(x, y))\ a)$
    c. $\pi_1 \pi_2((w, x), (y, z))$

The Curry–Howard correspondence (Girard *et al.*, 1989) is that intuitionistic natural deduction and typed lambda calculus are isomorphic. This *formulas-as-types* and *proofs-as-programs* correspondence exists at the following three levels:

(7)

intuitionistic natural deduction	typed lambda calculus
formulas:	types:
$A \rightarrow B$	$\tau_1 \rightarrow \tau_2$
$A \wedge B$	$\tau_1 \& \tau_2$
proofs:	terms:
E(limination of) $\rightarrow$	functional application
I(introduction of) $\rightarrow$	functional abstraction
E(limination of) $\wedge$	projection
I(ntroduction of) $\wedge$	ordered pair formation
normalization:	computation:
elimination of detours	lambda-reduction

Overall, the laws of lambda-reduction are the same laws as the natural deduction proof normalizations of Prawitz (1965). The β-reductions occur when the conclusion of the introduction rule for a connective is a premise of the elimination rule for that connective. The η-reductions occur when the conclusion of the elimination rule for a connective is a premise of the introduction rule for that connective. The β- and η-proof reductions for conjunction are as shown in Figs. 3.5 and 3.6 respectively and the β- and η-proof reductions for implication are as shown in Figs. 3.7 and 3.8 respectively.

$$
\begin{array}{ccc}
\phi \quad \psi & & \\
\vdots \quad \vdots & & \phi \\
\dfrac{A \quad B}{A \wedge B}\,I\wedge & \rightsquigarrow & \vdots \\
\dfrac{}{A}\,E\wedge_1 & & A
\end{array}
\qquad
\begin{array}{ccc}
\phi \quad \psi & & \\
\vdots \quad \vdots & & \psi \\
\dfrac{A \quad B}{A \wedge B}\,I\wedge & \rightsquigarrow & \vdots \\
\dfrac{}{B}\,E\wedge_2 & & B
\end{array}
$$

FIGURE 3.5. β-reduction for conjunction

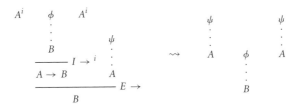

FIGURE 3.6. η-reduction for conjunction

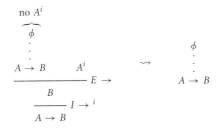

FIGURE 3.7. β-reduction for implication

$$
\begin{array}{c}
\text{no } A^i \\
\overbrace{\phi} \\
\vdots \\
\begin{array}{cc}
A \rightarrow B & A^i
\end{array} \\
\hline
\begin{array}{c}
B
\end{array} \; E \rightarrow \\
\hline
A \rightarrow B \quad I \rightarrow^i
\end{array}
\qquad \rightsquigarrow \qquad
\begin{array}{c}
\phi \\
\vdots \\
A \rightarrow B
\end{array}
$$

FIGURE 3.8. η-reduction for implication

3.3 Semantic readings of the Lambek calculus (derivational semantics)

Let us call a *(semantic) type map* a mapping T from syntactic types to semantic types satisfying:

(8) $\quad T(A\backslash B) = T(A) \rightarrow T(B)$
$\quad\quad T(B/A) = T(A) \rightarrow T(B)$
$\quad\quad T(A \bullet B) = T(A) \& T(B)$

The semantic reading of a Lambek derivation is its reading as an intuitionistic proof under this homomorphism. We formulate this as a mapping from Lambek sequent proofs to typed lambda terms. Given a type map T, a Lambek sequent proof δ of $A_1, \ldots, A_n \Rightarrow A$, and variables $x_1, \ldots, x_n$ of types $T(A_1), \ldots, T(A_n)$ respectively, the function $|\cdot|_{x_1,\ldots,x_n}$ defined in Fig. 3.9

$$|A \Rightarrow A|_{\phi} = \phi$$

$$\left| \begin{array}{cc} \overset{\delta_1}{\Gamma \Rightarrow A} & \overset{\delta_2}{\Delta(C) \Rightarrow D} \\ \hline \Delta(\Gamma, A\backslash C) \Rightarrow D \end{array} \backslash L \right|_{\mu(\nu, \phi)} = \left| \overset{\delta_2}{\Delta(C) \Rightarrow D} \right|_{\mu((\phi \mid \delta_1 \mid_{\nu}))}$$

$$\left| \begin{array}{c} \overset{\delta}{A, \Gamma \Rightarrow C} \\ \hline \Gamma \Rightarrow A\backslash C \end{array} \backslash R \right|_{\mu} = \lambda x \left| \overset{\delta}{A, \Gamma \Rightarrow C} \right|_{x, \mu} \text{ where } x \text{ is a new variable of type } T(A)$$

$$\left| \begin{array}{cc} \overset{\delta_1}{\Gamma \Rightarrow B} & \overset{\delta_2}{\Delta(C) \Rightarrow D} \\ \hline \Delta(C/B, \Gamma) \Rightarrow D \end{array} / L \right|_{\mu(\phi, \nu)} = \left| \overset{\delta_2}{\Delta(C) \Rightarrow D} \right|_{\mu((\phi \mid \delta_1 \mid_{\nu}))}$$

$$\left| \begin{array}{c} \overset{\delta}{\Gamma, B \Rightarrow C} \\ \hline \Gamma \Rightarrow C/B \end{array} / R \right|_{\mu} = \lambda x \left| \overset{\delta}{\Gamma, B \Rightarrow C} \right|_{\mu, x} \text{ where } x \text{ is a new variable of type } T(B)$$

$$\left| \begin{array}{c} \overset{\delta}{\Gamma(A, B) \Rightarrow D} \\ \hline \Gamma(A\bullet B) \Rightarrow D \end{array} \bullet L \right|_{\mu(\phi)} = \left| \overset{\delta}{\Gamma(A, B) \Rightarrow D} \right|_{\mu(\pi_1 \phi, \pi_2 \phi)}$$

$$\left| \begin{array}{cc} \overset{\delta_1}{\Gamma \Rightarrow A} & \overset{\delta_2}{\Delta \Rightarrow B} \\ \hline \Gamma, \Delta \Rightarrow A\bullet B \end{array} \bullet R \right|_{\mu, \nu} = (| \overset{\delta_1}{\Gamma \Rightarrow A} |_{\mu}, | \overset{\delta_2}{\Delta \Rightarrow B} |_{\nu})$$

$$\left| \begin{array}{cc} \overset{\delta_1}{\Gamma \Rightarrow A} & \overset{\delta_2}{\Delta(A) \Rightarrow B} \\ \hline \Delta(\Gamma) \Rightarrow B \end{array} Cut \right|_{\mu(\nu)} = | \overset{\delta_2}{\Delta(A) \Rightarrow B} |_{\mu(| \overset{\delta_1}{\Gamma \Rightarrow A} |_{\nu})}$$

FIGURE 3.9. Semantic readings of the Lambek sequent calculus

maps δ into an intuitionistic natural deduction proof notated as a typed lambda term under the Curry–Howard correspondence. When we write in the same context a configuration $\Delta(\Gamma)$ and a sequence of terms $\mu(\nu)$ it is to be understood that they are synchronized so that the distinguished subconfiguration Γ and the distinguished subsequence ν occur in the same list positions. Note that the image intuitionistic proofs are linear, always conditionalizing exactly one hypothesis, so that the lambda terms are single-bind.

For instance, recalling the example derivations of Chapter 2:

$$(9) \quad \left| \begin{array}{c} \dfrac{N \Rightarrow N \quad S \Rightarrow S}{\dfrac{N \Rightarrow N \quad N, N\backslash S \Rightarrow S}{N, (N\backslash S)/N, N \Rightarrow S}} \backslash L \\ \hspace{2cm} / L \end{array} \right|_{x_{\text{John}}, x_{\text{loves}}, x_{\text{Mary}}} = ((x_{\text{loves}} \, x_{\text{Mary}}) \, x_{\text{John}})$$

(10)
$$\cfrac{\cfrac{\cfrac{S \Rightarrow S \qquad S \Rightarrow S}{S, S \backslash S \Rightarrow S} \backslash L}{S/S, S, S\backslash S \Rightarrow S} /L}{} \Bigg|_{x_{\mathrm{tod}},\, x_{\mathrm{itrnd}},\, x_{\mathrm{amaz}}} \qquad = (x_{\mathrm{tod}}\,(x_{\mathrm{amaz}}\,x_{\mathrm{itrnd}}))$$

$$\cfrac{\cfrac{\cfrac{S \Rightarrow S \qquad S \Rightarrow S}{S/S, S \Rightarrow S} /L}{S/S, S, S\backslash S \Rightarrow S} \backslash L}{} \Bigg|_{x_{\mathrm{tod}},\, x_{\mathrm{itrnd}},\, x_{\mathrm{amaz}}} \qquad = (x_{\mathrm{amaz}}\,(x_{\mathrm{tod}}\,x_{\mathrm{itrnd}}))$$

(11)
$$\cfrac{\cfrac{CN \Rightarrow CN \qquad \cfrac{N \Rightarrow N \qquad S \Rightarrow S}{N, N\backslash S \Rightarrow S} \backslash L}{N/CN, CN, N\backslash S \Rightarrow S} /L}{} \Bigg|_{x_{\mathrm{the}},\, x_{\mathrm{cat}},\, x_{\mathrm{slept}}} \qquad =$$

$$\cfrac{\cfrac{\cfrac{CN \Rightarrow CN \qquad N \Rightarrow N}{N/CN, CN \Rightarrow N} /L \qquad S \Rightarrow S}{N/CN, CN, N\backslash S \Rightarrow S} \backslash L}{} \Bigg|_{x_{\mathrm{the}},\, x_{\mathrm{cat}},\, x_{\mathrm{slept}}} \qquad = (x_{\mathrm{slept}}\,(x_{\mathrm{the}}\,x_{\mathrm{cat}}))$$

And see Fig. 3.10.

3.4 Classical propositional logic

Derivational semantics is represented by a pure lambda term defining sentence meaning in terms of word meanings, but we want in addition to represent the logical properties (like entailment) of expressions of natural language. In this section we start to define classical logic, in order to incorporate it later into typed lambda calculus, and to use the resulting higher-order logic for categorial logical semantics.

The units of propositional logic are complete thoughts: states of affairs which may or may not hold. These correspond to declarative sentences in natural language and we call them *propositions*. Propositions are combined by sentential connectives like the unary connective 'not' and the binary connectives 'and', 'or', and 'if . . . then . . . '.

Given a set **P** of *propositional variables*, let us define the set **F** of *propositional formulas* by:

(12) $\mathbf{F} ::= \mathbf{P} \mid \neg \mathbf{F} \mid \mathbf{F} \wedge \mathbf{F} \mid \mathbf{F} \vee \mathbf{F} \mid \mathbf{F} \rightarrow \mathbf{F}$

In the standard model-theoretic semantics of classical propositional logic formulas are interpreted as one of the two truth values: true (which we mathematicize $\{\varnothing\}$ and write 1) or false (which we mathematicize $\varnothing$ and write 0). A *valuation* v is a mapping from propositional variables into truth values. Then the interpretation $[\![X]\!]$ of each formula X is given by:

$$CN \Rightarrow CN \quad N \Rightarrow N$$
$$\overline{}\,/L$$
$$N/CN, CN \Rightarrow N$$

$$\frac{N \Rightarrow N \quad PP \Rightarrow PP}{PP/N, N \Rightarrow PP}\,/L$$

$$\frac{CN \Rightarrow CN \quad N \Rightarrow N}{PP/N, N/CN, CN \Rightarrow PP}\,/L$$

$$\frac{N/CN, CN, PP/N, N/CN, CN \Rightarrow N\bullet PP}{}\,\bullet R$$

$$\frac{N \Rightarrow N \quad S \Rightarrow S}{N, N\backslash S \Rightarrow S}\,\backslash L$$

$$\frac{N\backslash S \Rightarrow N\backslash S}{}\,\backslash R$$

$$\frac{N \Rightarrow N \quad S \Rightarrow S}{N, N\backslash S \Rightarrow S}\,\backslash L$$

$$\frac{N, (N\backslash S)/(N\backslash S), N\backslash S \Rightarrow S}{}\,/L$$

$$N, (N\backslash S)/(N\backslash S), (N\backslash S)/(N\bullet PP), N/CN, CN, PP/N, N/CN, CN \Rightarrow S \quad /L$$

$$x_1, x_{have}, x_{set}, x_{my}, x_{bow}, x_{in}, x_{the}, x_{cloud}$$

$$= ((x_{have}\; \lambda x'((x_{set}\; ((x_{my}\; x_{bow}), (x_{in}\; (x_{the}\; x_{cloud})))\; x'))\; x_1)$$

FIGURE 3.10. Derivational semantics for *I have set my bow in the cloud*

(13) $[\![A]\!] = v(A)$ for $A \in \mathbf{P}$

        $[\![\neg A]\!] = \overline{[\![A]\!]}^{\{\emptyset\}}$ negation

        $[\![A \wedge B]\!] = [\![A]\!] \cap [\![B]\!]$ conjunction

        $[\![A \vee B]\!] = [\![A]\!] \cup [\![B]\!]$ disjunction

        $[\![A \rightarrow B]\!] = \overline{[\![A]\!]}^{\{\emptyset\}} \cup [\![B]\!]$ implication

We see from the set-theoretic interpretation that the *truth table* of, for example, the conjunction is:

(14)

A B	$A \wedge B$
0 0	0
0 1	0
1 0	0
1 1	1

Exercise 3.4. Compile the truth tables for negation, disjunction, and implication.

A formula A *entails* a formula B if and only if $[\![A]\!] \subseteq [\![B]\!]$ in every interpretation, which is the case if and only if every line of the truth table of A $\rightarrow$ B evaluates to true.

Gentzen (1934) gave a proof theory for classical logic in terms of sequent calculus. Let us define a *classical sequent* $\Gamma \Rightarrow \Delta$ as comprising an *antecedent* Γ and a *succedent* Δ which are finite, possibly empty, sequences of formulas. A sequent is read as asserting that the conjunction of the antecedent formulas (where the empty sequence is the conjunctive unit true) entails the disjunction of the succedent formulas (where the empty sequence is the disjunctive unit false). A sequent is called *valid* if and only if this assertion is true; otherwise it is called *invalid*. A sequent calculus for the propositional part of classical logic is presented in Fig. 3.11. As was the case for the Lambek sequent calculus, each rule has the form $\frac{\Sigma_1 \dots \Sigma_n}{\Sigma_0}$, $n \geq 0$ where the Σ_i are sequent schemata; $\Sigma_1, \dots, \Sigma_n$ are referred to as the *premises*, and Σ_0 as the *conclusion*.

The identity axiom id and the Cut rule in the *identity* group reflect the reflexivity and transitivity respectively of entailment as in the Lambek sequent calculus, except that the Cut rule is now generalized for multiple succedents. All the other rules are either left (L) rules, introducing or manipulating the active formula(s) on the left (antecedent) of the conclusion, or right (R) introduction rules, introducing or manipulating the active formula(s) on the right (succedent) of the conclusion.

The rules W (weakening), C (contraction), and P (permutation) are referred to as *structural* rules; they apply to properties of all formulas with respect to the metalinguistic comma (conjunction in the antecedent, disjunction in the succedent). Weakening corresponds to the *monotonicity*

$$\frac{}{A \Rightarrow A} \; id \qquad \frac{\Gamma_1 \Rightarrow \Delta_1, A \qquad A, \Gamma_2 \Rightarrow \Delta_2}{\Gamma_1, \Gamma_2 \Rightarrow \Delta_1, \Delta_2} \; Cut$$

$$\frac{\Delta_1, \Delta_2 \Rightarrow \Delta}{\Delta_1, A, \Delta_2 \Rightarrow \Delta} \; WL \qquad \frac{\Delta \Rightarrow \Delta_1, \Delta_2}{\Delta \Rightarrow \Delta_1, A, \Delta_2} \; WR$$

$$\frac{\Delta_1, A, A, \Delta_2 \Rightarrow \Delta}{\Delta_1, A, \Delta_2 \Rightarrow \Delta} \; CL \qquad \frac{\Delta \Rightarrow \Delta_1, A, A, \Delta_2}{\Delta \Rightarrow \Delta_1, A, \Delta_2} \; CR$$

$$\frac{\Delta_1, A, B, \Delta_2 \Rightarrow \Delta}{\Delta_1, B, A, \Delta_2 \Rightarrow \Delta} \; PL \qquad \frac{\Delta \Rightarrow \Delta_1, A, B, \Delta_2}{\Delta \Rightarrow \Delta_1, B, A, \Delta_2} \; PR$$

$$\frac{\Gamma \Rightarrow A, \Delta}{\neg A, \Gamma \Rightarrow \Delta} \; \neg L \qquad \frac{\Delta, A \Rightarrow \Gamma}{\Delta \Rightarrow \Gamma, \neg A} \; \neg R$$

$$\frac{\Delta_1, A, B, \Delta_2 \Rightarrow \Delta}{\Delta_1, A \wedge B, \Delta_2 \Rightarrow \Delta} \; \wedge L \qquad \frac{\Delta \Rightarrow \Delta_1, A, \Delta_2 \qquad \Delta \Rightarrow \Delta_1, B, \Delta_2}{\Delta \Rightarrow \Delta_1, A \wedge B, \Delta_2} \; \wedge R$$

$$\frac{\Delta_1, A, \Delta_2 \Rightarrow \Delta \qquad \Delta_1, B, \Delta_2 \Rightarrow \Delta}{\Delta_1, A \vee B, \Delta_2 \Rightarrow \Delta} \; \vee L \qquad \frac{\Delta \Rightarrow \Delta_1, A, B, \Delta_2}{\Delta \Rightarrow \Delta_1, A \vee B, \Delta_2} \; \vee R$$

$$\frac{\Gamma \Rightarrow A \qquad \Delta_1, B, \Delta_2 \Rightarrow \Delta}{\Delta_1, \Gamma, A \rightarrow B, \Delta_2 \Rightarrow \Delta} \; \rightarrow L \qquad \frac{\Delta_1, A, \Delta_2 \Rightarrow \Gamma_1, B, \Gamma_2}{\Delta_1, \Delta_2 \Rightarrow \Gamma_1, A \rightarrow B, \Gamma_2} \; \rightarrow R$$

FIGURE 3.11. Sequent calculus for classical propositional logic

of classical logic: that conjoining antecedents, or disjoining succedents, pre-serves validity. Together with Weakening, Contraction corresponds to the idempotency ($x + x = x$) of conjunction in the antecedent and disjunction in the succedent, and Permutation corresponds to the commutativity ($x + y = y + x$) of conjunction in the antecedent and disjunction in the succedent. The structural rules permit each side of a sequent to be read, if we wish, as a set rather than a list, of formulas.

Then there are the *logical* rules, dealing with the connectives themselves. As in the Lambek sequent calculus, for each connective there is a left rule and a right rule introducing single principle connective occurrences in the active formula in the antecedent (L) or the succedent (R) of the conclusion respectively.

A sequent which has a proof is a *theorem*. The sequent calculus is *sound* (every theorem is a valid sequent) and *complete* (every valid sequent is a theorem).

All the rules except Cut have the property that all the formulas in the premises are either in the conclusion (the side-formulas in the contexts

$\Gamma_{(i)}/\Delta_{(i)}$, and the active formulas of structural rules), or else are the (immediate) subformulas of the active formula (in the logical rules). In the Cut rule, the *Cut formula* A is a new unknown reading from conclusion to premises. As we remarked in Chapter 2, Gentzen proved as his *Haupsatz* that every proof has a Cut-free equivalent (Cut-elimination). Gentzen's Cut-elimination theorem has as a corollary that every theorem has a proof containing only its subformulas (the *subformula property*), namely any one of its Cut-free proofs.

Computationally, the Contraction rule is potentially problematic since it (as well as Cut) introduces material in a backward-chaining proof search reading from conclusion to premises. But such a Cut-free proof search becomes a decision procedure for classical propositional logic when antecedents and succedents are treated as sets.

3.5 Classical first-order logic

Whereas propositional logic deals only in complete thoughts or propositions, first-order logic incorporates also individuals and quantification, with properties, relations, and (usually) operations.

(15) DEFINITION (*language of first-order logic*). Let there be a set C of (individual) *constants*, a denumerably infinite set V of (individual) *variables*, a set F^i of *function letters* of arity i for each $i > 0$, and a set P^i of *predicate letters* of arity i for each $i \geq 0$. The set T of *first-order terms* and the set F of *first-order formulas* are defined recursively as follows:

$$T ::= C \mid V \mid F^i(T_1, \ldots, T_i)$$
$$F ::= P^i T_1 \ldots T_i \mid \neg F \mid F \wedge F \mid F \vee F \mid F \to F \mid \forall V F \mid \exists V F$$

The standard semantics of first-order logic was given by Tarski (1935). An *interpretation of first-order logic* is a structure (D, F) where *domain D* is a non-empty set (of *individuals*) and *valuation function F* is a function mapping each individual constant to an individual in D, each function letter of arity $i > 0$ to an i-ary operation in D^{D^i}, and each predicate letter of arity $i \geq 0$ to an i-ary relation in D^i. An *assignment function g* is a function mapping each individual variable to an individual in D. Each term or formula ϕ receives a semantic value $[\phi]^g$ relative to an interpretation (D, F) and an assignment g as shown in Fig. 3.12.

A formula A *entails* a formula B, or B is a *logical consequence* of A, if and only if $[A]^g \subseteq [B]^g$ in every interpretation and assignment. First-order logic is semidecidable but not decidable: there exist algorithms that determine for all pairs of formulas whether they stand in the entailment relation in the case that they do, but there is no algorithm that does so and also always terminates in the negative case.

$$[c]^g = F(c) \qquad\qquad\qquad\qquad\qquad\text{for } c \in C$$

$$[x]^g = g(x) \qquad\qquad\qquad\qquad\qquad\text{for } x \in V$$

$$[f(t_1, \ldots, t_i)]^g = F(f)([t_1]^g, \ldots, [t_i]^g) \qquad\qquad\text{for } f \in F^i, i > 0$$

$$[Pt_1 \ldots t_i]^g = \begin{cases} \{\emptyset\} \text{ if } \langle [t_1]^g, \ldots, [t_i]^g \rangle \in F(P) \\ \emptyset \quad \text{otherwise} \end{cases} \text{for } P \in P^i, i \geq 0$$

$$[\neg A]^g = \overline{[A]^g}^{\{\emptyset\}}$$

$$[A \wedge B]^g = [A]^g \cap [B]^g$$

$$[A \vee B]^g = [A]^g \cup [B]^g$$

$$[A \rightarrow B]^g = \begin{cases} \{\emptyset\} \text{ if } [A]^g \subseteq [B]^g \\ \emptyset \quad \text{otherwise} \end{cases}$$

$$[\forall x\, A]^g = \bigcap\nolimits_{d \in D} [A]^{(g - \{(x, g(x))\}) \cup \{(x, d)\}}$$

$$[\exists x\, A]^g = \bigcup\nolimits_{d \in D} [A]^{(g - \{(x, g(x))\}) \cup \{(x, d)\}}$$

FIGURE 3.12. Semantics of first-order logic

Second-order logic allows quantification not only over individuals (first-order quantification) but also over propositions and predicates (second-order quantification). For example, the principle of induction over the naturals can be expressed by second-order universal quantification:

(16) $\forall^2 P((P0 \wedge \forall x (Px \rightarrow Psucc(x))) \rightarrow \forall x Px)$

Second-order logic is not even semidecidable. Hence also third-order logic (allowing quantification over properties of sets) and all higher-order logics are non-semidecidable.

3.6 Classical higher-order logic

We can express indefinitely high-order logic (ω-order logic) simply by adding logical constants to typed lambda calculus (Church, 1940). Let us assume basic types e for entities ($d(e)$ a non-empty set) and t for truth values ($d(t) = \{1, 0\}$). Logical constants are typed constants as usual, except that their denotations are constrained. For example, we may assume a logical constant $\wedge$ for conjunction of type $t \rightarrow (t \rightarrow t)$. But as a constant which is logical, rather than considering valuations in which it is interpreted as any function of type $(\{1, 0\}^{\{1,0\}})^{\{1,0\}}$, we include only those valuations in which it is interpreted specifically as the function $[0 \mapsto [0 \mapsto 0, 1 \mapsto 0], 1 \mapsto [0 \mapsto 0, 1 \mapsto 1]]$.

Similarly, we may assume a logical constant ι for definite descriptions of type $(e \rightarrow t) \rightarrow e$ for which we only consider valuations f such that when

TABLE 3.1. Logical constants

constant	type	constraint
$\neg$	$t \to t$	$f(\neg)(m) = \overline{m}^{\{\emptyset\}}$
$\wedge$	$t \to (t \to t)$	$f(\wedge)(m)(m') = m \cap m'$
$\vee$	$t \to (t \to t)$	$f(\vee)(m)(m') = m \cup m'$
$\to$	$t \to (t \to t)$	$f(\to)(m)(m') = \overline{m}^{\{\emptyset\}} \cup m'$
$=$	$e \to (e \to t)$	$f(=)(m)(m') = \{\emptyset\}$ if $m = m'$ else $\emptyset$
$\forall$	$(e \to t) \to t$	$f(\forall)(m) = \bigcap_{m' \in d(e)} m(m')$
$\exists$	$(e \to t) \to t$	$f(\exists)(m) = \bigcup_{m' \in d(e)} m(m')$
ι	$(e \to t) \to e$	$f(\iota)(\{m\}) = m$

$$|x| = x \qquad \text{for individual variable } x$$
$$|a| = a \qquad \text{for individual constant } a$$
$$|f(t_0, \ldots, t_n)| = (\cdots (f\ |t_0|) \cdots |t_n|)$$
$$|P t_1 \ldots t_n| = (\cdots (P\ |t_1|) \cdots |t_n|)$$
$$|\neg A| = (\neg\ A)$$
$$|A \wedge B| = ((\wedge\ |A|)\ |B|)$$
$$|A \vee B| = ((\vee\ |A|)\ |B|)$$
$$|A \to B| = ((\to\ |A|)\ |B|)$$
$$|\forall x\, A| = (\forall\ \lambda x |A|)$$
$$|\exists x\, A| = (\exists\ \lambda x |A|)$$

FIGURE 3.13. Translation from first-order logic notation into higher-order logic

$m \in D_{e \to t}$ is the characteristic function of a singleton set, then $f(\iota)(m)$ is the unitary member of that set.[1]

Let us assume the logical constants in Table 3.1. There is the translation $|\cdot|$ given in Fig. 3.13 from the first-order logic notation defined in (15) into our higher-order logic.

3.7 Lexical semantics

We will represent a reading of an expression of syntactic type A by a closed term of higher-order logic of semantic type $T(A)$. We have already seen in Section 3.3 how a derivation of a sequent $A_1, \ldots, A_n \Rightarrow A$ is associated with a pure lambda term of type $T(A)$ with free variables of types $T(A_1), \ldots, T(A_n)$: the *derivational semantics*. The lexicon will associate closed terms of higher-order logic with basic expressions, the *lexical semantics*. A *lexical entry* $\alpha : A : \phi$ will comprise a syntactical semigroup term α, a lexical

---

[1] Cf. Carpenter (1996). Of course this does not capture the presuppositional nature of the definite article whereby its use presupposes the unicity of the extension of its noun in the domain of discourse.

syntactic type A, and a closed higher-order lexical semantic term ϕ of semantic type $T(A)$.

Sometimes lexical semantics will be unstructured, consisting simply of a non-logical constant, for example:

(17) **John** : $N : j$
      loves : $(N \backslash S)/N : love$
      Mary : $N : m$

A *lexical selection* for a derivation of $A_1, \ldots, A_n \Rightarrow A$ is a choice of lexical entries, $\alpha_1 : A_1 : \phi_1, \ldots, \alpha_n : A_n : \phi_n$. A derivation plus a lexical selection determines the semantics that is the substitution of the lexical semantics into the derivational semantics. For example, recall from above the derivation and derivational semantics:

(18)
$$
\begin{array}{|c}
\dfrac{\dfrac{N \Rightarrow N \quad S \Rightarrow S}{N, N\backslash S \Rightarrow S}\ \backslash L}{\dfrac{N \Rightarrow N \quad N, N\backslash S \Rightarrow S}{N, (N\backslash S)/N, N \Rightarrow S}\ /L}
\end{array}
\quad
\begin{array}{|l}
\\[2pt]
x_{\text{John}}, x_{\text{loves}}, x_{\text{Mary}}
\end{array}
= ((x_{\text{loves}}\ x_{\text{Mary}})\ x_{\text{John}})
$$

Then substituting in the lexical semantics in (17), *John loves Mary* is assigned semantics:

(19) $((x_{\text{loves}}\ x_{\text{Mary}})\ x_{\text{John}})\{j/x_{\text{John}}, love/x_{\text{loves}}, m/x_{\text{Mary}}\} = ((love\ m)\ j)$

In other cases lexical semantics will be represented by a structured term, encoding denotational constraints and hence logical semantic properties of the lexical expression. For example, the following lexical assignment to a reflexive pronoun encodes its duplicating semantics:

(20) **himself** : $((N\backslash S)/N)\backslash(N\backslash S) : \lambda x \lambda y ((x\ y)\ y)$

For *John loves himself* there is the following derivation and derivational semantics:

(21)
$$
\begin{array}{|c}
\dfrac{(N\backslash S)/N \Rightarrow (N\backslash S)/N \quad \dfrac{\dfrac{N \Rightarrow N \quad S \Rightarrow S}{N, N\backslash S \Rightarrow S}\ \backslash L}{}}{N, (N\backslash S)/N, ((N\backslash S)/N)\backslash(N\backslash S) \Rightarrow S}\ \backslash L
\end{array}
\quad
\begin{array}{|l}
\\[2pt]
x_{\text{John}}, x_{\text{loves}}, x_{\text{himself}}
\end{array}
=
$$

$$((x_{\text{himself}}\ x_{\text{loves}})\ x_{\text{John}})$$

Substituting in the lexical semantics and simplifying, we obtain:

(22) $((x_{\text{himself}}\ x_{\text{loves}})\ x_{\text{John}})\{\lambda x \lambda y ((x\ y)\ y)/x_{\text{himself}}, love/x_{\text{loves}}, j/x_{\text{John}}\} =$
      $((\lambda x \lambda y ((x\ y)\ y)\ love)\ j) = (\lambda y ((love\ y)\ y)\ j) = ((love\ j)\ j)$

Finally, lexical semantics may be structured and/or contain constants which can be logical, for example:

(23) **and** : $(S \backslash S)/S : \wedge$
bachelor : $CN : \lambda x((\wedge (man\ x)) (\neg (married\ x)))$
the : $N/CN : \iota$

Exercise 3.5. Analyse the syntax and semantics of *The bachelor loves himself* according to these lexical assignments.

3.8 Natural deduction for the Lambek calculus

A sequent is a simple arrangement of formulas, and we have noted how, in sequent calculus, rules have a perfectly modular form, centred on a single main connective occurrence in the antecedent or succedent of the conclusion. Lambek sequent calculus, like that of classical and intuitionistic logic, enjoys the Cut-elimination property.

Typically, proofs of Cut-elimination are *constructive*, meaning that they not only show the existence of a Cut-free counterpart to a proof, but show algorithmically how to transform proofs into Cut-free proofs, eliminating the Cuts. This constructivity is of computational importance (Girard *et al.*, 1989), but even the dry fact of Cut-elimination alone has good consequences: the subformula property and decidability. The latter follows from the finiteness of the space of Cut-free backward chaining sequent proof-search. This same finiteness also entails for Lambek categorial grammar the *finite reading property* (van Benthem, 1991): that any sequent only ever has at most a finite number of semantic readings, because of the finiteness of the number of possible Cut-free proofs together with *semantic Cut-elimination* (Hendriks, 1993): that the Cut-elimination algorithm preserves semantic readings. The finite reading property is consistent with the observation that natural language only ever appears to be finitely ambiguous.

However, the sequent calculus notation for proofs, taken exactly as it appears, is highly redundant because all side formulas are duplicated in premises and conclusion at every inference step. And although Cut-elimination provides a partial normalization, there are (as we have seen) still multiple equivalent Cut-free proofs (spurious ambiguity). In the interests of elegance, economy, and efficiency, we would like canonicality or unicity whereby there is a unique (normal form) derivation for each reading. Furthermore, such a representation could be interpreted linguistically as the actual syntactic structure or structural description corresponding to a sentence and a reading. König (1989), Hepple (1990), and Hendriks (1993) present normalization of the Cut-free Lambek calculus which succeeds in establishing unicity,

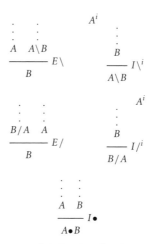

$$
\begin{array}{cc}
\begin{array}{cc}
\vdots & \vdots \\
A & A\backslash B
\end{array} & \\
\overline{ B } \; E\backslash & \\
\end{array}
\qquad
\begin{array}{c}
A^i \\
\vdots \\
B \\
\overline{A\backslash B} \; I\backslash^i
\end{array}
$$

$$
\begin{array}{cc}
\begin{array}{cc}
\vdots & \vdots \\
B/A & A
\end{array} & \\
\overline{ B } \; E/ & \\
\end{array}
\qquad
\begin{array}{c}
A^i \\
\vdots \\
B \\
\overline{B/A} \; I/^i
\end{array}
$$

$$
\begin{array}{c}
\begin{array}{cc}
\vdots & \vdots \\
A & B
\end{array} \\
\overline{ A\bullet B } \; I\bullet
\end{array}
$$

FIGURE 3.14. Natural deduction for the Lambek calculus

except for the rule of product on the left. However, this still suffers from the redundancy of the representation of side-formulas in sequent calculus.

In sequent calculus proofs are trees with the nodes labelled by entire sequents. We have seen how in natural deduction for intuitionistic logic proofs are represented by trees (with some coindexing) the nodes of which are labelled by just single formulas. This both removes the side formula redundancy of sequent calculus, and provides a notation which is strongly normalizing and Church–Rosser. So it is natural to seek a natural deduction representation for the Lambek calculus (Barry *et al.*, 1991; van Benthem, 1991; Tiede, 1999).

Standard natural deduction is unordered, but in natural deduction for the Lambek calculus it is straightforward to represent the order of the premises by the order on the page. Then we can give the rules shown in Fig. 3.14. In the rules of \ introduction and / introduction it is required that exactly one hypothesis A be conditionalized (closed), and that it be the undischarged assumption dominated by B which is leftmost in the case of $\backslash I$ and rightmost in the case of $/I$. We disallow conditionalization of a last remaining assumption because the Lambek calculus does not allow empty antecedents. Note that we are lacking a $\bullet$ elimination rule (see below).

By way of illustration, forward type lifting and forward composition are derived as follows:

$$
(24) \quad \dfrac{\dfrac{A \qquad A\backslash B^i}{B} \; E\backslash}{B/(A\backslash B)} \; I/^i
$$

(25)
$$\frac{\displaystyle\frac{B/A \qquad A^i}{\displaystyle\frac{C/B \qquad B}{\displaystyle\frac{C}{C/A}\ I/^i}\ E/}}{}$$

We define normal forms in the same way as for intuitionistic natural deduction by normalizing detours comprising introduction and elimination, or elimination and introduction, of the same connective.

In linguistic derivations represented by natural deduction we may write lexical expressions above their open leaf types. For example, for *John loves Mary*:

(26)
$$\frac{\text{John} \quad \dfrac{\dfrac{\text{loves}}{(N\backslash S)/N} \quad \dfrac{\text{Mary}}{N}}{N\backslash S}\ E/}{\dfrac{S}{}}\ E\backslash$$

For *The cat slept* we get one (normal form) natural deduction derivation, in contrast to the two Cut-free sequent derivations:

(27)
$$\frac{\dfrac{\dfrac{\text{the}}{N/CN} \quad \dfrac{\text{cat}}{CN}}{N}\ E/ \qquad \dfrac{\text{slept}}{N\backslash S}}{S}\ E\backslash$$

For *I have set my bow in the cloud* there is the natural deduction derivation given in Fig. 3.15.

Exercise 3.6. Give natural deduction proofs of backward type lifting, backward composition, forward and backward division, and associativity and other laws such as those in Fig. 2.2.

Giving a • elimination rule in ordered natural deduction for the Lambek calculus is problematic. It is tempting to write something like:

(28)
$$\frac{\begin{array}{c}\vdots\\ A \bullet B\end{array}}{A \qquad B}\ \bullet E$$

However this spoils the single-mother (tree) property of natural deduction and would make it complicated to define correctly for all cases what would be

$$
\dfrac{
  \dfrac{
    I \quad \dfrac{(N\backslash S)/(N\backslash S)}{N}
  }{N}
  \quad
  \dfrac{
    \dfrac{\text{have}}{(N\backslash S)/(N\backslash S)}
    \quad
    \dfrac{
      \dfrac{\text{set}}{(N\backslash S)/(N\bullet PP)}
      \quad
      \dfrac{
        \dfrac{\dfrac{\text{my}}{N/CN}\quad\dfrac{\text{bow}}{CN}}{N}\;E/
        \quad
        \dfrac{
          \dfrac{\text{in}}{PP/N}
          \quad
          \dfrac{\dfrac{\text{in}}{PP/N}\quad\dfrac{\dfrac{\text{the}}{N/CN}\quad\dfrac{\text{cloud}}{CN}}{N}E/}{PP}
        }{N\bullet PP}\bullet I
      }{N\backslash S}E/
    }{N\backslash S}E/
  }{N\backslash S}
}{S}E\backslash
$$

FIGURE 3.15. Natural deduction derivation of *I have set my bow in the cloud*

meant by leftmost or rightmost undischarged assumption in order to regulate the division introduction rules. Alternatively we might try something like:

(29)
$$
\begin{array}{c}
\vdots \\
A\bullet B \\
\hline
A \quad B \\
\vdots \\
\vdots \\
C
\end{array}\;\bullet E
$$

But this spoils the property whereby natural deduction proofs are only adjoined and extended at the roots. The issue is not clear. But in any case, we shall settle in Chaper 4 on a final proof syntax, proof nets, which on the one hand is even deeper than natural deduction, and on the other hand treats all the rules of inference, including the rule of use of product, in a uniform way. Thus the question of how to treat product elimination in ordered natural deduction does not seem to matter much in the end.

3.9 Natural deduction for the Lambek calculus with semantic annotation

An ordered Lambek calculus natural deduction proof is annotated with lambda terms representing the semantic reading as shown in Fig. 3.16.

For semantics with sequent calculus we had to first obtain the entire derivational semantics, then substitute in the lexical semantics, and then normalize.

$$
\cfrac{A:\phi \quad A\backslash B:\chi}{B:(\chi\;\phi)}\;E\backslash
\qquad
\cfrac{\begin{array}{c}\overset{A\,:\,x^{i}}{\vdots}\\[2pt]B:\psi\end{array}}{A\backslash B:\lambda x\psi}\;I\backslash^{i}
$$

$$
\cfrac{B/A:\chi \quad A:\phi}{B:(\chi\;\phi)}\;E/
\qquad
\cfrac{\begin{array}{c}\overset{A\,:\,x^{i}}{\vdots}\\[2pt]B:\psi\end{array}}{B/A:\lambda x\psi}\;I/^{i}
$$

$$
\cfrac{A:\phi \quad B:\psi}{A\bullet B:(\phi,\psi)}\;I\bullet
$$

FIGURE 3.16. Natural deduction for the Lambek calculus with semantic annotation

If we annotate natural deduction assumptions with (distinct) variables, the semantic annotation built up at the root of a proof represents its derivational semantics. However, in natural deduction we may annotate open assumptions with their lexical semantics and then build up (and possibly normalize) semantics as we work from leaves to root. For example:

(30)
$$
\cfrac{N:j \quad \cfrac{\overline{(N\backslash S)/N:love} \quad \overline{N:m}}{N\backslash S:(love\;m)}\;E/}{S:((love\;m)\;j)}\;E\backslash
$$

$$
\begin{array}{cc}\text{loves} & \text{Mary}\\ \text{John}\end{array}
$$

(31)
$$
\cfrac{\cfrac{\overline{N/CN:\iota} \quad \overline{CN:cat}}{N:(\iota\;cat)}\;E/ \quad \overline{N\backslash S:slept}}{S:(slept\;(\iota\;cat))}\;E\backslash
$$

$$
\begin{array}{cc}\text{the} & \text{cat}\end{array}\qquad \text{slept}
$$

(32)
$$
\cfrac{N:j \quad \cfrac{\overline{(N\backslash S)/N:love} \quad \overline{((N\backslash S)/N)\backslash(N\backslash S):\lambda x\lambda y((x\;y)\;y)}}{N\backslash S:(\lambda x\lambda y((x\;y)\;y)\;love)=\lambda y((love\;y)\;y)}\;E\backslash}{S:(\lambda y((love\;y)\;y)\;j)=((love\;j)\;j)}\;E\backslash
$$

$$
\begin{array}{cc}\text{loves} & \text{himself}\\ \text{John}\end{array}
$$

Categorial grammar handles subcategorization, that is the classification of the categorial contexts in which expressions expect to find themselves, quite naturally. In Part II of this book we look at extensions of Lambek calculus of the kind that seem to be required to treat extraction, discontinuity, polymorphism, and intensionality. But in the final section of this chapter we look at a phenomenon for which Lambek categorial grammar alone already provides a notable treatment of both the syntax and semantics: coordination, including the coordination of non-standard constituents.

3.10 Coordination of standard and non-standard constituents

As is well known, Boolean coordination can be treated in categorial grammar by assigning say *or* types of the form $(X\backslash X)/X$ with semantics $\lambda x\lambda y\lambda z_1 \ldots \lambda z_n[(y\ z_1\ \ldots\ z_n) \vee (x\ z_1\ \ldots\ z_n)]$ where $T(X) = \tau_1 \to \cdots \to \tau_n \to t$. Something further would be required for group readings of conjunction, and there are complications with agreement in subject noun phrase coordination in, for example, *John (m) or Mary (f) arrived* and *John (sg) and Mary (sg) are/*is arriving*, but we leave these issues aside here.

As is also well-known, this generalized coordination extends automatically in combinatory categorial grammar to coordination of non-standard constituents as in right node raising (*John likes and Mary dislikes linguistics*) and left node raising (*John saw Bill yesterday and Mary today*) (Steedman 1985; 1987; Dowty 1988). The same is true in type logical categorial grammar. Here we survey the coordination in natural deduction Lambek categorial grammar of standard and non-standard constituents by means of the assignment schema above.

In derivations here and henceforth we allow ourselves to assume a convention of left-association of function application so that $((\phi\ \psi)\ \chi)$ may be abbreviated $(\phi\ \psi\ \chi)$, and so forth. Where ϕ is a binary logical operator such as $\wedge$, we also allow ourselves to write this in infix notation: $[\psi \wedge \chi]$. We abbreviate $(A\backslash A)/A$ as $\frac{1}{A}$. Fig. 3.17 shows the derivation of the verb phrase coordination

$$\dfrac{\dfrac{\text{John}}{N:j}\qquad \dfrac{\dfrac{\dfrac{\text{praises}}{(N\backslash S)/N:praise}\quad\dfrac{\text{Mary}}{N:m}}{N\backslash S:(praise\ m)}E/ \qquad \dfrac{\dfrac{\text{and}}{\frac{1}{N\backslash S}:\lambda x\lambda y\lambda z[(y\ z)\wedge(x\ z)]}\quad \dfrac{\text{laughs}}{N\backslash S:laugh}}{(N\backslash S)\backslash(N\backslash S):\lambda y\lambda z[(y\ z)\wedge(laugh\ z)]}E/}{N\backslash S:\lambda z[(praise\ m\ z)\wedge(laugh\ z)]}E\backslash}{S:(praise\ m\ j)\wedge(laugh\ j)}E\backslash$$

FIGURE 3.17. Verb phrase coordination

love

$$(N\backslash S)/N : love \qquad \overline{N : x}^{\,i}$$
$$\cfrac{}{N\backslash S : (love\ x)}\ E/$$

will

$$(N\backslash S)/(N\backslash S) : will$$
$$\cfrac{}{N\backslash S : (will\ (love\ x))}\ E/$$
$$\cfrac{}{(N\backslash S)/N : \lambda x(will\ (love\ x))}\ I/^{\,i}$$

and

$$\cfrac{1}{(N\backslash S)/N} : \lambda xyzw[(y\ z\ w) \wedge (x\ z\ w)]$$
$$\cfrac{}{((N\backslash S)/N)\backslash((N\backslash S)/N)/N : \lambda yzw[(y\ z\ w) \wedge (will\ (love\ z)\ w)]}\ E/$$

likes

$$(N\backslash S)/N : like$$

$$\cfrac{}{(N\backslash S)/N : \lambda zw[(like\ z\ w) \wedge (will\ (love\ z)\ w)]}\ E\backslash$$

London

$$\cfrac{N : l}{}\ E/$$

John

$$N : j$$

$$\cfrac{}{N\backslash S : \lambda w[(like\ l\ w) \wedge (will\ (love\ l)\ w)]}\ E/$$

$$S : (like\ l\ j) \wedge (will\ (love\ l)\ j)$$

FIGURE 3.18. Transitive verb phrase coordination with non-standard constituent

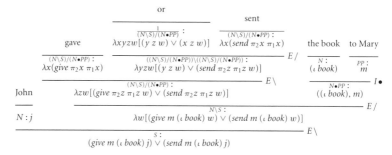

FIGURE 3.19. Coordination of prepositional ditransitive verbs

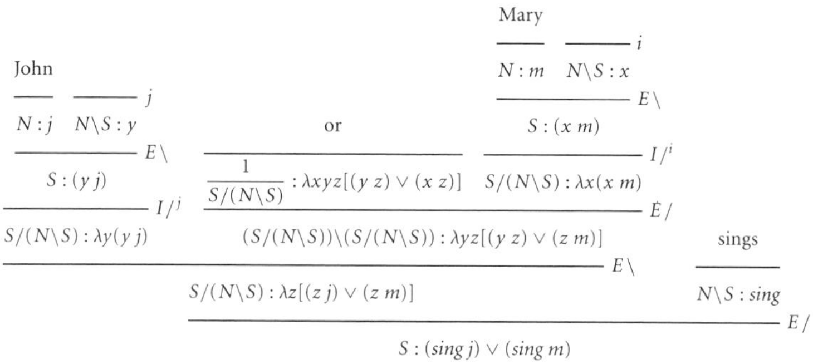

FIGURE 3.20. Subject coordination

John praises Mary and laughs. Fig. 3.18 shows the transitive verb phrase coordination of *likes* with the non-standard constituent *will love*. Fig. 3.19 shows coordination of prepositional ditransitive verbs.

Fig. 3.20 shows coordination of subjects. Observe the subject type lifting necessary in order to predicate *sings* of both disjuncts. In the analysis of *John loves Mary and himself* in Fig. 3.21 we see object coordination, which also requires derivational type lifting in general, but in this case the second conjunct is a reflexive pronoun which already has the lifted type lexically. Fig. 3.22 shows right node raising, that is to say, coordination of non-standard constituents in which a shared object of the conjuncts appears to the right outside the coordinate structure.

Fig. 3.23 shows the derivation of a conjunct in a coordination such as *John gave the book and sent the record to Mary*, which is coordination of a non-standard constituent according to our prepositional ditransitive type. The

$$\frac{}{(N\backslash S)/N : x}\,i \qquad \frac{\text{Mary}}{N : m}$$

$$\frac{(N\backslash S)/N : x \qquad N : m}{N\backslash S : (x\ m)}\,E/$$

$$\frac{N\backslash S : (x\ m)}{((N\backslash S)/N)\backslash(N\backslash S) : \lambda x(x\ m)}\,I\backslash^{i}$$

$$\frac{\text{and}}{\dfrac{1}{((N\backslash S)/N)\backslash(N\backslash S)} : \lambda xyzw[(y\ z\ w) \wedge (x\ z\ w)]} \qquad \frac{\text{himself}}{((N\backslash S)/N)\backslash(N\backslash S) : \lambda xy(x\ y\ y)}$$

$$\frac{\dfrac{1}{((N\backslash S)/N)\backslash(N\backslash S)} : \lambda xyzw[(y\ z\ w) \wedge (x\ z\ w)] \qquad ((N\backslash S)/N)\backslash(N\backslash S) : \lambda xy(x\ y\ y)}{(((N\backslash S)/N)\backslash(N\backslash S))\backslash(((N\backslash S)/N)\backslash(N\backslash S)) : \lambda yzw[(y\ z\ w) \wedge (z\ w\ w)]}\,E/$$

$$\frac{((N\backslash S)/N)\backslash(N\backslash S) : \lambda x(x\ m) \qquad (((N\backslash S)/N)\backslash(N\backslash S))\backslash(((N\backslash S)/N)\backslash(N\backslash S)) : \lambda yzw[(y\ z\ w) \wedge (z\ w\ w)]}{((N\backslash S)/N)\backslash(N\backslash S) : \lambda zw[(z\ m\ w) \wedge (z\ w\ w)]}\,E\backslash$$

$$\frac{\text{loves}}{(N\backslash S)/N : love}$$

$$\frac{(N\backslash S)/N : love \qquad ((N\backslash S)/N)\backslash(N\backslash S) : \lambda zw[(z\ m\ w) \wedge (z\ w\ w)]}{N\backslash S : \lambda w[(love\ m\ w) \wedge (love\ w\ w)]}\,E\backslash$$

$$\frac{\text{John}}{N : j}$$

$$\frac{N : j \qquad N\backslash S : \lambda w[(love\ m\ w) \wedge (love\ w\ w)]}{S : (love\ m\ j) \wedge (love\ j\ j)}\,E\backslash$$

FIGURE 3.21. Object coordination

$$
\begin{array}{c}
\text{loves} \\
\hline
\end{array}
$$

likes

$$\quad\quad\quad\quad\quad\quad\quad\quad\quad\quad\quad\quad\quad\quad\quad\quad\quad j$$

Mary $\quad (N\backslash S)/N : love \quad N : y$

John $\quad (N\backslash S)/N : like \quad N : x$

$$\quad\quad\quad\quad\quad\quad\quad\quad\quad\quad\quad\quad\quad\quad E/$$

$$\frac{}{\quad\quad} \; i$$

$$N : j \quad\quad N\backslash S : (like\ x)$$

$$N : m \quad\quad N\backslash S : (love\ y)$$

$$\frac{}{} E/$$

and

$$\frac{}{} E\backslash$$

$$S : (like\ x\ j)$$

$$\frac{1}{S/N} : \lambda xyz[(y\ z) \wedge (x\ z)] \quad\quad S/N : \lambda y(love\ y\ m)$$

$$S : (love\ y\ m)$$

$$\frac{}{} I/^{j}$$

$$\frac{}{} I/^{i}$$

$$S/N : \lambda x(like\ x\ j)$$

$$(S/N)\backslash(S/N) : \lambda yz[(y\ z) \wedge (love\ z\ m)]$$

$$\frac{}{} E/$$

$$\frac{}{} E\backslash$$

London

$$S/N : \lambda z[(like\ z\ j) \wedge (love\ z\ m)]$$

$$N : l$$

$$\frac{}{} E/$$

$$S : (like\ l\ j) \wedge (love\ l\ m)$$

FIGURE 3.22. Right node raising

$$
\begin{array}{c}
\text{the book}
\end{array}
$$

gave

$$N : (\iota\ book) \quad PP : x$$

$$\frac{}{} i$$

$$(N\backslash S)/(N\bullet PP) : \lambda x(give\ \pi_2 x\ \pi_1 x) \quad N\bullet PP : ((\iota\ book), x)$$

$$\frac{}{} I\bullet$$

$$\frac{}{} E/$$

$$N\backslash S : (give\ x\ (\iota\ book))$$

$$\frac{}{} I/^{i}$$

$$(N\backslash S)/PP : \lambda x(give\ x\ (\iota\ book))$$

FIGURE 3.23. Derivation of one conjunct in *John gave the book and sent the record to Mary*

$$
\begin{array}{cc}
\text{the book} & \text{to Mary}
\end{array}
$$

$$N : (\iota\ book) \quad PP : m$$

$$\frac{}{} i$$

$$\frac{}{} I\bullet$$

$$(N\backslash S)/(N\bullet PP) : x \quad N\bullet PP : ((\iota\ book), m)$$

$$\frac{}{} E/$$

$$N\backslash S : (x\ ((\iota\ book), m))$$

$$\frac{}{} I\backslash^{i}$$

$$((N\backslash S)/(N\bullet PP))\backslash(N\backslash S) : \lambda x(x\ ((\iota\ book), m))$$

FIGURE 3.24. Derivation of one conjunct in *John gave the book to Mary and the record to Suzy*

$$
\cfrac{
  \cfrac{
    \cfrac{\cfrac{\overline{\quad}^{\,j}}{TV:y}\quad \cfrac{\text{Mary}}{N:m}}{VP:(y\,m)}\;E/ \quad \cfrac{\text{today}}{VP\backslash VP:today}
  }{
    \cfrac{\cfrac{VP:(today\,(y\,m))}{E\backslash}}{TV\backslash VP:\lambda y(today\,(y\,m))}\;I\backslash^{j}
  }
}{}
$$

$$
\cfrac{\text{and}}{\cfrac{1}{TV\backslash VP}:\lambda xyzw[(y\,z\,w)\wedge(x\,z\,w)]}
$$

$$
\text{Bill}
$$
$$
\cfrac{
  \cfrac{\cfrac{\overline{\quad}^{\,i}}{TV:x}\quad \cfrac{}{N:b}\;E/}{VP:(x\,b)}\quad \cfrac{\text{yesterday}}{VP\backslash VP:yesterday}\;E\backslash
}{
  \cfrac{VP:(yesterday\,(x\,b))}{TV\backslash VP:\lambda x(yesterday\,(x\,b))}\;I\backslash^{i}
}
$$

$$(TV\backslash VP)\backslash(TV\backslash VP):\lambda yzw[(y\,z\,w)\wedge(yesterday\,(z\,b)\,w)]\quad E/$$

$$TV\backslash VP:\lambda zw[(today\,(z\,m)\,w)\wedge(yesterday\,(z\,b)\,w)]\quad E\backslash$$

$$\cfrac{\text{saw}}{N:see}$$

$$VP:\lambda w[(today\,(see\,m)\,w)\wedge(yesterday\,(see\,b)\,w)]\quad E\backslash$$

$$\cfrac{\text{John}}{N:j}$$

$$S:(today\,(see\,m)\,j)\wedge(yesterday\,(see\,b)\,j)\quad E\backslash$$

FIGURE 3.25. Left node raising

derivation of *John gave the book to Mary and the record to Suzy* on the other hand is, according to our prepositional ditransitive type, constituent coordination, but it requires lifting in order to distribute the verb; see Fig. 3.24. Derivation of true left node raising, which we name by analogy with right node raising, is shown in Fig. 3.25, where *TV* abbreviates $(N\backslash S)/N$ and *VP* abbreviates $N\backslash S$.

4

Processing

'*Take complexity-based accounts. . . . Here, the idea is to establish a nonarbitrary metric for complexity, one that makes reference to structure. These metrics are rarely spelled out explicitly or motivated theoretically.*'

Grodzinsky 2000: 56

'*. . . the complexity of the component processes in sentence processing does not lend itself well to developing [computational] models that make close contact with empirical data without making numerous ancillary assumptions.*'

Tanenhaus 2003: 1145

Accounts of linguistic competence rest on abstractions and idealizations which, however fruitful, must eventually be integrated in a full account of language with human computational performance in language use. Here we advocate the modelling of language processing on the basis of an incremental synthesis of categorial proof nets, therein obtaining a wide-ranging complexity metric which is nonarbitrary, simple, explicit, free of ancillary assumptions, and theoretically motivated.[1]

Centre embedding unacceptability is illustrated by the fact that while the nested subject relativizations of (1) exhibit little variation in acceptability,

---

[1] This chapter is a reworking of material from Morrill (2000) Incremental Processing and Acceptability. *Computational Linguistics*, 26(3), 319–338, used with permission of the Association for Computational Linguistics.

the increasingly nested object relativizations (2) are increasingly unacceptable (Chomsky 1965, ch. 1).

(1) a. The dog that chased the cat barked.
     b. The dog that chased the cat that saw the rat barked.
     c. The dog that chased the cat that saw the rat that ate the cheese barked.

(2) a. The cheese that the rat ate stank.
     b. ?The cheese that the rat that the cat saw ate stank.
     c. ??The cheese that the rat that the cat that the dog chased saw ate stank.

Gibson (1998) analyses such phenomena in terms of a dependency locality theory according to which the resources required for storing a partially processed structure are proportional to the number of incomplete syntactic dependencies at that point in processing the structure. Taking inspiration from Gibson, Johnson (1998) analyses centre embedding in terms of categorial proof nets, relating the maximal nesting of axiom links to the degree of unacceptability. Morrill (2000), on which this chapter is based, implements and rationalizes these ideas in terms of syntactic structures as proof nets and a complexity metric derived from the load on memory of an incremental algorithm of language processing.

4.1 Introduction

Girard (1987) introduced linear logic. Linear logic preserves from standard logic the freely applying structural rule of permutation, but not freely applying structural rules of contraction and weakening. The Lambek calculus lacks all three structural rules. Thus the Lambek calculus and linear logic are instances of what has come to be known as *substructural logic* (Restall, 2000). Just as the Lambek calculus is a *sequence logic*, linear logic is an *occurrence* logic.

Occurrence logics had been studied before under the rubric of BCI-logic.[2] However, Girard's linear logic established in a clear and unprecedented way the concepts of additive, multiplicative, and exponential connective.[3] We consider additives in Chapter 7. Examples of multiplicative connectives are the

---

[2] It is called 'BCI' after the names of the combinators (pure lambda terms) the type schemata of which are the axiom schemata of a Hilbert-style presentation of the logic:

(i) Combinator   Lambda term   Type/axiom schema
    B $\lambda x \lambda y \lambda z (x\,(y\,z))$ $(B \to C) \to ((A \to B) \to (A \to C))$
    C $\lambda x \lambda y \lambda z ((x\,z)\,y)$ $(A \to (B \to C)) \to (B \to (A \to C))$
    I $\lambda x x$ $A \to A$

[3] The arithmetic terms refer to the complexity of Cut-elimination of the connective classes.

times and divisions of the Lambek calculus, which is a non-commutative intuitionistic linear logic. Exponential connectives were entirely new kinds of modalities licensing controlled use of structural rules. We consider a variation in Chapter 5.

In addition, Girard (1987) introduced a new proof format, *proof nets* (for multiplicative classical linear logic). Proof nets are a deeper representation than both sequent calculus and natural deduction.[4] They form a graphical syntax which, as Girard *et al.* (1989) observe, captures the *essence même* of a proof. Roorda (1991) adapted proof nets to multiplicative non-commutative intuitionistic linear logic, that is, to the Lambek calculus. Proof nets are an ideal proof format for categorial logic: they are the syntactic structures of logical categorial grammar. The format of proof nets, unlike the format of sequent calculus, exhibits no spurious ambiguity and proof nets play the role in logical categorial grammar that parse trees play in phrase structure grammar. In this chapter we present, in terms of proof net synthesis, a non-deterministic incremental parsing algorithm for Lambek categorial grammar which consists purely in lexical choice and the complementization of syntactic valencies by shift/reduce syntactic choice. Furthermore, we associate with it a simple metric of complexity, the maximum number of unresolved valencies at any point in an analysis, that is the working memory stack-depth required for analysis according to the algorithm. We discuss how this complexity metric correctly predicts a wide variety of performance phenomena.

In Section 4.2 we define proof nets for the Lambek calculus. In Section 4.3 we define the extraction of semantics from a proof net analysis. In Section 4.4 we specify the natural nondeterministic incremental parsing algorithm and complexity metric for the proof net syntactic structures. We illustrate by reference to garden-pathing. In Section 4.5 we compare with human performance the predictions of logical categorial grammar and the complexity metric in relation to centre embedding unacceptability, left to right quantifier scope preference, preference for the lower attachment of adverbial phrases and of possessive clitics, heavy noun phrase shift, and preference for the passivization of nested sentential subjects.

4.2 Proof nets for the Lambek calculus

A proof net packs a proof into a minimal graphical structure. In sequent calculus logical inference rules for each connective decompose formulas into subformulas. Consider for example the following sequent proof:

---

[4] Or rather, it is sometimes said that proof nets are the natural deduction of linear logic.

(3)
$$\cfrac{\cfrac{N \Rightarrow N \qquad S \Rightarrow S}{N \Rightarrow N \qquad N, N\backslash S \Rightarrow S} \backslash L}{N, (N\backslash S)/N, N \Rightarrow S} /L$$

At the leaves, identity axioms relate antecedent and succedent atoms. In the corresponding proof net types and subtypes, marked by • and ○ for antecedent and succedent respectively, are unfolded into formula trees and complementary atomic leaves are connected. First, we obtain a *proof frame* by unfolding the endsequent types:

(4)

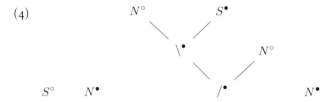

Each local tree in a proof frame corresponds to a sequent inference. We obtain a *proof structure* by connecting each atomic leaf with another complementary atomic leaf, corresponding to an identity axiom. Proof structures must satisfy further correctness criteria in order to qualify as well-formed representations of proofs, in which case they are called *proof nets*, so the proof nets are a proper subset of the proof structures. Continuing our example, the proof structure in Fig. 4.1 is also a proof net.

Exercise 4.1. The following two sequent proofs are represented by a single proof net. What do you think it is?

$$\cfrac{\cfrac{N \Rightarrow N \qquad S \Rightarrow S}{CN \Rightarrow CN \qquad N, N\backslash S \Rightarrow S} \backslash L}{N/CN, CN, N\backslash S \Rightarrow S} /L \qquad \cfrac{\cfrac{CN \Rightarrow CN \qquad N \Rightarrow N}{N/CN, CN \Rightarrow N} /L \qquad S \Rightarrow S}{N/CN, CN, N\backslash S \Rightarrow S} \backslash L$$

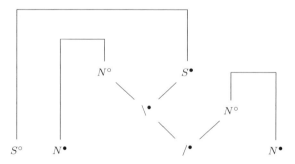

FIGURE 4.1. Proof net for $N, (N\backslash S)/N, N \Rightarrow S$

A *polar type* A^p comprises a type A together with a *polarity* $p = \bullet$ (*input*) or $\circ$ (*output*). In relating proof nets to sequent calculus and natural deduction, polarities indicate sequent sidedness: a type of input polarity corresponds to an antecedent type, and a type of output polarity corresponds to a succedent type.

The *polar type tree* $|A^p|$ of a polar type A^p is the ordered tree defined by the following polar translation function:

(5) $|P^P| = P^P$ if P is atomic

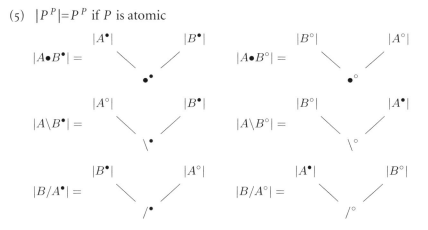

We see that the polar type tree of a polar type is basically its parse tree/formula tree decorated with polarities. Observe that the polar translation function transmits polarity from a mother node to its daughters according to the distribution in the corresponding sequent rule of the corresponding active type and its subtypes in the conclusion and the premise(s). For example, the translation of $A \bullet B^\bullet$ corresponds to the $\bullet L$ sequent rule. In that rule, both the subtypes of the active type have antecedent occurrences in the premise. Accordingly, the daughters in the image of the translation function are both of input polarity.

Exercise 4.2. Check that in the other five clauses of the translation function, the distributions of polarities also follow the sequent rules.

Let us recall that the sequents of the Lambek calculus are intuitionistic, having always a single succedent type, and always have non-empty antecedents, so that, for example, there is no inference from $A \Rightarrow A$ to $\Rightarrow A \backslash A$ (the latter is not even well-formed as a sequent). We define the *proof frame* of a sequent $A_0, \ldots, A_n \Rightarrow A$ as the sequence of polar type trees $\langle |A^\circ|, |A_0{}^\bullet|, \ldots, |A_n{}^\bullet| \rangle$. For example, the proof frame of the sequent (6) is given in Fig. 4.2, where we have additionally numbered the leaves.

(6) $S/(N\backslash S), (N\backslash S)/N, (S/N)\backslash S \Rightarrow S$

FIGURE 4.2. Proof frame of $S/(N\backslash S), (N\backslash S)/N, (S/N)\backslash S \Rightarrow S$

As we shall see, two proof nets can be built on this proof frame.

The local tree unfolded in a clause of the definition of the translation function (2) is called a *logical link*. A logical link in a proof net corresponds to a sequent inference rule, but it represents only the active types themselves. In a non-commutative system we also need to take order into account. The daughters of the logical links are ordered, but observe that in the unfoldings of output types, the order of the subtypes is commuted in the daughters. This is because polarities are read as affirmative or negative and in a non-commutative logic negation commutes the subformulas in the de Morgan laws. Philippe de Groote (p.c.) provides the following intuition. Consider going from a to c via b: first from a to b and then from b to c. The reverse (negation) of this is not to go from b to a and then from c to b, but to go first from c to b (the negation of the second operand) and then from b to a (the negation of the first operand). That is, the subformulas/operands are commuted.[5]

We define the *complement* $\overline{X}$ of a polar type X by $\overline{A^{\bullet}} = A^{\circ}$ and $\overline{A^{\circ}} = A^{\bullet}$. Two polar types are *complementary* if and only if they are the complements of each other. An *axiom link* on a proof frame is a pair of complementary leaves. We draw one thus as a connecting line, corresponding to an id axiom instance $P \Rightarrow P$ in sequent calculus:

(7)

$$P^p \qquad P^{\overline{p}}$$

An *axiom linking* for a proof frame is a set of axiom links with at most one axiom link per leaf and which is *planar*, that is there are no two axiom links (i, k) and (j, l) such that $i < j < k < l$. Geometrically, planarity means that where the polar type trees are ordered on a line, the axiom links can be drawn in the half-plane (on top) without crossing lines. Planarity corresponds to non-commutative order.

A *partial proof structure* (PPS) is a proof frame with zero or more axiom links. A *proof structure* is a (proof) frame together with an axiom linking that

---

[5] By symmetry we could have chosen to commute the input unfoldings instead, but then our word order would have appeared from right to left on the page.

links every leaf. Thus an *axiom linking* of a proof structure is a partitioning of its leaves into complementary pairs where the connections of paired leaves do not cross. Not every proof structure represents a proof. To do so a proof structure must further satisfy certain proof net conditions, but these conditions are not very transparent.

To take into account the arities of sequent rules, that is whether the active subtypes go into the same subproof (unary rules) or different subproofs (binary rules) we will need a global correctness condition on proof nets that makes reference to the arities of rules. We define here the $\wp$-*links* as those which are unary, that is those with mother $\bullet^\bullet$, $\backslash^\circ$ or $/^\circ$.[6]

A *switching* of a PPS is a graph resulting from removing one of the edges from each $\wp$-link. A *proof net* is a proof structure in which (i) every switching is a connected and acyclic graph (Danos–Regnier acyclicity and connectedness; see Danos and Regnier 1989), and (ii) no axiom link connects the leftmost and rightmost descendent leaves of an output division (we call this Retoré no subtending; see de Groote and Retoré 2003). Danos–Regnier (DR) connectedness and acyclicity takes care of rule arity. Retoré no subtending prohibits empty antecedents.

(8) THEOREM. A sequent is a theorem of (i.e., derivable in) the Lambek
     sequent calculus if and only if there is an axiom linking which forms a
     proof net on its frame.

Figs. 4.3 and 4.4 show the two proof nets that can be built on the frame of Fig. 4.2.

Actually, DR connectedness can be omitted because Fadda and Morrill (2005) show that in view of the intuitionistic nature of Lambek sequents (that there is exactly one root of output polarity), every proof structure which satisfies DR acyclicity also satisfies DR connectedness. Therefore we need only check for DR acyclicity (and no subtending). We call a partial proof structure *correct* if and only if it satisfies DR acyclicity and no subtending.

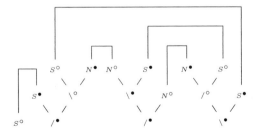

FIGURE 4.3. A proof net for $S/(N\backslash S), (N\backslash S)/N, (S/N)\backslash S \Rightarrow S$

[6] These are the cases which compile into linear multiplicative disjunction $\wp$ ('par'), which has a unary rule.

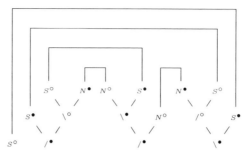

FIGURE 4.4. Another proof net for $S/(N\backslash S), (N\backslash S)/N, (S/N)\backslash S \Rightarrow S$

(9) COROLLARY. A sequent is a theorem of the Lambek calculus if and only if there is an axiom linking which forms a correct proof structure on its frame.

Therefore we can carry out Lambek theorem-proving by building up proof nets incrementally, checking for correctness (DR acyclicity and no subtending) at each step. We have a Lambek theorem if and only if we succeed in linking all the leaves while satisfying these criteria.

4.3 The semantic trip and the semantic reading of a proof net

The semantics associated with a categorial proof net, that is the proof as a lambda term (intuitionistic natural deduction proof, under the Curry–Howard correspondence) is extracted by associating a distinct index with each output division node and travelling as follows, starting by going up at the unique output root (De Groote and Retoré, 1996):

(10) • travelling up at the mother of an output division link, perform the lambda abstraction with respect to the associated index of the result of travelling up at the daughter of output polarity;
    • travelling up at the mother of an output product link, form the ordered pair of the result of travelling up at the right daughter (first component) and the left daughter (second component);
    • travelling up at one end of an axiom link, continue down at the other end;
    • travelling down at an (input) daughter of an input division link, perform the functional application of the result of travelling down at the mother to the result of travelling up at the other (output) daughter;

- travelling down at the left (resp. right) daughter of an input product link, take the first (resp. second) projection of the result of travelling down at the mother;
- travelling down at the (input) daughter of an output division link, return the associated index and bounce;
- travelling down at a root, return the associated lexical semantics and bounce.

We call this special trip around the proof net by which the semantics is extracted the 'semantic trip'. The semantic trip begins at the unique root of polarity output (the 'origin'), starting by travelling upwards. Edges are followed in a uniform direction until we come to logical links. Then the travel instructions are followed, which we illustrate diagrammatically in Fig. 4.5. The labels of edges taken generate the successive symbols of the semantic form. Lambda variables are unique to their link. When we arrive down at an input polarity root, the associated lexical semantics is inserted, and the trip 'bounces' back up. The trip visits each node twice, once travelling upwards and once travelling downwards, and crosses each edge twice, once in each direction. It ends when it arrives back down at the origin.

For example, where we associate with the three left-to-right input roots of Fig. 4.1 the lexical semantics *j*, *love*, and *m* respectively, the semantic trip yields ((*love m*) *j*). And where we associate with the three left-to-right roots of Figs. 4.3 and 4.4 the lexical semantics *someone*, *love*, and *everyone* respectively, the semantic trip yields for Fig. 4.3 (*someone* λ*x*(*everyone* λ*y*((*love y*) *x*))).

Exercise 4.3. What does the semantic trip yield for Fig. 4.4?

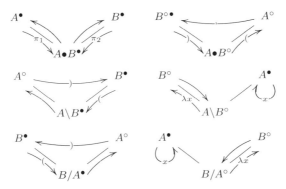

FIGURE 4.5. Semantic trip travel instructions

4.4 Incremental parsing algorithm and complexity metric

4.4.1 Parsing algorithm

We present a stack-based incremental parsing algorithm for Lambek categorial grammar. There is nondeterminism in respect of lexical choice (lexical ambiguity) and in respect of syntactic shift or reduce choice (syntactic ambiguity).

The algorithm works left-to-right through a buffer representing the successive words in the input speech stream. There are two stacks, a global stack and a local stack. When a next segment of the buffer is chosen as a lexical expression, the leaves of the polar tree of its lexical type are put on the local stack. Each such leaf L is then considered in turn, either reducing with a complementary leaf on the top of the global stack (establishing an axiom link ending at L), or pushing it onto the global stack (meaning that an axiom link will have to be established later starting at L).

We present the algorithm as a state transition system. A state comprises five components:

(11)   • A **global stack** G. This is the main stack, containing unresolved syntactic valencies. We define the complexity of a parse as the maximum depth of the global stack.
   • A **local stack** Ls. This is an auxiliary stack, containing the remaining valencies of the lexical type most recently inserted by lexical lookup.
   • A **buffer** a. The words remaining in the input speech stream.
   • A **frame** F. The proof frame built by lexical choice so far.
   • A set of **axiom links** X. The set of axiom links (syntactic dependencies) established so far on the proof frame.

We represent a state:

(12) G, Ls, a, F, X

The parsing algorithm is given in Fig. 4.6. We use Prolog notation for lists/stacks, thus $[]$ is the empty list and $[H|T]$ is the list with head H and tail T. $\oplus$ is list concatenation. $\#(F)$ is the total number of atomic type occurrences in the types of F; this is for numbering the leaves of the proof frame. $|A^{\bullet}|_n$ is like $|A^{\bullet}|$ but in addition numbers the leaves of the polar type tree from left to right starting from n. Where T is a (numbered) polar type tree, fringe(T) is the list of its leaves from left to right (product or yield). Note how the sideconditions on *REDUCE* incrementally ensure no subtending and DR acyclicity, i.e. correctness.

4.4.2 Parsing examples (garden pathing) and complexity metric

By way of illustration of the parsing algorithm and the complexity metric we consider garden pathing (Bever, 1970):

$$\frac{process\ \alpha}{[S^\circ{}_0],[],\alpha,[S^\circ{}_0],\emptyset}\ START$$

$$\frac{G,[],\alpha\oplus\alpha',F,X}{G,\mathrm{fringe}(|A^\bullet|_{\#(F)}),\alpha',F\oplus[|A^\bullet|_{\#(F)}],X}\ LEX,\ where\ \alpha:A$$

$$\frac{G,[L_i|Ls],\alpha,F,X}{[L_i|G],Ls,\alpha,F,X}\ SHIFT$$

$$\frac{[L_i|G],[L_j|Ls],\alpha,F,X}{G,Ls,\alpha,F,X\cup\{(i,j)\}}\ REDUCE,$$ where L_i and L_j are complementary and do not subtend in frame F, and every path between them in F together with axiom links X crosses both edges of some $\wp$-link.

$$\frac{[],[],[],F,X}{accept}\ END$$

FIGURE 4.6. Parsing algorithm for Lambek categorial grammar

(13) a. The horse raced past the barn.
    b. ?The horse raced past the barn fell.

(14) a. The boat floated down the river.
    b. ?The boat floated down the river sank.

(15) a. The dog that knew the cat disappeared.
    b. ?The dog that knew the cat disappeared was rescued.

Typically, although the (b) sentences are perfectly well-formed they are perceived of as being ungrammatical apparently due to a strong tendency to interpret their initial segments as in the (a) sentences.

Let us assume the following lexical assignments:

(16) **barn** : CN : *barn*
    horse : CN : *horse*
    past : $((N\backslash St)\backslash(N\backslash St))/N$: $\lambda x\lambda y\lambda z(past\ x\ (y\ z))$
    raced : $N\backslash S+$: *race*
    the   : N/CN : *the*

The feature + on S marks the projection of a tensed verb form; a verb phrase modified by 'past' need not be tensed and the feature is marked with a variable t in that lexical entry. Let us consider the incremental processing of (13a) as proof net construction. We assume initially that an S is expected; after perception of the word 'the' there is the following partial proof net (for simplicity we omit features, included in lexical entries, from proof nets):

(17)

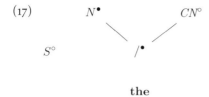

the

Here there are three unmatched valencies/unresolved dependencies; no axiom links can yet be placed, but after 'horse' we can build:

(18)

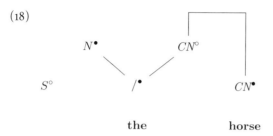

the   horse

Now there are only two unmatched valencies. After 'raced' we have, on the correct analysis, the following:

(19)

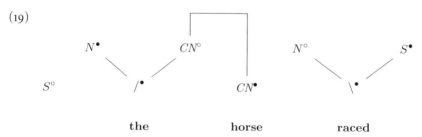

the   horse   raced

Note that linking the Ns is possible, but we are interested in the history of the analysis which turns out to be correct, and in that analysis the verb valencies are matched by the adverb that follows:

(20)

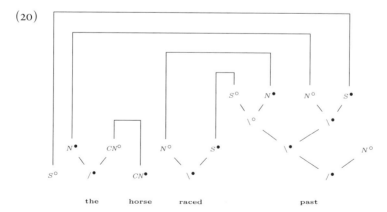

the   horse   raced   past

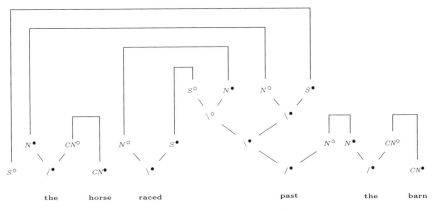

FIGURE 4.7. *the horse raced past the barn*

Observe that a cycle is created, but as required it crosses both edges of a ℘-link. At the penultimate step we have:

(21)

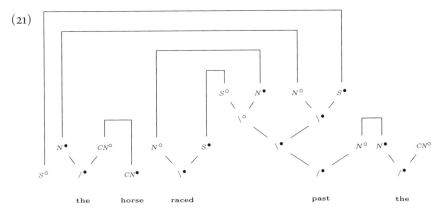

The final proof net analysis is given in Fig. 4.7. Carrying out the semantic trip we obtain (22a), which is logically equivalent to (22b).

(22) a. $(\lambda x \lambda y \lambda z (past\ x\ (y\ z))\ (the\ barn)\ \lambda w (race\ w)\ (the\ horse))$
      b. $(past\ (the\ barn)\ (race\ (the\ horse)))$

The analysis of (13b) is less straightforward. Whereas in (13a) 'raced' expresses a one-place predication ('go quickly'), in (13b) it expresses a two-place predication (there was some agent racing the horse); 'horse' is modified by an agentless passive participle, but the adverbial 'past the barn' is modifying 'race'. Within the confines of the Lambek calculus the characterization we offer assumes the lexical assignment to the passive participle given in the following.[7]

---

[7] In general grammar requires the expressivity of more powerful categorial logics than just Lambek calculus (see Part II); however, so far as we are aware, the characterizations we offer within the Lambek calculus bear the same properties with regard to our processing considerations as their more

(23) **fell**   : $N \backslash S+$: *fall*

      raced : $((CN \backslash CN)/(N \backslash (N \backslash S-))) \bullet (N \backslash (N \backslash S-))$

               : $(\lambda x \lambda y \lambda z [(y\ z) \wedge \exists w (x\ z\ w)],\ race2)$

Here 'raced' is classified as the product of an untensed transitive verbal type, which can be modified by the adverbial 'past the barn' by composition, and an adnominalizer of this transitive verbal type. According to this, (13b) has the proof net analysis given in Fig. 4.8. The semantics extracted is (24a), equivalent to (24b)

(24) a. $(fall\ (the\ (\pi_1 (\lambda x \lambda y \lambda z [(y\ z) \wedge \exists w (x\ z\ w)],\ race2)\ \lambda n \lambda o (\lambda u \lambda v \lambda w (past\ u\ (v\ w))$
         $(the\ barn)\ \lambda r (((\pi_2 (\lambda p \lambda s \lambda t [(s\ t) \wedge \exists q (p\ t\ q)],\ race2)\ n\ r)\ o) horse))))$

      b. $(fall\ (the\ \lambda x [(horse\ x) \wedge \exists y (past\ (the\ barn)\ (race2\ x\ y))]))$

Let us assign to each proof net analysis a complexity profile which indicates, before and after each word, the number of unmatched literals, that is unresolved valencies or dependencies, according to the processing up to that point. This is a measure of the course of memory load in optimal incremental processing. We are not concerned here with the resolution of lexical ambiguity or serial backtracking: we are supposing sufficient resources that the non-determinism of selection of lexical entries and their parallel consideration is not the critical burden. Rather, the question is: which among parallel competing analyses places the least load on memory?

    The complexity profile is easily read off a completed proof net: the complexity in between two words is the number of axiom links bridging over at that point. Thus for (13a) and (13b) analysed in Figs. 4.7 and 4.8 the complexity profiles are as follows:

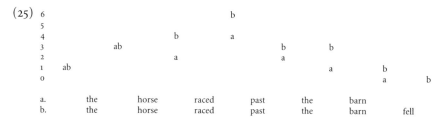

We see that after the first words the complexity of the correct analysis of (13b) is consistently higher than that of its garden path (13a), just as would be expected on the assumption that in (13b) the less costly but incorrect analysis is salient.

sophisticated categorial logic refinements, because the latter concern principally generalizations of word order, whereas the semantic dependencies on which our complexity metric depends remain the same.

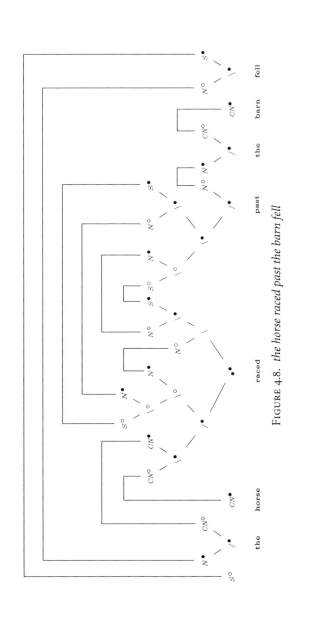

FIGURE 4.8. *the horse raced past the barn fell*

4.5 Predicting performance

4.5.1 Centre embedding unacceptability

Turning now to the performance phenomenon mentioned at the beginning of the chapter, for subject and object relativization we assume the relative pronoun lexical assignments (26).

(26) **that** : $(CN\backslash CN)/(N\backslash S+)$: $\lambda x \lambda y \lambda z[(y\ z) \wedge (x\ z)]$
　　　that : $(CN\backslash CN)/(S+/N)$: $\lambda x \lambda y \lambda z[(y\ z) \wedge (x\ z)]$

Sentence (1b) is analysed in Fig. 4.9. Sentence (2b) is analysed in Fig. 4.10. Let us compare the complexities:

(27)
```
9                                          b
8                                      b
7                       b   b
6                   b
5                                          b
4           ab  ab              a   a
3       ab              a   a           a   a
2                                               ab
1   ab
0                                                   ab

    a. the  dog   that chased the cat  that saw the rat  barked
    b. the  cheese that the   rat that the  cat saw ate  stank
```

Again, the profile of (2b) is higher.[8] We suggest that this is what causes the unacceptability of centre embedding.

4.5.2 Left-to-right quantifier scope preference

Left-to-right quantifier scope preference is illustrated by:

(28) a. Someone loves everyone.
　　　b. Everyone is loved by someone.

Both sentences exhibit both quantifier scopings:

(29) a. $\exists x \forall y (love\ y\ x)$
　　　b. $\forall y \exists x (love\ y\ x)$

However, while the dominant reading of (28a) is (29a), that of (28b) is (29b), that is, the preference is for the first quantifier to have wider scope. Note that the same effect is observed when the quantifiers are swapped:

(30) a. Everyone loves someone.
　　　b. Someone is loved by everyone.

---

[8] Indeed it rises above 7–8, thus reaching what are usually taken to be the limits of short-term memory.

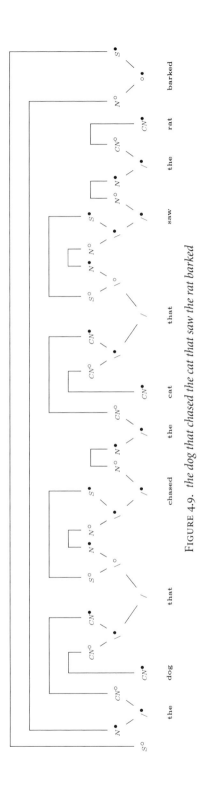

FIGURE 4.9. *the dog that chased the cat that saw the rat barked*

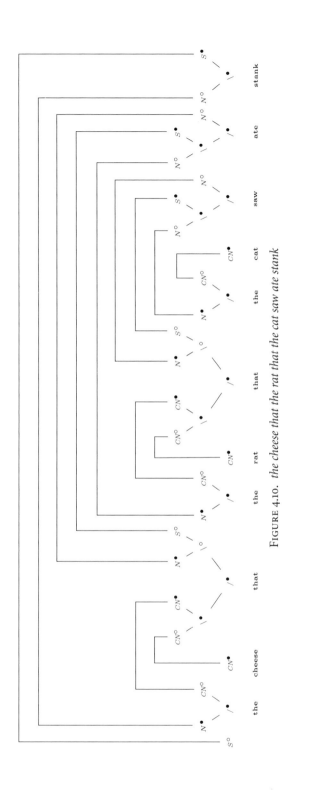

FIGURE 4.10. *the cheese that the rat that the cat saw ate stank*

While both sentences in (30) have both quantifier scopings, the preferred readings give the first quantifier wide scope.

A rudimentary account of sentence-peripheral quantifier phrase scoping is obtained in Lambek categorial grammar by means of lexical assignments such as the following (for a more refined treatment, without lexical ambiguity, see Chapter 6):

(31)   **everyone** : $St/(N\backslash St)$: $\lambda x \forall y(x\ y)$
       everyone : $(St/N)\backslash St$: $\lambda x \forall y(x\ y)$
       someone : $St/(N\backslash St)$: $\lambda x \exists y(x\ y)$
       someone : $(St/N)\backslash St$: $\lambda x \exists y(x\ y)$

Then one analysis of (28a) is that given in Fig. 4.11. This is the subject wide scope analysis: its extracted and simplified semantics is as in (32).

(32)   a. $(\lambda x \exists y(x\ y)\ \lambda u(\lambda x \forall y(x\ y)\ \lambda v(love\ v\ u)))$
       b. $\exists x \forall y(love\ y\ x)$

A second analysis is that given in Fig. 4.12. This is the object wide scope analysis: its extracted and simplified semantics is as in (33).

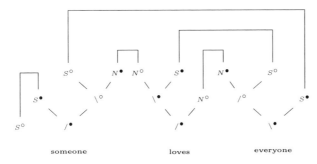

FIGURE 4.11. *someone loves everyone* ($\exists\forall$)

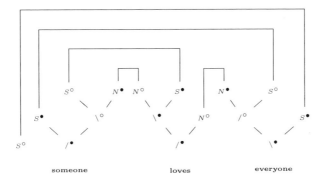

FIGURE 4.12. *someone loves everyone* ($\forall\exists$)

(33) a. $(\lambda x \forall y(x \ y) \ \lambda v(\lambda x \exists y(x \ y) \ \lambda u(love \ v \ u)))$
      b. $\forall y \exists x (love \ y \ x)$

Let us compare the complexity profiles of the two readings:

(34) 4   b
      3   ab
      2   a
      1   ab
      0   ab

      a.   ∃∀ (subject wide scope, Fig. 4.11)
            someone   loves   everyone
      b.   ∀∃ (object wide scope, Fig. 4.12)

At the only point of difference the subject wide scope reading, the preferred reading, has the lower complexity.

For the passive (28b) let there be assignments as in (35). The preposition 'by' projects an agentive adverbial phrase; 'is' is a functor over (post-)nominal modifiers (*the man outside, John is outside*, etc.) and passive 'loved' is treated exactly like passive 'raced' in (23).

(35) **by** : $((N\backslash S-)\backslash (N\backslash S-))/N$: $\lambda x \lambda y \lambda z[[z = x] \wedge (y \ z)]$
      is : $(N\backslash S+)/(CN\backslash CN)$: $\lambda x \lambda y(x \ \lambda z[z = y] \ y)$
      loved : $((CN\backslash CN)/(N\backslash (N\backslash S-)))\bullet (N\backslash (N\backslash S-))$
            : $(\lambda x \lambda y \lambda z[(y \ z) \wedge \exists w(x \ z \ w)], \ love)$

A ∀∃ analysis of (28b) is given in Fig. 4.13. This has semantics, after some simplification, as in (36), which is equivalent to (33).

(36) $\forall x \exists y \exists z[[y = z] \wedge (love \ x \ y)]$

An ∃∀ analysis of (28b) is given in Fig. 4.14. This has semantics, after some simplification, as in (37), which is equivalent to (32).

(37) $\exists y \forall x \exists z[[z = y] \wedge (love \ x \ z)]$

Again, the preferred reading has the lower complexity profile:

(38) 6   b
      5
      4   b   b   a
      3   ab
      2   a   a
      1   ab
      0   ab

      a.   ∀∃ (Fig. 4.13)
            everyone   is   loved   by   someone
      b.   ∃∀ (Fig. 4.14)

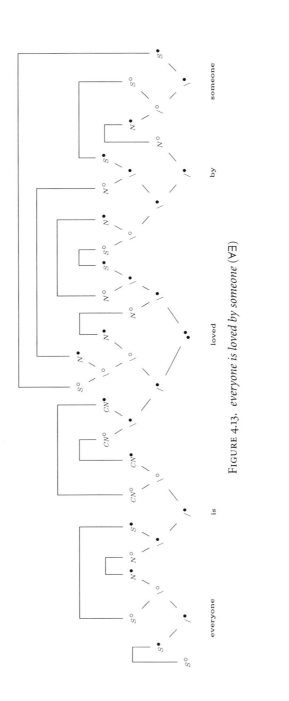

FIGURE 4.13. *everyone is loved by someone* (∃∀)

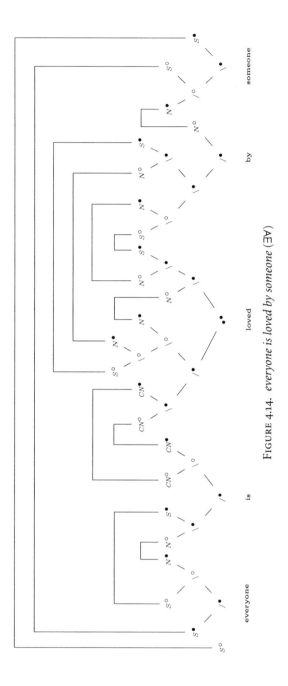

FIGURE 4.14. *everyone is loved by someone* (∀∃)

4.5.3 Preference for lower attachment

Kimball (1973: 27) observes that in a sentence such as (39), three ways ambiguous according to the attachment of the adverb, the lower the attachment is, the higher the preference (what he terms 'Right Association').

(39)   Joe said that Martha believed that Ingrid fell today.

In Fig. 4.15 we give the analyses for the highest, the middle, and the lowest attachments. (We now abbreviate proof nets by flattening formula trees into their linear representations; since this conceals the order switching of output links in this notation the axiom links may cross, belying the underlying planarity.) The complexity profiles are:

```
(40)  6                              c                    bc
      5                  c    c              bc    bc
      4                                                   abc
      3
      2          abc              ab                a
      1   abc         ab    ab              a    a
      0                                                        abc

      a.                                                  lowest attachment
      b. Joe  said  that  Martha  believed  that  Ingrid  fell  today   middle attachment
      c.                                                  highest attachment
```

The same effect occurs strongly in (41), where the preferred reading is the one given by the lowest attachment, even though that one is the nonsensical reading.

(41)   the book that shocked Mary's title

The analyses are given in Fig. 4.16. The complexities are thus:

```
(42)  4                      a    a
      3              a                  a
      2                 b    b               ab
      1       ab   b                b         ab
      0                                           ab

      a.                                       sensical
         the  book  that  shocked  Mary  's  title
      b.                                       nonsensical
```

4.5.4 Heavy noun phrase shift

Our account appears to explain the preference for heavy noun phrases to appear at the end of the verb phrase (heavy noun phrase shift). Of the following the second is more acceptable:

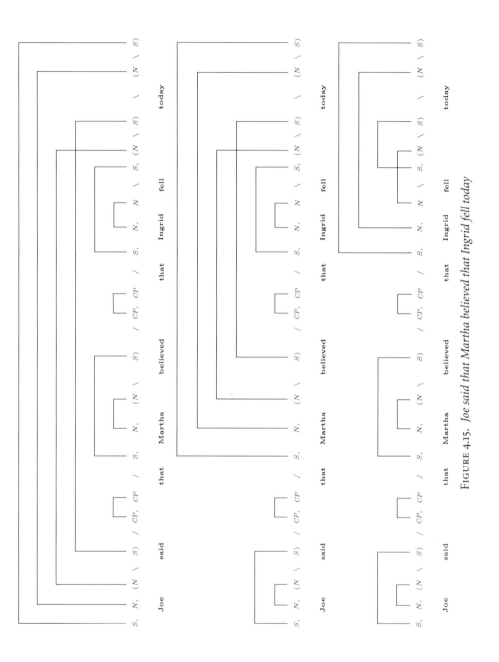

FIGURE 4.15. *Joe said that Martha believed that Ingrid fell today*

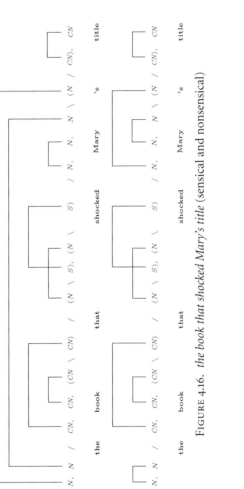

FIGURE 4.16. *the book that shocked Mary's title* (sensical and nonsensical)

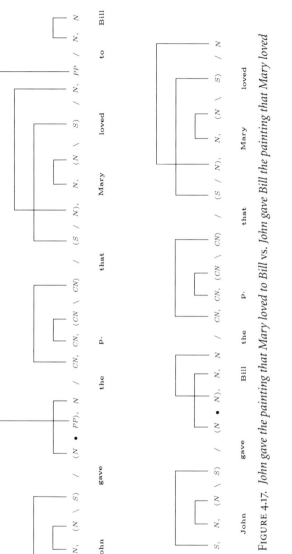

FIGURE 4.17. *John gave the painting that Mary loved to Bill vs. John gave Bill the painting that Mary loved*

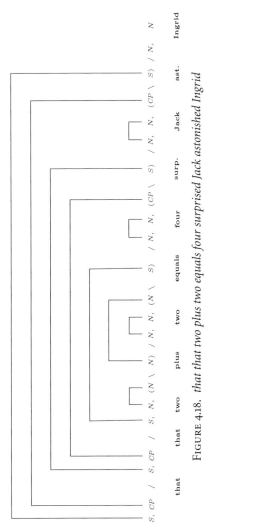

FIGURE 4.18. *that that two plus two equals four surprised Jack astonished Ingrid*

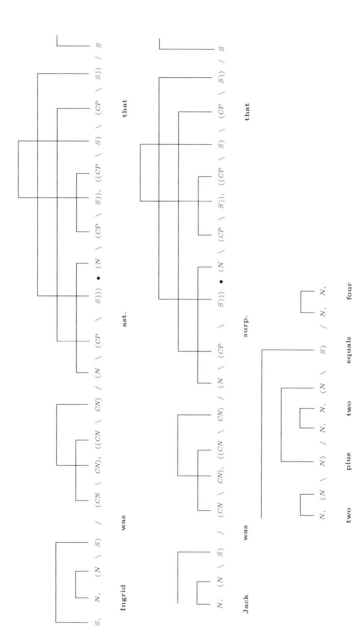

FIGURE 4.19. *Ingrid was astonished that Jack was surprised that two plus two equals four*

7													
6													
5			a										
4		a	b	a		a							
3							ab		b				
2	a	b			a			a	ab	b			
1	b			b		b				a	a	b	
0	ab											a	b	b

a. | that | two | plus | two | equals | four | surp. | jack | ast. | Ingrid |
| | was | ast. | that | Jack | was | surp. | that | two | plus | two | equals | four |

b. | that | was | that | Jack | was | surp. | that | two | plus | two | equals | four |

FIGURE 4.20. Complexity profiles for active and passive nested sentential subjects

(43) a. ?John gave the painting that Mary loved to Bill.
      b. John gave Bill the painting that Mary loved.

The analyses are given in Fig. 4.17. The complexities are thus:

(44)
```
4                                         a
3                       a       a              b
2        ab    ab    a               b    b
1    ab              b    b                    a     a
0                                         b    a
     a.  John  gave  the   painting  that   Mary  loved  to    Bill
     b.  John  gave  Bill  the       painting  that   Mary  loved
```

4.5.5 Preference for passivization of nested sentential subjects

A final dramatic example of unacceptability is provided by the following:

(45) a. That two plus two equals four surprised Jack.
      b. ?That that two plus two equals four surprised Jack astonished Ingrid.
      c. ??That that that two plus two equals four surprised Jack astonished Ingrid bothered Frank.

The passive paraphrases, however, seem more or less equally acceptable:

(46) a. Jack was surprised that two plus two equals four.
      b. Ingrid was astonished that Jack was surprised that two plus two equals four.
      c. Frank was bothered that Ingrid was astonished that Jack was surprised that two plus two equals four.

This is puzzling, since just about any theory of processing would expect passives to be no more acceptable than actives. For example, Clark and Clark (1977: 144) cite such examples as reasons for the abandonment of the theory of derivational complexity in transformational grammar.

Let us consider the predictions of our theory. In Fig. 4.18 we give the analysis of (45b) and in Fig. 4.19 that of (46b). It is very interesting to observe that in accordance with the actual acceptabilities the complexity profile of the latter is in general lower even though the analysis has more than twice the total number of links; the complexity profiles are given in Fig. 4.20.

Part II
Logical Categorial Grammar

The Lambek calculus is multiplicative non-commutative intuitionistic linear logic without empty antecedents. As a logic it enjoys good properties, but its range of linguistic application is restricted. Therefore we want to extend the calculus whilst keeping its good properties. To increase the range of application of categorial grammar, it is natural to enrich the Lambek calculus with other non-commutative intuitionistic linear connectives. We call the result of so doing *logical categorial grammar*.

In Chapter 5 we consider non-normal modalities (bracket operators) for islands and extraction, including parasitic extraction. Chapter 6 presents *discontinuous Lambek calculus*, containing discontinuity operators for syntax/semantics mismatch. Chapter 7 presents additives for polymorphism. Chapter 8 presents normal modalities for intensionality.

5

Bracket operators for extraction

The following examples illustrate subject relativization, right-peripheral object relativization, and medial relativization, respectively:

(1) a. man who loves Mary
     b. woman who John loves
     c. man who Mary saw today

Relativization exemplifies extraction non-adjacency in grammar. The Lambek calculus can handle cases of the kind in (1a) by assigning the relative pronoun type $(CN \backslash CN)/(N \backslash S)$ and cases of the kind in (1b) by assigning the relative pronoun type $(CN \backslash CN)/(S/N)$. However, cases of the kind in (1c) resist characterization in the unextended Lambek calculus. Still more complex is parasitic extraction as follows, where the filler binds more than one gap:

(2) paper which I filed without reading

Morrill (1992), Moortgat (1995), and Fadda and Morrill (2005) define what we call here bracket operators for Lambek calculus.[1] These are kinds of non-normal modalities.[2] In this chapter we present, in terms of bracket operators, a general account of extraction as exemplified by relativization.

In Section 5.1 we outline the theory of bracket operators and in Section 5.2 we describe a first application of basic bracket operators, namely to defining

---

[1] Moortgat (1995) corrects Morrill (1992) which erroneously invoked antibracket configurations for $[]^{-1}L$.

[2] 'Non-normal' because they do not obey distribution: $\Box(A \rightarrow B) \Rightarrow \Box A \rightarrow \Box B$.

island constraints. In Section 5.3 we describe how a generalization to *structural* bracket operators enables medial extraction. In Section 5.4 we discuss how a grammar may be attuned to assign degrees of grammaticality in relation to island constraints. In Section 5.5 we extend our account of relativization to include parasitic extraction.

5.1 Theory

Let us extend the definition of types $\mathbf{F}$ with two unary modalities $\langle\rangle$ ('bracket') and $[\,]^{-1}$ ('antibracket'); in terms of a set $\mathbf{P}$ of atomic type formulas:

(3) $\mathbf{F} ::= \mathbf{P} \mid \mathbf{F}{\bullet}\mathbf{F} \mid \mathbf{F}\backslash\mathbf{F} \mid \mathbf{F}/\mathbf{F} \mid \langle\rangle\mathbf{F} \mid [\,]^{-1}\mathbf{F}$

We allow ourselves to omit parentheses under the convention that unary connectives bind more tightly than binary connectives. Partially ordered algebraic models for the Lambek calculus were proposed in Došen (1985), which proves completeness of $\mathbf{L}$ for partially ordered semigroups. Buszkowski (1986) provides a simplified proof of the same result, (and a strengthening to the case of plain semigroups). Here we shall consider such syntactical models for the Lambek calculus with brackets.

(4)   DEFINITION (*Partially ordered bracket semigroup*). A *partially ordered bracket semigroup* (p.o. b-semigroup) is a structure $(L, +, b; \leq)$ of arity $(2, 1; 2)$ such that:

- $(L, +)$ is a semigroup, i.e.
  $$s_1+(s_2+s_3) = (s_1+s_2)+s_3 \qquad \text{associativity}$$

- $(L; \leq)$ is a partial order, i.e.
  $$s \leq s \qquad\qquad\qquad\qquad\qquad \text{reflexivity}$$
  $$s_1 \leq s_3 \quad \text{if } s_1 \leq s_2 \text{ and } s_2 \leq s_3 \quad \text{transitivity}$$
  $$s_1 = s_2 \quad \text{if } s_1 \leq s_2 \text{ and } s_2 \leq s_1 \quad \text{antisymmetry}$$

- $\leq$ is compatible with $+$ and b, i.e.
  $$s_1+s_3 \leq s_2+s_4 \text{ if } s_1 \leq s_2 \text{ and } s_3 \leq s_4$$
  $$b(s_1) \leq b(s_2) \text{ if } s_1 \leq s_2$$

We say that a subset D of the domain L is *downward closed* if and only if for all $s, s' \in L$, if $s \in D$ & $s' \leq s$ then $s' \in D$.

    An *interpretation* comprises a p.o. b-semigroup $(L, +, b; \leq)$ and a valuation F mapping from $\mathbf{P}$ into $\leq$-downward closed subsets of L. Then the value $[\![A]\!]_F$ induced for each type A is:

(5) $[[P]]_F = F(P)$ for atomic P

$[[A \bullet B]]_F = \{s_3 | \exists s_1 \in [[A]]_F, s_2 \in [[B]]_F, s_3 \le s_1 + s_2\}$

$[[A \backslash C]]_F = \{s_2 | \forall s_1 \in [[A]]_F, s_1 + s_2 \in [[C]]_F\}$

$[[C/B]]_F = \{s_1 | \forall s_2 \in [[B]]_F, s_1 + s_2 \in [[C]]_F\}$

$[[\langle \rangle A]]_F = \{s_2 | \exists s_1 \in [[A]]_F, s_2 \le b(s_1)\}$

$[[[\ ]^{-1}B]]_F = \{s_1 | b(s_1) \in [[B]]_F\}$

Let us extend the definition of antecedent configurations **O** to include brackets:

(6) **O** ::= **F** | **O**, **O** | [**O**]

Then the Gentzen sequent calculus of the Lambek calculus with brackets **Lb** is as shown in Fig. 5.1. Moortgat (1995) proves that this calculus enjoys Cut-elimination. Just as the structure $(\mathbf{F}, \backslash, \bullet, /; \Rightarrow)$ of arity $(2, 2, 2; 2)$ forms a *residuated triple* (see Appendix A), the structure $(\mathbf{F}, \langle \rangle, [\ ]^{-1}; \Rightarrow)$ of arity $(1, 1; 2)$ forms a *residuated pair* since it satifies the residuation property $A \Rightarrow \langle \rangle B$ if and only if $[\ ]^{-1} A \Rightarrow B$, or equivalently:

(7) $\langle \rangle [\ ]^{-1} A \Rightarrow A \Rightarrow [\ ]^{-1} \langle \rangle A$

$$\frac{}{A \Rightarrow A} id \qquad \frac{\Gamma \Rightarrow A \quad \Delta(A) \Rightarrow B}{\Delta(\Gamma) \Rightarrow B} Cut$$

$$\frac{\Gamma \Rightarrow A \quad \Delta(C) \Rightarrow D}{\Delta(\Gamma, A \backslash C) \Rightarrow D} \backslash L \qquad \frac{A, \Gamma \Rightarrow C}{\Gamma \Rightarrow A \backslash C} \backslash R$$

$$\frac{\Gamma \Rightarrow B \quad \Delta(C) \Rightarrow D}{\Delta(C/B, \Gamma) \Rightarrow D} /L \qquad \frac{\Gamma, B \Rightarrow C}{\Gamma \Rightarrow C/B} /R$$

$$\frac{\Delta(A, B) \Rightarrow D}{\Delta(A \bullet B) \Rightarrow D} \bullet L \qquad \frac{\Gamma \Rightarrow A \quad \Delta \Rightarrow B}{\Gamma, \Delta \Rightarrow A \bullet B} \bullet R$$

$$\frac{\Delta([A]) \Rightarrow B}{\Delta(\langle \rangle A) \Rightarrow B} \langle \rangle L \qquad \frac{\Gamma \Rightarrow A}{[\Gamma] \Rightarrow \langle \rangle A} \langle \rangle R$$

$$\frac{\Delta(A) \Rightarrow B}{\Delta([[\ ]^{-1} A]) \Rightarrow B} [\ ]^{-1} L \qquad \frac{[\Gamma] \Rightarrow A}{\Gamma \Rightarrow [\ ]^{-1} A} [\ ]^{-1} R$$

FIGURE 5.1. The Lambek calculus with brackets **Lb**

Exercise 5.1. Prove the residuation triple and residuation pair laws in the sequent calculus of **Lb**.

Kurtonina (1995) (cf. Morrill 1992) proves that the following translation faithfully embeds the non-associative Lambek calculus **NL** of Lambek (1961) into the Lambek calculus with brackets **Lb**, i.e. $\vdash_{NL} \Gamma \Rightarrow A$ if and only if $\vdash_{Lb} |\Gamma| \Rightarrow |A|$:

(8) $|[\Gamma, \Delta]| = [|\Gamma|, |\Delta|]$

  $|A\backslash B| = |A|\backslash [\;]^{-1}|B|$

  $|B/A| = [\;]^{-1}|B|/|A|$

  $|A \bullet B| = \langle\rangle(|A|\bullet|B|)$

The sequent calculus is sound with respect to the plain (and partially ordered) syntactical models. Fadda and Morrill (2005) prove that it is complete with respect to the partially ordered models. So far as we know, it is an open question whether it is complete with respect to the plain syntactical models.

5.2 Application

Left extraction such as interrogativization, topicalization, and relativization is unbounded in distance:

(9)   a. man who Mary loves
  b. man who John knows that Mary loves
  c. man who Bill knows that John knows that Mary loves
  d. man who John knows that Bill knows that John knows that Mary loves ...

The relative pronoun type $(CN\backslash CN)/(S/N)$ admits the unboundedness of relativization.

Exercise 5.2. Derive (9b).

5.2.1 Island brackets

However, although left extraction such as relativization can take place over an unboundedly long distance, it is not unconstrained. Certain constituents are *islands* to extraction (Ross, 1967). For example, adverbial phrases (Adverbial Island Constraint), coordinate structures (Coordinate Structure Constraint), and relative clauses themselves (*wh*-Island Constraint) are islands:

(10)   a. ?the paper that$_i$ John slept [without reading e_i]
  b. ??the man that$_i$ [John laughed and Mary likes e_i]
  c. ??the man that$_i$ Bill met the woman [who loves e_i]

Adverbial phrases are referred to as *weak* islands, since extraction from them is semi-acceptable. Coordinate structures and relative clauses are referred to as *strong* islands, since extraction from them is distinctly still less acceptable. Morrill (1992) proposed projecting islands using bracket operators. For example:

(11) **without** : $((N\backslash S)\backslash(N\backslash S))/\langle\rangle(N\backslash S)$
     and   : $(S\backslash[\,]^{-1}[\,]^{-1}S)/S$
     who   : $(CN\backslash CN)/\langle\rangle\langle\rangle(N\backslash S)$

Here, we encode weak islandhood and strong islandhood by projecting single bracketing and double bracketing respectively. Thus, for example, to be generated, *John walks without reading Ulysses* must have the (single) bracketing as follows:

(12)
$$\cfrac{\cfrac{\cfrac{\cfrac{N\Rightarrow N \quad N\backslash S\Rightarrow N\backslash S}{(N\backslash S)/N,\,N\Rightarrow N\backslash S}\,/L}{[(N\backslash S)/N,\,N]\Rightarrow\langle\rangle(N\backslash S)}\,\langle\rangle R \quad\quad \cfrac{N\backslash S\Rightarrow N\backslash S \quad \cfrac{N\Rightarrow N \quad S\Rightarrow S}{N,\,N\backslash S\Rightarrow S}\,\backslash L}{N,\,N\backslash S,\,(N\backslash S)\backslash(N\backslash S)\Rightarrow S}\,\backslash L}{\underset{\underset{\text{John, walks,}}{N\quad N\backslash S}\quad\underset{\text{without}}{((N\backslash S)\backslash(N\backslash S))/\langle\rangle(N\backslash S)}\quad\underset{\text{, [reading, Ulysses]}}{(N\backslash S)/N\quad N}}{}\Rightarrow S}\,/L}$$

But then (10a) is not generated because the island bracketing blocks the associativity by which the hypothetical gap subtype projected by the relative pronoun would have to position itself to be able to satisfy the valency within the adverbial phrase; where R abbreviates $CN\backslash CN$:

(13)
$$\cfrac{\cfrac{\cfrac{N,\,N\backslash S,\,((N\backslash S)\backslash(N\backslash S))/\langle\rangle(N\backslash S),\,[(N\backslash S)/N,\,N]\Rightarrow S}{N,\,N\backslash S,\,((N\backslash S)\backslash(N\backslash S))/\langle\rangle(N\backslash S),\,[(N\backslash S)/N],\,N\Rightarrow S}\,*}{N,\,N\backslash S,\,((N\backslash S)\backslash(N\backslash S))/\langle\rangle(N\backslash S),\,[(N\backslash S)/N]\Rightarrow S/N}\,/R \quad\quad R\Rightarrow R}{\underset{\underset{\text{that , John, slept,}}{R/(S/N)\quad N\quad N\backslash S}\quad\underset{\text{without}}{((N\backslash S)\backslash(N\backslash S))/\langle\rangle(N\backslash S)}\quad\underset{\text{, [reading]}}{(N\backslash S)/N}}{}\Rightarrow R}\,/L$$

5.3 Medial extraction

In the 1990s there was much interest within categorial grammar in the recourse of 'multimodality' (Moortgat, 1997; Oehrle, 1999; Morrill, 1994). This technique consists in multiplying residuated families of (unary or binary) connectives, perhaps with varying structural rules. In this section we adopt this strategy in relation to bracket operators, obtaining a variant structural bracket operator for medial extraction.

The relative pronoun type $(CN\backslash CN)/(S/N)$ fails to generate non-peripheral (*medial*) extraction:

(14)   the man who$_i$ John saw e_i today

(15)
$$\cfrac{\cfrac{\cfrac{\cfrac{N, (N\backslash S)/N, N, (N\backslash S)\backslash(N\backslash S) \Rightarrow S}{N, (N\backslash S)/N, (N\backslash S)\backslash(N\backslash S), N \Rightarrow S} \, *}{N, (N\backslash S)/N, (N\backslash S)\backslash(N\backslash S) \Rightarrow S/N} \, /R \qquad N/CN, CN, CN\backslash CN \Rightarrow N}{N/CN, CN, (CN\backslash CN)/(S/N), N, (N\backslash S)/N, (N\backslash S)\backslash(N\backslash S) \Rightarrow N}} \, /L$$

To obtain medial extraction we will assume another family $\{\langle_i\rangle, [_i]^{-1}\}$ of bracket operators, but this time with structural properties (Moortgat, 1999; cf. Barry *et al.*, 1991). We now assume types and configurations as follows:

(16) $\mathbf{F} ::= \mathbf{P} \mid \mathbf{F} \bullet \mathbf{F} \mid \mathbf{F} \backslash \mathbf{F} \mid \mathbf{F}/\mathbf{F} \mid \langle \rangle F \mid [\,]^{-1}F \mid \langle_i\rangle F \mid [_i]^{-1}F$

(17) $\mathbf{O} ::= \mathbf{F} \mid \mathbf{O}, \mathbf{O} \mid [\mathbf{O}] \mid [_i\mathbf{O}]$

The two families of unary operators will be interpreted by unary residuation with respect to the two unary functions in a syntactical frame $(L, +, b, i; \leq)$ of arity $(2, 1, 1; 2)$. The new structural bracket operator has the logical rules of bracket operators, conditioned on its own structural connector $[_i \cdot]$:

(18)
$$\cfrac{\Delta([_i A]) \Rightarrow B}{\Delta(\langle_i\rangle A) \Rightarrow B} \, \langle_i\rangle L \qquad\qquad \cfrac{\Gamma \Rightarrow A}{[_i\Gamma] \Rightarrow \langle_i\rangle A} \, \langle_i\rangle R$$

$$\cfrac{\Delta(A) \Rightarrow B}{\Delta([_i[_i]^{-1}A]) \Rightarrow B} \, [_i]^{-1}L \qquad\qquad \cfrac{[_i\Gamma] \Rightarrow A}{\Gamma \Rightarrow [_i]^{-1}A} \, [_i]^{-1}R$$

However, in addition we have structural rules, corresponding to the frame condition $i(s_1)+s_2 = s_2+i(s_1)$:

(19)
$$\cfrac{\Delta([_i\Gamma_1], \Gamma_2) \Rightarrow A}{\Delta(\Gamma_2, [_i\Gamma_1]) \Rightarrow A} \, P_i \qquad\qquad \cfrac{\Delta(\Gamma_2, [_i\Gamma_1]) \Rightarrow A}{\Delta([_i\Gamma_1], \Gamma_2) \Rightarrow A} \, P_i$$

We now assign the relative pronoun type $(CN\backslash CN)/(S/\langle_i\rangle[_i]^{-1}N)$. This continues to generate peripheral extraction:

(20)   the son who$_i$ the father loves e_i

(21)
$$\dfrac{\dfrac{\dfrac{\dfrac{N/CN, CN, (N\backslash S)/N, N \Rightarrow S}{N/CN, CN, (N\backslash S)/N, [_{i}[_{i}]^{-1}N] \Rightarrow S}\; [_{i}]^{-1}L}{N/CN, CN, (N\backslash S)/N, \langle_{i}\rangle[_{i}]^{-1}N \Rightarrow S}\; \langle_{i}\rangle L}{N/CN, CN, (N\backslash S)/N \Rightarrow S/\langle_{i}\rangle[_{i}]^{-1}N}\; /R \qquad N/CN, CN, CN\backslash CN \Rightarrow N}{N/CN, CN, (CN\backslash CN)/(S/\langle_{i}\rangle[_{i}]^{-1}N), N/CN, CN, (N\backslash S)/N \Rightarrow S}\; /L$$

However, it now additionally generates medial extraction as in (14):

(22)
$$\dfrac{\dfrac{\dfrac{\dfrac{\dfrac{N, (N\backslash S)/N, N, (N\backslash S)\backslash(N\backslash S) \Rightarrow S}{N, (N\backslash S)/N, [_{i}[_{i}]^{-1}N], (N\backslash S)\backslash(N\backslash S) \Rightarrow S}\; \langle_{i}\rangle L}{N, (N\backslash S)/N, (N\backslash S)\backslash(N\backslash S), [_{i}[_{i}]^{-1}N] \Rightarrow S}\; P_{i}}{N, (N\backslash S)/N, (N\backslash S)\backslash(N\backslash S), \langle_{i}\rangle[_{i}]^{-1}N \Rightarrow S}\; \langle_{i}\rangle L}{N, (N\backslash S)/N, (N\backslash S)\backslash(N\backslash S) \Rightarrow S/\langle_{i}\rangle[_{i}]^{-1}N}\; /R \qquad N/CN, CN, CN\backslash CN \Rightarrow N}{N/CN, CN, (CN\backslash CN)/(S/\langle_{i}\rangle[_{i}]^{-1}N), N, (N\backslash S)/N, (N\backslash S)\backslash(N\backslash S) \Rightarrow N}\; /L$$

5.4 Semigrammaticality

Ordinary subjects are weak islands (Subject Condition; Chomsky, 1973) and sentential subjects are strong islands:

(23) a. ?the man who$_i$ [the friends of e_i] went to Paris
        b. ??the man who$_i$ [that Mary loves e_i] surprises Bill

Thus we henceforth mark ordinary subjects with single island brackets and sentential subjects with double island brackets:

(24) **went** : $(\langle\rangle N\backslash S)/PP$
       surprises : $(\langle\rangle\langle\rangle CP)/N$

To account for the semi-acceptability of extraction from weak islands, we assume further structural semirules:

(25) $\dfrac{\Delta([[_{i}\Gamma_{1}], \Gamma_{2}]) \Rightarrow A}{\Delta([_{i}\Gamma_{1}], [\Gamma_{2}]) \Rightarrow A}\; ? \qquad \dfrac{\Delta([\Gamma_{1}, [_{i}\Gamma_{2}]]) \Rightarrow A}{\Delta([\Gamma_{1}], [_{i}\Gamma_{2}]) \Rightarrow A}\; ?$

We assume that these rules are not strictly grammatical and that their use incurs a cost in ungrammaticality. As we are defining weak islands with single brackets, extraction from a weak island requires one structural semirule application, but as we are defining strong islands with double brackets, extraction from a strong island requires two structural semirule applications, hence its greater ungrammaticality.

Extraction from within two weak islands is similarly characterized as ??-:

(26) a. ??man who$_i$ [the fact that [the friends of e_i] slept] annoys John
      b. ??man who$_i$ [the fact that Mary left [without meeting e_i]] annoys John

Correspondingly, (27) are characterized as ???-:

(27) a. ???man who$_i$ [that Mary slept [without meeting e_i]] annoys John
      b. ???man who$_i$ [that [the friends of e_i] slept] annoys John

And so forth.

5.4.1 Subject extraction

The projection of island brackets on subjects predicts the *that*-trace effect (Fixed Subject Constraint; Bresnan, 1972; Chomsky and Lasnik, 1977):

(28) a. *man who$_i$ Mary believes that e_i walks
      b. $CN, (CN\backslash CN)/(S/\langle_i\rangle[_i]^{-1}N), [N], ((\langle\rangle N\backslash S)/CP, CP/S, \langle\rangle N\backslash S \Rightarrow N$

Because the entire embedded subject is missing, there is nowhere to put the brackets required by the subordinate verb. The structural semirules do not help since the problem is not one of penetrating island brackets, but of not having anywhere to place them at all.[3] Hence the total ungrammaticality of extraction of the subject of a complementized clause. On the other hand, extraction from the subject of a complementized clause is predicted to be semigrammatical, by one application of a structural semirule:

(29) a. ?the man who$_i$ Mary believes that [the friends of e_i] walk
      b. $N/CN, CN, (CN\backslash CN)/(S/\langle_i\rangle[_i]^{-1}N), [N], ((\langle\rangle N\backslash S)/CP, CP/S,$
         $[N/CN, CN, (CN\backslash CN)/N], \langle\rangle N\backslash S \Rightarrow N$

Extraction of the subject of an uncomplementized embedded clause is grammatical:

(30) the man who$_i$ Mary believes e_i walks

To license this we assume that the lexical entry of an equi raising verb is as follows:

(31) **believes** : $((\langle\rangle N\backslash S)/(N\bullet((\langle\rangle N\backslash S)) : \lambda x(believe\,(\pi_2 x\,\pi_1 x))$

---

[3] We do not have empty configurations, so we cannot have '$N/CN, CN, (CN\backslash CN)/(S/\langle_i\rangle[_i]^{-1}N), [N], ((\langle\rangle N\backslash S)/CP, CP/S, [\epsilon], \langle\rangle N\backslash S \Rightarrow N$'.

This predicts that extraction which is from the subject of an uncomplementized embedded clause is also fully grammatical:

(32)   the man who$_i$ Mary believes the friends of e_i walk

5.5 Parasitic extraction

Extraction from weak islands can become fully acceptable when accompanied by a cobound non-island extraction:

(33)   a. the man that$_i$ [the friends of e_i] admire e_i
       b. the paper that$_i$ John filed e_i [without reading e_i]

This is known as *parasitic extraction* (Ross, 1967; Taraldsen, 1979; Engdahl, 1983; Sag, 1983). The term comes from the idea that the gaps in the islands are licensed by or dependent or parasitic on the non-island host gaps. Note that in judging (10a) we even experience the pressure of parasiticy to force a transitive reading on the intransitive verb.

We assume here that as the term 'parasitic' suggests, a parasitic gap must fall within an island:

(34)   *the slave that$_i$ John sold e_i to e_i

To obtain parasitic extraction we further assume the following two structural rules (cf. Morrill, 2002a):

(35) $$\frac{\Delta([_i[_i\Gamma]], [_i\Gamma]) \Rightarrow A}{\Delta([_i\Gamma]) \Rightarrow A} C_i \qquad \frac{\Delta([\Gamma_1, [_i\Gamma_2]]) \Rightarrow A}{\Delta([[\Gamma_1]], [_i[_i[\Gamma_2]]]) \Rightarrow A} D_i$$

These correspond to the frame conditions $i(s) \le i(i(s))+i(s)$ and $b(b(s_1))+i(i(s_2)) \le b(s_1+i(s_2))$ respectively.

For example, (33a) is then generated as shown in Fig. 5.2. From root to leaf in our analysis, the controlled structural rule of contraction C_i first generates from a host gap subconfiguration $[_i[_i]^{-1}N]$ a second parasitic gap subconfiguration $[_i[_i[_i]^{-1}N]]$, while preserving the host gap configuration. The parasitic gap subconfiguration permutes to the periphery of a weak island, which must be marked by double brackets, and then the structural rule of distribution D_i cancels an island bracket against a structural bracket of the parasitic gap subconfiguration and in the process distributes the remaining island bracket over the parasitic gap subconfiguration, which has now become another host gap subconfiguration within the island. There it may satisfy a valency (as in Fig. 5.2), but it also may itself undergo C_i, so we predict that one parasitic gap can in turn be host to another:

$$\cfrac{\cfrac{\cfrac{\cfrac{\cfrac{\cfrac{\cfrac{\cfrac{[N/CN, CN, (CN\backslash CN)/N, N], (\langle\rangle N\backslash S)/N, N \Rightarrow S}{[N/CN, CN, (CN\backslash CN)/N, N], (\langle\rangle N\backslash S)/N, [_i[_i]^{-1}N] \Rightarrow S}\;[_i]^{-1}L}{[N/CN, CN, (CN\backslash CN)/N, [_i[_i]^{-1}N], (\langle\rangle N\backslash S)/N, [_i[_i]^{-1}N] \Rightarrow S}\;[_i]^{-1}L}{[[N/CN, CN, (CN\backslash CN)/N]], [_i[_i[_i]^{-1}N]], (\langle\rangle N\backslash S)/N, [_i[_i]^{-1}N] \Rightarrow S}\;D_i}{[[N/CN, CN, (CN\backslash CN)/N]], (\langle\rangle N\backslash S)/N, [_i[_i[_i]^{-1}N]], [_i[_i]^{-1}N] \Rightarrow S}\;P_i}{[[N/CN, CN, (CN\backslash CN)/N]], (\langle\rangle N\backslash S)/N, [_i[_i]^{-1}N] \Rightarrow S}\;C_i}{[[N/CN, CN, (CN\backslash CN)/N]], (\langle\rangle N\backslash S)/N, \langle_i\rangle[_i]^{-1}N \Rightarrow S}\;\langle_i\rangle L}{[[N/CN, CN, (CN\backslash CN)/N]], (\langle\rangle N\backslash S)/N \Rightarrow S/\langle_i\rangle[_i]^{-1}N}\;/R \qquad R \Rightarrow R}{R/(S/\langle_i\rangle[_i]^{-1}N), [[N/CN, CN, (CN\backslash CN)/N]], (\langle\rangle N\backslash S)/N \Rightarrow R}\;/L$$

FIGURE 5.2. Sequent derivation of parasitic extraction *that_i* [*the friends of e_i*] *admire e_i*

$$\left|\cfrac{\Delta([A]) \Rightarrow B}{\Delta(\langle\rangle A) \Rightarrow B}\;\langle\rangle L\right|_\phi \quad = \quad \left|\;\Delta([A]) \Rightarrow B\;\right|_\phi$$

$$\left|\cfrac{\Gamma \Rightarrow A}{[\Gamma] \Rightarrow \langle\rangle A}\;\langle\rangle R\right|_\phi \quad = \quad \left|\;\Gamma \Rightarrow A\;\right|_\phi$$

$$\left|\cfrac{\Delta(A) \Rightarrow B}{\Delta([[\,]^{-1}A]) \Rightarrow B}\;[\,]^{-1}L\right|_\phi \quad = \quad \left|\;\Delta(A) \Rightarrow B\;\right|_\phi$$

$$\left|\cfrac{[\Gamma] \Rightarrow A}{\Gamma \Rightarrow [\,]^{-1}A}\;[\,]^{-1}R\right|_\phi \quad = \quad \left|\;[\Gamma] \Rightarrow A\;\right|_\phi$$

FIGURE 5.3. Semantic readings of the island bracket proofs

(36) a. man who_i [the fact that [the friends of e_i] admire e_i] surprises e_i
      b. paper that_i the editor published e_i [without [the author of e_i] re-
          checking e_i]
      c. man who_i [the fact that [the friends of e_i] admire e_i [without prais-
          ing e_i]] surprises e_i

$$\left| \begin{array}{c} \vdots \\ \dfrac{\varDelta([_{\mathsf{i}}A]) \Rightarrow B}{\varDelta(\langle_{\mathsf{i}}\rangle A) \Rightarrow B} \; \langle_{\mathsf{i}}\rangle L \end{array} \right|_{\phi} = \mid \varDelta([_{\mathsf{i}}A]) \Rightarrow B \mid_{\phi}$$

$$\left| \begin{array}{c} \vdots \\ \dfrac{\Gamma \Rightarrow A}{[_{\mathsf{i}}\Gamma] \Rightarrow \langle_{\mathsf{i}}\rangle A} \; \langle_{\mathsf{i}}\rangle R \end{array} \right|_{\phi} = \mid \Gamma \Rightarrow A \mid_{\phi}$$

$$\left| \begin{array}{c} \vdots \\ \dfrac{\varDelta(A) \Rightarrow B}{\varDelta([_{\mathsf{i}}[_{\mathsf{i}}]^{-1}A]) \Rightarrow B} \; [_{\mathsf{i}}]^{-1}L \end{array} \right|_{\phi} = \mid \varDelta(A) \Rightarrow B \mid_{\phi}$$

$$\left| \begin{array}{c} \vdots \\ \dfrac{[_{\mathsf{i}}\Gamma] \Rightarrow A}{\Gamma \Rightarrow [_{\mathsf{i}}]^{-1}A} \; [_{\mathsf{i}}]^{-1}R \end{array} \right|_{\phi} = \mid [_{\mathsf{i}}\Gamma] \Rightarrow A \mid_{\phi}$$

$$\left| \begin{array}{c} \vdots \\ \dfrac{\varDelta([_{\mathsf{i}}\Gamma_1], \Gamma_2) \Rightarrow A}{\varDelta(\Gamma_2, [_{\mathsf{i}}\Gamma_1]) \Rightarrow A} \; P_{\mathsf{i}} \end{array} \right|_{\phi(\mu,\, \nu)} = \mid \varDelta([_{\mathsf{i}}\Gamma_1], \Gamma_2) \Rightarrow A \mid_{\phi(\nu,\mu)}$$

$$\left| \begin{array}{c} \vdots \\ \dfrac{\varDelta(\Gamma_2, [_{\mathsf{i}}\Gamma_1]) \Rightarrow A}{\varDelta([_{\mathsf{i}}\Gamma_1], \Gamma_2) \Rightarrow A} \; P_{\mathsf{i}} \end{array} \right|_{\phi(\mu,\, \nu)} = \mid \varDelta(\Gamma_2, [_{\mathsf{i}}\Gamma_1]) \Rightarrow A \mid_{\phi(\nu,\mu)}$$

$$\left| \begin{array}{c} \vdots \\ \dfrac{\varDelta([_{\mathsf{i}}[_{\mathsf{i}}\Gamma]], _{\mathsf{i}}[\Gamma]) \Rightarrow A}{\varDelta([_{\mathsf{i}}\Gamma]) \Rightarrow A} \; C_{\mathsf{i}} \end{array} \right|_{\phi(\mu)} = \mid \varDelta([_{\mathsf{i}}[_{\mathsf{i}}\Gamma]], _{\mathsf{i}}[\Gamma]) \Rightarrow A \mid_{\phi(\mu,\mu)}$$

$$\left| \begin{array}{c} \vdots \\ \dfrac{\varDelta([\Gamma_1, [_{\mathsf{i}}\Gamma_2]]) \Rightarrow A}{\varDelta([[\Gamma_1]], [_{\mathsf{i}}[_{\mathsf{i}}\Gamma_2]]) \Rightarrow A} \; D_{\mathsf{i}} \end{array} \right|_{\phi} = \mid \varDelta([\Gamma_1, [_{\mathsf{i}}\Gamma_2]]) \Rightarrow A \mid_{\phi}$$

FIGURE 5.4. Semantic readings of the structural bracket proofs

However, because of the resource-consciousness of the cancellation of the structural rule of distribution $D_\uparrow$, according to our account successive parasitic gaps must each be within their own island, and cannot be within the same island. This prediction appears to be correct:

(37) *slave who$_i$ [the fact that John sold e_i to e_i] surprised e_i

We predict that strong islands do not allow parasitic gaps:

(38) ?man who$_i$ [that Mary likes e_i] surprises e_i

Postal (1993, (8a)) has an example of cobound traces where there does not appear to be an island:

(39) man who$_i$ Mary convinced e_i that John wanted to visit e_i

For such an example, we might assume an additional licensing lexical entry **convinced** : $[\,]^{-1}((N\backslash S)/CP)/N$.[4]

5.5.1 Semantics

We assume that the bracket operators are semantically transparent, thus:

(40) $T(\langle\,\rangle A) = T([\,]^{-1}A) = T(\langle_\uparrow\rangle A) = T([_\uparrow]^{-1}A) = T(A)$

We give the semantic readings of the bracket operators in Figs. 5.3 and 5.4.
  For example, where Π is the derivation of Fig. 5.2:

(41) $|\Pi|_{x_{\text{that}}, x_{\text{the}}, x_{\text{friends}}, x_{\text{of}}, x_{\text{admire}}} = (x_{\text{that}}\; \lambda x((x_{\text{admire}}\; x)\; (x_{\text{the}}\; ((x_{\text{of}}\; x)\; x_{\text{friends}}))))$

Substituting in lexical semantics and evaluating:

(42) $(\lambda x\lambda y\lambda z[(y\; z) \wedge (x\; z)]\; \lambda x((\textit{admire}\; x)\; (\textit{the}\; (\textit{of}\; x)\; \textit{friends}))) =$
    $\lambda y\lambda z[(y\; z) \wedge (\textit{admire}\; z\; (\textit{the}\; (\textit{of}\; z)\; \textit{friends}))]$

---

[4] Thanks to Tom Roeper (p.c.) for suggesting for this case that 'although there need not be an island, there could be one'.

6

Discontinuity operators

In this chapter we present a calculus for discontinuity, $(\omega\text{-})\mathbf{DL}$: discontinuous Lambek calculus. The calculus allows an unbounded number of points of discontinuity (hence the prefix ω-) and includes both deterministic and nondeterministic discontinuous connectives. We believe that it constitutes a general and natural extension of the Lambek calculus $\mathbf{L}$. Like the Lambek calculus it has a sequent calculus which is a sequence logic without structural rules, and it enjoys such properties as Cut-elimination, the subformula property and decidability.

By $n\text{-}\mathbf{DL}$ we refer to $\omega\text{-}\mathbf{DL}$ restricted to at most n points of discontinuity. $0\text{-}\mathbf{DL}$ is the original Lambek calculus $\mathbf{L}$. Of particular interest is $1\text{-}\mathbf{DL}$ in which the unicity of the point of discontinuity means that the deterministic and nondeterministic discontinuous connectives coincide. We illustrate $1\text{-}\mathbf{DL}$ with linguistic applications to medial extraction, discontinuous idioms, parentheticals, gapping, VP ellipsis, reflexivization, quantification, pied-piping, appositive relativization, comparative subdeletion, null operators, and right extraposition.[1] We further illustrate deterministic $2\text{-}\mathbf{DL}$ with linguistic application to anaphora, and nondeterministic $2\text{-}\mathbf{DL}$ with linguistic application to particle shift and complement alternation.

6.1 Introduction

A critical issue in natural grammar is 'discontinuity': syntax–semantics mismatch. Lambek categorial grammar is continuous, as is reflected in the planarity of its proof nets. Our aim here is to give a technically natural and

---

[1] For cross-serial dependencies see Morrill *et al.* (2009).

empirically wide-ranging adaptation of the continuous model of Lambek categorial grammar to discontinuity.

Ojeda (2006) identifies two early approaches to discontinuity as being 'permutation' (Chomsky, 1955: 405)[2] and 'wrapping' (Yngve 1960: 448). We have considered permutation via structural modalities in the previous chapter. In this chapter we develop the wrapping approach to discontinuity in logical categorial grammar. In Section 6.2 we present the theory of the discontinuous Lambek calculus, and hypersequent calculus and labelled natural deduction for **DL**. In Section 6.3 we present linguistic applications of discontinuous Lambek calculus.

6.2 Theory of discontinuous Lambek calculus

The key to our treatment of discontinuity is the notion of a 'separator' (Morrill, 2002b):

(1) DEFINITION (*graded syntactical algebra*). A *graded syntactical algebra* is a free algebra $(L, +, 0, 1)$ of arity $(2, 0, 0)$ such that $(L, +, 0)$ is a monoid and 1 is a prime. I.e. L is a set, $0, 1 \in L$ and $+$ is a binary operation on L such that for all $s_1, s_2, s_3, s \in L$,

$$s_1 + (s_2 + s_3) \quad = \quad (s_1 + s_2) + s_3 \text{ associativity}$$
$$0 + s = s = s + 0$$

The distinguished constant 1 is called a *separator*.

(2) DEFINITION (*sorts*). The *sorts* of discontinuous Lambek calculus are the naturals $0, 1, \ldots$. The sort $\sigma(s)$ of an element s of a graded syntactical algebra $(L, +, 0, 1)$ is defined by the morphism of monoids σ to the additive monoid of naturals defined thus:

$$\sigma(1) = 1$$
$$\sigma(a) = 0 \qquad \text{for a prime } a \neq 1$$
$$\sigma(s_1 + s_2) = \sigma(s_1) + \sigma(s_2)$$

That is, the sort of a syntactical element is simply the number of separators it contains; we require the separator 1 to be a prime and the graded syntactical algebra to be free in order to ensure the well-definedness of this definition by induction on the sort of syntactical objects. The fact that there is a homomorphism from a graded syntactical algebra to the additive monoid of naturals means that a graded syntactical algebra is an instance of what is known as a *graded* algebra, in particular a *graded monoid*.

[2] Chomsky (1965) revoked permutation in favour of copying and deletion.

(3) DEFINITION (*sorts*). The *sorts* of discontinuous Lambek calculus are the
naturals $0, 1, \ldots .$.

(4) DEFINITION (*sort domains*). Where $(L, +, 0, 1)$ is a graded syntactical
algebra, the *sort domains* L_i of sort i of discontinuous Lambek calculus
are defined as follows:

$$L_i = \{s \in L \mid \sigma(s) = i\}\ i \geq 0$$

(5) DEFINITION (*discontinuous syntactical structure*). The *discontinuous syntactical structure* defined by a graded syntactical algebra $(L, +, 0, 1)$ is the
ω-sorted structure

$$(\{L_i\}_{i \in \mathbb{N}}, \{U_k\}_{k \in \mathbb{Z}^+}, +, \{W_k\}_{k \in \mathbb{Z}^+}; U, W)$$

where:

operation or relation	is such that
$U_k : L_{i+1} \to L_i$	for all $s \in L$, $U_k(s)$ is the result of erasing the k-th separator from s
$+ : L_i \times L_j \to L_{i+j}$	as in the graded syntactical algebra
$W_k : L_{i+1} \times L_j \to L_{i+j}$	for all $s, t \in L$, $W_k(s, t)$ is the result of replac-ing the k-th separator in s by t
$U : L_{i+1} \times L_i$	it is the smallest relation such that for all $s_1, s_2 \in L$, $U(s_1 + 1 + s_2, s_1 + s_2)$
$W : L_{i+1} \times L_j \times L_{i+j}$	it is the smallest relation such that for all $s_1, s_2, s_3 \in L$, $W(s_1 + 1 + s_3, s_2, s_1 + s_2 + s_3)$

The types of discontinuous Lambek calculus are to be interpreted as subsets
of L according to a sorting discipline: a type of sort i will be interpreted as a
subset of L_i. The connectives and their syntactical interpretations are shown
in Fig. 6.1.[3] Note the constraints ensuring that no complex type contains the
empty element 0.[4]

The functionalities and relationalities of the operations and relations with
respect to which the connectives are defined fix the pattern between the types
and the sorts. Sets $\mathbf{F}_i$ of types of sort i for each sort i are defined on the
basis of sets $\mathbf{P}_i$ of primitive types of sort i for each sort i. Fig. 6.2 gives
both the grammar defining the sorted types by mutual recursion, and the
homomorphic *syntactic sort map S* sending types to their sorts. The syntactic

---

[3] Modulo sorting, $\{^{\backprime k}, {}^{\backprime k}\}, k > 0$ and $\{^{\backprime}, {}^{\backprime}\}$ are residuated pairs and $\{\backslash, \bullet, /\}$, $\{\downarrow_k, \odot_k, \uparrow_k\}, k > 0$, and $\{\downarrow, \odot, \uparrow\}$ are residuated triples.

[4] A version of discontinuous type logical connectives was first proposed in Moortgat (1988). Ver-sions of the unary operators $\hat{}$ ('bridge') and $\check{}$ ('split') were introduced in Morrill and Merenciano (1996). Generalized binary discontinuous connectives were given in Morrill (2002b) and Morrill *et al.* (2007).

$$[\![^{\wedge_k} A]\!] = \{U_k(s) \neq 0 \mid s \in [\![A]\!]\} \qquad\qquad k > 0$$
deterministic bridge
$$[\![^{\vee_k} B]\!] = \{s \mid U_k(s) \in [\![B]\!]\} \qquad\qquad k > 0$$
deterministic split

$$[\![^{\wedge} A]\!] = \{s \neq 0 \mid \exists s_1 \in [\![A]\!], U(s_1, s)\}$$
nondeterministic bridge
$$[\![^{\vee} B]\!] = \{s_1 \mid \forall s, U(s_1, s) \Rightarrow s \in [\![B]\!]\}$$
nondeterministic split

$$[\![A \bullet B]\!] = \{s_1 + s_2 \mid s_1 \in [\![A]\!] \,\&\, s_2 \in [\![B]\!]\}$$
(continuous) product
$$[\![A \backslash C]\!] = \{s_2 \neq 0 \mid \forall s_1 \in [\![A]\!], s_1 + s_2 \in [\![C]\!]\}$$
under
$$[\![C / B]\!] = \{s_1 \neq 0 \mid \forall s_2 \in [\![B]\!], s_1 + s_2 \in [\![C]\!]\}$$
over

$$[\![A \odot_k B]\!] = \{W_k(s_1, s_2) \mid s_1 \in [\![A]\!] \,\&\, s_2 \in [\![B]\!]\} \qquad\qquad k > 0$$
deterministic discontinuous product
$$[\![A \downarrow_k C]\!] = \{s_2 \neq 0 \mid \forall s_1 \in [\![A]\!], W_k(s_1, s_2) \in [\![C]\!]\} \qquad\qquad k > 0$$
deterministic infix
$$[\![C \uparrow_k B]\!] = \{s_1 \mid \forall s_2 \in [\![B]\!], W_k(s_1, s_2) \in [\![C]\!]\} \qquad\qquad k > 0$$
deterministic extract

$$[\![A \odot B]\!] = \{s \mid \exists s_1 \in [\![A]\!] \,\&\, \exists s_2 \in [\![B]\!], W(s_1, s_2, s)\}$$
nondeterministic discontinuous product
$$[\![A \downarrow C]\!] = \{s_2 \neq 0 \mid \forall s_1 \in [\![A]\!], \forall s, W(s_1, s_2, s) \Rightarrow s \in [\![C]\!]\}$$
nondeterministic infix
$$[\![C \uparrow B]\!] = \{s_1 \mid \forall s_2 \in [\![B]\!], \forall s, W(s_1, s_2, s) \Rightarrow s \in [\![C]\!]\}$$
nondeterministic extract

FIGURE 6.1. Syntactical interpretation of DL types

sort map is to syntax what the semantic type map is to semantics: both homomorphisms mapping syntactic types to the datatypes of the respective components of their inhabiting signs in the dimensions of language: syntactic sort for form/signifier and semantic type for meaning/signified.

6.2.1 Hypersequent calculus for DL

We define the *components* of a syntactical object as its maximal sub-parts not containing 1. Morrill (1997) introduced sequent calculus for (sorted) discontinuity in which a single discontinuous type has multiple

$$F_i ::= P_i \qquad\qquad S(A) = i \qquad\qquad\qquad \text{for } A \in P_i$$

$$\begin{aligned}
F_i &::= {}^{\wedge k}F_{i+1} & S({}^{\wedge k}A) &= S(A) - 1 & 1 &\le k \le i+1 \\
F_{i+1} &::= {}^{\vee k}F_i & S({}^{\vee k}A) &= S(A) + 1 & 1 &\le k \le i+1
\end{aligned}$$

$$\begin{aligned}
F_i &::= {}^{\wedge}F_{i+1} & S({}^{\wedge}A) &= S(A) - 1 \\
F_{i+1} &::= {}^{\vee}F_i & S({}^{\vee}A) &= S(A) + 1
\end{aligned}$$

$$\begin{aligned}
F_{i+j} &::= F_i \bullet F_j & S(A \bullet B) &= S(A) + S(B) \\
F_j &::= F_i \backslash F_{i+j} & S(A \backslash C) &= S(C) - S(A) \\
F_i &::= F_{i+j}/F_j & S(C/B) &= S(C) - S(B)
\end{aligned}$$

$$\begin{aligned}
F_{i+j} &::= F_{i+1} \odot_k F_j & S(A \odot_k B) &= S(A) + S(B) - 1 & 1 &\le k \le i+1 \\
F_j &::= F_{i+1} \downarrow_k F_{i+j} & S(A \downarrow_k C) &= S(C) + 1 - S(A) & 1 &\le k \le i+1 \\
F_{i+1} &::= F_{i+j} \uparrow_k F_j & S(C \uparrow_k B) &= S(C) + 1 - S(B) & 1 &\le k \le i+1
\end{aligned}$$

$$\begin{aligned}
F_{i+j} &::= F_{i+1} \odot F_j & S(A \odot B) &= S(A) + S(B) - 1 \\
F_j &::= F_{i+1} \downarrow F_{i+j} & S(A \downarrow C) &= S(C) + 1 - S(A) \\
F_{i+1} &::= F_{i+j} \uparrow F_j & S(C \uparrow B) &= S(C) + 1 - S(B)
\end{aligned}$$

FIGURE 6.2. Sorted **DL** types and syntactic sort map for **DL**

manifestations at the loci of its expressions' components, punctuated by surds. This is called 'hypersequent calculus' in the appendix of Morrill (2003), although in a usage of the term hypersequent calculus distinct from that of Avron (1987). The spirit is to maintain everything in evaluated/spelt-out linearized form.

The surd notation is meant to be suggestive of the (commutative) numeric law:

$$(6) \quad \underbrace{\sqrt[i]{A} \times \cdots \times \sqrt[i]{A}}_{i \text{ times}} = A$$

For us, non-commutatively:[5]

---

[5] Since elements of graded syntactical algebras are in bijection with tuples, it could also be reasonable to punctuate the components of discontinuous types in hypersequents with projections $\pi_i A$. However, in logical categorial grammar with bracket operators for domains (Chapter 5), it seems that eventually we will need to allow separators within bracketed domains (e.g. $s_1+b(s_2+1+s_3)+s_4$, e.g. for quantifier phrases which outscope *wh*-islands). In this case, 'components' would not be projective since they would not always correspond to elements of the (bracketed graded) syntactical algebra. It seems we will need surded subparts of configurations which are not well-formed terms of the configuration algebra and do not denote well-formed syntactical objects, but only 'parts' of them; for example, containing the left boundary of a unary operation of bracketing, but not the right boundary. And sorts themselves would seem to have to be extended to say bracketed sequences of 1's to control for when a separator is or is not within a bracketed domain and thus is not or is available to some mode of discontinuity. Therefore we prefer to keep the surd notation, which does not seem to imply as much as would a projective notation that there will always be projectivity, cf. that $\sqrt{-1}$ is a number which is imaginary although not a number which is real: in the complex number system a general nth degree equation has exactly n roots; for us, a syntactical object of sort i has $i + 1$ components. It seems that for brackets, which can perhaps be seen as a kind of negation, we could need a noncommutative monoidal analogue of the complex numbers defining roots of negative numbers.

(7) $\sqrt[0]{A}\bullet\{1\}\cdots\{1\}\bullet {}^{S(A)}\!\sqrt{A} = A$

(8) DEFINITION (*figures, configurations and hypersequents of hypersequent cal-culus*). In hypersequent calculus the *figures* $\mathbf{Q}_i$ of sort i for each sort i are defined as follows ([] is our *metalinguistic separator*):

$$\mathbf{Q}_0 ::= A \qquad\qquad\qquad\qquad\qquad \text{for } S(A) = 0$$
$$\mathbf{Q}_{S(A)} ::= \sqrt[0]{A}, [], \sqrt[1]{A}, \ldots, {}^{S(A)-1}\!\sqrt{A}, [], {}^{S(A)}\!\sqrt{A} \text{ for } S(A) > 0$$

By the vectorial notation $\overrightarrow{A}$ we mean the figure of sorted type A, i.e.

$$\overrightarrow{A} =_{df.} \begin{cases} A & \text{if } S(A) = 0 \\ \sqrt[0]{A}, [], \sqrt[1]{A}, \ldots, {}^{S(A)-1}\!\sqrt{A}, [], {}^{S(A)}\!\sqrt{A} & \text{if } S(A) > 0 \end{cases}$$

The *configurations* $\mathbf{O}_i$ of sort i for each sort i are defined unambiguously by mutual recursion as follows, where Λ is the empty string:

$$\mathbf{O}_0 ::= \Lambda$$
$$\mathbf{O}_i ::= A, \mathbf{O}_i \text{ for } S(A) = 0$$
$$\mathbf{O}_{i+1} ::= [], \mathbf{O}_i$$
$$\mathbf{O}_{\sum_{k=0}^{S(A)} j_k} ::= \sqrt[0]{A}, \mathbf{O}_{j_0}, \sqrt[1]{A}, \ldots, {}^{S(A)-1}\!\sqrt{A}, \mathbf{O}_{j_{S(A)-1}}, {}^{S(A)}\!\sqrt{A}, \mathbf{O}_{j_{S(A)}}$$
$$\text{for } S(A) > 0$$

Note that figures are a particular case of configurations. Not every substring of a configuration is a (well-formed) configuration because a configuration must contain all the segments of discontinuous types. We define the *components* of a configuration as its maximal substrings not containing the metalinguistic separator [] (components indeed are correct configurations).

The *hypersequents* Σ_i of sort i for each sort i are defined as follows:

$$\Sigma_0 ::= \mathbf{O}_0 - \{\Lambda\} \Rightarrow \mathbf{Q}_0$$
$$\Sigma_i ::= \mathbf{O}_i \Rightarrow \mathbf{Q}_i \quad i \geq 0$$

$\mathbf{O}_i$ is called the *antecedent* configuration and $\mathbf{Q}_i$ is called the *succedent* figure. Note that we do not have empty antecedents in hypersequents.

Observe that the components of discontinuous types are well-nested in configurations, that is that there are no crossing discontinuities, so that in con-figurations the enumeration of components is sufficient to define their depen-dencies. This corresponds to the fact that under wrapping, the infix is always kept intact within the circumfix. With a 'shuffle' discontinuous operation this would no longer be true, and components which belong together would need to be coindexed in some way, as in Morrill (2003).

(9) DEFINITION (*syntactical interpretation of configurations and validity of sequents in hypersequent calculus*). In hypersequent calculus we extend the interpretation of types to include configurations, as follows:

$$[\![\Lambda]\!] = \{0\}$$
$$[\![A, \Gamma]\!] = \{s_1 + s_2 \mid s_1 \in [\![A]\!] \ \& \ s_2 \in [\![\Gamma]\!] \}$$
$$[\![[], \Gamma]\!] = \{1 + s \mid s \in [\![\Gamma]\!] \}$$
$$[\![\sqrt[0]{A}, \Gamma_0, \dots, \Gamma_{S(A)-1}, \sqrt[S(A)]{A}, \Gamma_{S(A)}]\!] = \{s_0 + t_0 + \dots + t_{S(A)-1} + s_{S(A)} + t_{S(A)} \mid$$
$$s_0 + 1 + \dots + 1 + s_{S(A)} \in [\![A]\!]$$
$$\& \ t_j \in [\![\Gamma_j]\!], 0 \le j \le S(A) \}$$

A hypersequent $\Gamma \Rightarrow X$ is *valid* iff in every interpretation, $[\![\Gamma]\!] \subseteq [\![X]\!]$.

The hypersequent calculus for **DL** is given in Figs. 6.3 and 6.4. $\Delta(\Gamma)$ means a configuration Δ in which in some distinguished positions the components of Γ appear in the given order and such that parts of Δ appearing between components of Γ are well-formed configurations. $\Delta|_k \Gamma$, $k > 0$ is the result of replacing the k-th separator in Δ by Γ. We require that the antecedent of the conclusion be non-empty in $\hat{}^k R$, $\hat{}R$, $\backslash R$, $/R$, $\downarrow_k R$, and $\downarrow R$.

$$\frac{}{\overrightarrow{A} \Rightarrow \overrightarrow{A}} id \qquad \frac{\Gamma \Rightarrow \overrightarrow{A} \quad \Delta(\overrightarrow{A}) \Rightarrow \overrightarrow{B}}{\Delta(\Gamma) \Rightarrow \overrightarrow{B}} Cut$$

$$\frac{\Delta(\overrightarrow{B}) \Rightarrow \overrightarrow{C}}{\Delta(\check{}^k\overrightarrow{B}|_k \Lambda) \Rightarrow \overrightarrow{C}} \check{}^k L \qquad \frac{\Delta|_k \Lambda \Rightarrow \overrightarrow{B}}{\Delta \Rightarrow \check{}^k\overrightarrow{B}} \check{}^k R$$

$$\frac{\Delta(\overrightarrow{A}|_k \Lambda) \Rightarrow \overrightarrow{C}}{\Delta(\hat{}^k\overrightarrow{A}) \Rightarrow \overrightarrow{C}} \hat{}^k L \qquad \frac{\Delta \Rightarrow \overrightarrow{A}}{\Delta|_k \Lambda \Rightarrow \hat{}^k\overrightarrow{A}} \hat{}^k R$$

$$\frac{\Delta(\overrightarrow{B}) \Rightarrow \overrightarrow{C}}{\Delta(\check{}\overrightarrow{B}|_k \Lambda) \Rightarrow \overrightarrow{C}} \check{}L \qquad \frac{\Delta|_1 \Lambda \Rightarrow \overrightarrow{B} \quad \cdots \quad \Delta|_{S(B)} \Lambda \Rightarrow \overrightarrow{B}}{\Delta \Rightarrow \check{}\overrightarrow{B}} \check{}R$$

$$\frac{\Delta(\overrightarrow{A}|_1 \Lambda) \Rightarrow \overrightarrow{C} \quad \cdots \quad \Delta(\overrightarrow{A}|_{S(A)} \Lambda) \Rightarrow \overrightarrow{C}}{\Delta(\hat{}\overrightarrow{A}) \Rightarrow \overrightarrow{C}} \hat{}L \qquad \frac{\Delta \Rightarrow \overrightarrow{A}}{\Delta|_k \Lambda \Rightarrow \hat{}\overrightarrow{A}} \hat{}R$$

FIGURE 6.3. Hypersequent calculus for **DL**, part I

$$\frac{\Gamma \Rightarrow \vec{A} \qquad \Delta(\vec{C}) \Rightarrow \vec{D}}{\Delta(\Gamma, \overrightarrow{A\backslash C}) \Rightarrow \vec{D}} \,\backslash L \qquad\qquad \frac{\vec{A}, \Gamma \Rightarrow \vec{C}}{\Gamma \Rightarrow \overrightarrow{A\backslash C}} \,\backslash R$$

$$\frac{\Gamma \Rightarrow \vec{B} \qquad \Delta(\vec{C}) \Rightarrow \vec{D}}{\Delta(\overrightarrow{C/B}, \Gamma) \Rightarrow \vec{D}} \,/L \qquad\qquad \frac{\Gamma, \vec{B} \Rightarrow \vec{C}}{\Gamma \Rightarrow \overrightarrow{C/B}} \,/R$$

$$\frac{\Delta(\vec{A}, \vec{B}) \Rightarrow \vec{D}}{\Delta(\overrightarrow{A\bullet B}) \Rightarrow \vec{D}} \,\bullet L \qquad\qquad \frac{\Gamma_1 \Rightarrow \vec{A} \qquad \Gamma_2 \Rightarrow \vec{B}}{\Gamma_1, \Gamma_2 \Rightarrow \overrightarrow{A\bullet B}} \,\bullet R$$

$$\frac{\Gamma \Rightarrow \vec{A} \qquad \Delta(\vec{C}) \Rightarrow \vec{D}}{\Delta(\Gamma|_k \overrightarrow{A\downarrow_k C}) \Rightarrow \vec{D}} \,\downarrow_k L \qquad\qquad \frac{\vec{A}|_k \Gamma \Rightarrow \vec{C}}{\Gamma \Rightarrow \overrightarrow{A\downarrow_k C}} \,\downarrow_k R$$

$$\frac{\Gamma \Rightarrow \vec{B} \qquad \Delta(\vec{C}) \Rightarrow \vec{D}}{\Delta(\overrightarrow{C\uparrow_k B}|_k \Gamma) \Rightarrow \vec{D}} \,\uparrow_k L \qquad\qquad \frac{\Gamma|_k \vec{B} \Rightarrow \vec{C}}{\Gamma \Rightarrow \overrightarrow{C\uparrow_k B}} \,\uparrow_k R$$

$$\frac{\Delta(\vec{A}|_k \vec{B}) \Rightarrow \vec{D}}{\Delta(\overrightarrow{A\odot_k B}) \Rightarrow \vec{D}} \,\odot_k L \qquad\qquad \frac{\Gamma_1 \Rightarrow \vec{A} \qquad \Gamma_2 \Rightarrow \vec{B}}{\Gamma_1|_k \Gamma_2 \Rightarrow \overrightarrow{A\odot_k B}} \,\odot_k R$$

$$\frac{\Gamma \Rightarrow \vec{A} \qquad \Delta(\vec{C}) \Rightarrow \vec{D}}{\Delta(\Gamma|_k \overrightarrow{A\downarrow C}) \Rightarrow \vec{D}} \,\downarrow L \qquad\qquad \frac{\vec{A}|_1 \Gamma \Rightarrow \vec{C} \quad \cdots \quad \vec{A}|_{S(A)} \Gamma \Rightarrow \vec{C}}{\Gamma \Rightarrow \overrightarrow{A\downarrow C}} \,\downarrow R$$

$$\frac{\Gamma \Rightarrow \vec{B} \qquad \Delta(\vec{C}) \Rightarrow \vec{D}}{\Delta(\overrightarrow{C\uparrow B}|_k \Gamma) \Rightarrow \vec{D}} \,\uparrow L \qquad\qquad \frac{\Gamma|_1 \vec{B} \Rightarrow \vec{C} \quad \cdots \quad \Gamma|_{S(\Gamma)} \vec{B} \Rightarrow \vec{C}}{\Gamma \Rightarrow \overrightarrow{C\uparrow B}} \,\uparrow R$$

$$\frac{\Delta(\vec{A}|_1 \vec{B}) \Rightarrow \vec{D} \quad \cdots \quad \Delta(\vec{A}|_{S(A)} \vec{B}) \Rightarrow \vec{D}}{\Delta(\overrightarrow{A\odot B}) \Rightarrow \vec{D}} \,\odot L \qquad\qquad \frac{\Gamma_1 \Rightarrow \vec{A} \qquad \Gamma_2 \Rightarrow \vec{B}}{\Gamma_1|_k \Gamma_2 \Rightarrow \overrightarrow{A\odot B}} \,\odot R$$

FIGURE 6.4. Hypersequent calculus for **DL**, part II

Observe that the interpretation of our distinguished occurrence notation is such that the rules for continuous connectives in hypersequent calculus look just like those of the original Lambek calculus, but with the vectorial notation on the active types. Observe also that the rules for the deterministic discontinuous connectives in hypersequent calculus look just like the rules for the continuous connectives, but with metalinguistic wrapping '|' instead of metalinguistic concatenation ','. We consider that these symmetries give some of the substance to our claim that discontinuous Lambek calculus is a natural generalization of (continuous) Lambek calculus. But unlike the case of deterministic discontinuity, the rules for nondeterministic discontinuity no longer follow exactly the same pattern as those for continuity because nondeterministic wrapping is no longer functional but only relational. There are an infinite number of rule schemata in the calculus since the number of premises is unbounded in $\downarrow R$, $\uparrow R$, and $\odot L$, although every instance is finite, and (Cut-free) only a finite number of instances can apply in derivations from a given (finite) lexicon.

(10)   PROPOSITION (*soundness of* DL).
          In DL, every theorem is valid.

Proof. By induction on the length of proofs.   □

(11)   THEOREM (*Cut-elimination for* DL).
          In DL, every theorem has a Cut-free hypersequent proof.

Proof. See the appendix of Morrill *et al.* (2008).   □

(12)   COROLLARY (*subformula property for* DL).
          In DL, every theorem has a hypersequent proof containing only its subformulas.

Proof. Every rule except Cut has the property that all the types in the premises are either in the conclusion (side formulas) or are the immediate subtypes of the active formula, and Cut itself is eliminable.   □

(13)   COROLLARY (*decidability of* DL).
          In DL, it is decidable whether a hypersequent is a theorem.

Proof. By backward-chaining in the finite Cut-free hypersequent search space.   □

The question of completeness of DL, that is whether every valid hypersequent is a theorem, remains open. The question of the generative power of DL also remains open. Valentín (2006) observes that 1-DL can generate the non-context free but mildly context sensitive language $a^n b^n c^n$.

The *semantic type map* T for DL is given in Fig. 6.5. The unary connectives are interpreted as semantically inert. The semantic type map sends derivations into intuitionistic proofs so the usual Curry–Howard categorial type-logical semantics comes for free.

M. Moortgat has placed much emphasis on the possibility of interpreting type-logical connectives relationally (e.g. Moortgat 1997), as we do here for the nondeterministic discontinuity operators. Such models can be rather austere, as van Benthem (2005) puts it; being more general than functional models

$$T(^{\vee k}B) = T(B)$$
$$T(^{\wedge k}A) = T(A)$$
$$T(^{\vee}B) = T(B)$$
$$T(^{\wedge}A) = T(A)$$
$$T(A\backslash C) = T(A) \to T(C)$$
$$T(C/B) = T(B) \to T(C)$$
$$T(A\bullet B) = T(A)\&T(B)$$
$$T(A\downarrow_k C) = T(A) \to T(C)$$
$$T(C\uparrow_k B) = T(B) \to T(C)$$
$$T(A\odot_k B) = T(A)\&T(B)$$
$$T(A\downarrow C) = T(A) \to T(C)$$
$$T(C\uparrow B) = T(B) \to T(C)$$
$$T(A\odot B) = T(A)\&T(B)$$

FIGURE 6.5. Semantic type map for **DL**

they are less contentful ontologically: a scientific theory should make the strongest claims possible which are not yet refuted. But in the present case we think the nondeterministic wrapping relational interpretation of discontinuity operators is motivated by its applicability to particle shift and complement alternation (see later), and perhaps to other phenomena of semi-free word order. Reape (1993) appears to have been the first to propose what is (in our terms) a nondeterministic mode of discontinuous syntactical composition (a kind of shuffle, for the German Mittelfeld), in the alternative categorial-like approach of Head-driven Phrase Structure Grammar.[6]

6.2.2 Labelled natural deduction for DL

We can present type-logical calculi in a labelled deductive system (LDS) of natural deduction in which syntactical terms α and semantic terms ϕ label types A thus: $\alpha : A : \phi$; see Figs. 6.6, 6.7, and 6.8. As in the hypersequent calculus, syntactic terms are kept in evaluated/spelt-out forms with atoms only of sort 0. The vectorial notation $\overrightarrow{a}$ means $a_0+1+a_1+\cdots+a_{i-1}+1+a_i$ where i is the sort of a; $a|_k\beta$, $k > 0$ is the result of replacing the k-th separator in a by β.

---

[6] The extension of the present proposals to some such shuffle is problematic in that the sort of the output of the shuffle might not be deterministically fixed by the sorts of its inputs; e.g. the shuffles of $s_1+1+s_2+1+s_3$ and t_1+1+t_2 could include $s_1+t_1+1+t_2+s_2+1+s_3$ and $s_1+1+s_2+t_1+1+t_2+s_3$ of sort 2, as well as $s_1+t_1+s_2+t_2+s_3$ of sort 0. Perhaps the 'cards' of the shuffle should not be divided by separators, but just be the factors of continuous (bracketed) strings.

$$\frac{\vdots \quad a : {}^{\vee k} B : \phi}{a|_k 0 : B : \phi}\ E^{\vee k} \qquad \frac{\vdots \quad a|_k 0 : B : \phi}{a : {}^{\vee k} B : \phi}\ I^{\vee k}$$

$$\overrightarrow{a} : A : x^i$$

$$\frac{\vdots \qquad \qquad \vdots}{\beta : {}^{\wedge k} A : \phi \quad \gamma(\overrightarrow{a}|_k 0) : C : \chi(x)}{\gamma(\beta) : C : \chi(\phi)}\ E^{\wedge k i} \qquad \frac{\vdots \quad a : A : \phi}{a|_k 0 : {}^{\wedge k} A : \phi}\ I^{\wedge k}$$

$$\frac{\vdots \quad a : {}^{\vee} B : \phi}{a|_k 0 : B : \phi}\ E^{\vee} \qquad \frac{\vdots \qquad \qquad \vdots}{a|_1 0 : B : \phi \quad \cdots \quad a|_{S(B)} 0 : B : \phi}{a : {}^{\vee} B : \phi}\ I^{\vee}$$

$$\overrightarrow{a} : A : x^i \qquad \qquad \overrightarrow{a} : A : x^i$$

$$\frac{\vdots \qquad \vdots \qquad \qquad \vdots}{\beta : {}^{\wedge} A : \phi \quad \gamma(\overrightarrow{a}|_1 0) : C : \chi(x) \quad \cdots \quad \gamma(\overrightarrow{a}|_{S(A)} 0) : C : \chi(x)}{\gamma(\beta) : C : \chi(\phi)}\ E^{\wedge i} \qquad \frac{\vdots \quad a : A : \phi}{a|_k 0 : {}^{\wedge} A : \phi}\ I^{\wedge}$$

FIGURE 6.6. Labelled natural deduction for DL, part I

6.3 Applications of discontinuous Lambek calculus

6.3.1 *Linguistic applications of* BDLC

By Basic discontinuous Lambek calculus **BDLC** we mean **DL** in which the discontinuous syntactical structure is restricted to just $+ : L_0 \times L_0 \rightarrow L_0$ and $W : L_1 \times L_0 \rightarrow L_0$. Therefore the only discontinuous connectives it contains are sort non-polymorphic operators which we notate $\downarrow$, $\odot$, and $\uparrow$. In this section we list accounts of linguistic phenomena falling within the scope of this minimal discontinuity calculus.

6.3.1.1 Discontinuous idioms   Idioms are complex expressions which have a meaning not compositionally attributable to the meanings of their parts (e.g. *red herring*). In grammar delivering logical semantics, they must be listed in the lexicon, because there is no other place in which to specify their meaning. In discontinuous idioms, the idiomatic material is interpolated by non-idiomatic dependents, for example:

(14)   Mary *gave* John/the man/. . . *the cold shoulder.*

Let there be the following lexical assignment:

(15)   **gave**+1+**the**+**cold**+**shoulder** : *shun* : $(N\backslash S)\uparrow N$

$$\frac{a:A:\phi \quad \gamma:A\backslash C:\chi}{a+\gamma:C:(\chi\,\phi)}\,E\backslash$$

$$\frac{\overset{\cdot}{\overset{\cdot}{\overset{\cdot}{\overrightarrow{a}:A:x^i}}}}{\underset{\cdot}{\overset{\cdot}{\overset{\cdot}{\cdot}}}}$$

$$\frac{\overrightarrow{a}+\gamma:C:\chi}{\gamma:A\backslash C:\lambda x\chi}\,I\backslash^i$$

$$\frac{\gamma:C/B:\chi \quad \beta:B:\psi}{\gamma+\beta:C:(\chi\,\psi)}\,E/$$

$$\frac{\overrightarrow{b}:B:y^i}{\gamma+\overrightarrow{b}:C:\chi}{\gamma:C/B:\lambda y\chi}\,I/^i$$

$$\frac{\gamma:A\bullet B:\chi \quad \delta(\overrightarrow{a}+\overrightarrow{b}):D:\omega(x,y)}{\delta(\gamma):D:\omega(\pi_1\chi,\pi_2\chi)}\,E\bullet^i$$

$$\frac{a:A:\phi \qquad \beta:B:\psi}{a+\beta:A\bullet B:(\phi,\psi)}\,I\bullet$$

$$\frac{a:A:\phi \quad \gamma:A\!\downarrow_k\!C:\chi}{a|_k\gamma:C:(\chi\,\phi)}\,E\!\downarrow_k$$

$$\frac{\overrightarrow{a}|_k\gamma:C:\chi}{\gamma:A\!\downarrow_k\!C:\lambda x\chi}\,I\!\downarrow_k^i$$

$$\frac{\gamma:C\!\uparrow_k\!B:\chi \quad \beta:B:\psi}{\gamma|_k\beta:C:(\chi\,\psi)}\,E\!\uparrow_k$$

$$\frac{\gamma|_k\overrightarrow{b}:C:\chi}{\gamma:C\!\uparrow_k\!B:\lambda y\chi}\,I\!\uparrow_k^i$$

$$\frac{\gamma:A\odot_k B:\chi \quad \delta(\overrightarrow{a}|_k\overrightarrow{b}):D:\omega(x,y)}{\delta(\gamma):D:\omega(\pi_1\chi,\pi_2\chi)}\,E\odot_k^i$$

$$\frac{a:A:\phi \qquad \beta:B:\psi}{a|_k\beta:A\odot_k B:(\phi,\psi)}\,I\odot_k$$

FIGURE 6.7. Labelled natural deduction for **DL**, part II

Then our example is derived as follows in the hypersequent calculus and the labelled natural deduction calculus respectively:

(16)

$$\frac{N\Rightarrow N}{\dfrac{N\Rightarrow N \quad \dfrac{N\Rightarrow N \quad S\Rightarrow S}{N,\,N\backslash S\Rightarrow S}\,\backslash L}{N,\,\sqrt[0]{(N\backslash S)\!\uparrow\!N},\,N,\,\sqrt[0]{(N\backslash S)\!\uparrow\!N}\Rightarrow S}}\,\uparrow L$$

$$
\begin{array}{c}
\vec{a}:A:x^i \\
\vdots \\
\vec{a}|_1\gamma:C:\chi \quad \cdots \quad \vec{a}|_{S(A)}\gamma:C:\chi \\
\hline
\gamma:A{\downarrow}C:\lambda x\chi
\end{array}\; I{\downarrow}^i
$$

$$
\begin{array}{c}
a:A:\phi \quad \gamma:A{\downarrow}C:\chi \\
\hline
a|_k\gamma:C:(\chi\,\phi)
\end{array}\; E{\downarrow}
$$

$$
\begin{array}{c}
\vec{b}:B:y^i \\
\vdots \\
\gamma|_1\vec{b}:C:\chi \quad \cdots \quad \gamma|_{S(C)}\vec{b}:C:\chi \\
\hline
\gamma:C{\uparrow}B:\lambda y\chi
\end{array}\; I{\uparrow}^i
$$

$$
\begin{array}{c}
\gamma:C{\uparrow}B:\chi \quad \beta:B:\psi \\
\hline
\gamma|_i\beta:C:(\chi\,\psi)
\end{array}\; E{\uparrow}
$$

$$
\begin{array}{c}
\vec{a}:A:x^i \quad \vec{b}:B:y^i \\
\vdots \\
\gamma:A{\odot}B:\chi \quad \delta(\vec{a}|_1\vec{b}):D:\omega(x,y) \quad \cdots \quad \delta(\vec{a}|_{S(A)}\vec{b}):D:\omega(x,y) \\
\hline
\delta(\gamma):D:\omega(\pi_1\chi,\pi_2\chi)
\end{array}\; E{\odot}^i
$$

$$
\begin{array}{c}
a:A:\phi \quad \beta:B:\psi \\
\hline
a|_k\beta:A{\odot}B:(\phi,\psi)
\end{array}\; I{\odot}
$$

FIGURE 6.8. Labelled natural deduction for **DL**, part III

(17)

$$
\begin{array}{c}
\dfrac{\text{gave} \ldots \text{the cold shoulder}}{\text{gave}+1+\text{the}+\text{cold}+\text{shoulder}:(N\backslash S){\uparrow}N:shun} \quad \text{John}:N:j \\[2pt]
\dfrac{\text{Mary} \qquad \text{gave}+\text{John}+\text{the}+\text{cold}+\text{shoulder}:N\backslash S:(shun\,j)}{} \\[2pt]
\end{array}
$$

$$
\begin{array}{c}
\dfrac{\text{Mary}:N:m \qquad \text{gave}+\text{John}+\text{the}+\text{cold}+\text{shoulder}:N\backslash S:(shun\,j)}{\text{Mary}+\text{gave}+\text{John}+\text{the}+\text{cold}+\text{shoulder}:S:(shun\,j\,m)}\; E\backslash
\end{array}
$$

6.3.1.2 Quantification Quantification is a classical instance of discontinuity, that is of syntactic–semantic mismatch: quantifier phrases occupy nominal positions syntactically but take sentential scope semantically, for example:

(18)   a. John gave every book to Mary.
       b. $\forall x[(book\ x) \rightarrow (give\ m\ x\ j)]$

We treat quantification by type assignments such as the following:

(19)   **every** : $((S{\uparrow}N){\downarrow}S)/CN$: $\lambda x\lambda y\forall z[(x\ z) \rightarrow (y\ z)]$

Such a composite of extraction and infixation to treat quantification was suggested in Moortgat (1991), but he did not have a calculus ensuring that the extraction and infixation points would be one and the same. The first proposals to remedy this were those of Versmissen (1991) and Solias (1992).

An example like (18) is derived (with the right semantics) as follows, where *PTV* abbreviates $(N\backslash S)/(N \bullet PP)$.

(20)
$$
\cfrac{
  \cfrac{
    \cfrac{N, PTV, N, PP \Rightarrow S}{N, PTV, [\,], PP \Rightarrow \sqrt[0]{S{\uparrow}N}, [\,], \sqrt[1]{S{\uparrow}N}} \uparrow R
    \qquad S \Rightarrow S
  }{N, PTV, (S{\uparrow}N){\downarrow}S, PP \Rightarrow S} \downarrow L
}{N, PTV, ((S{\uparrow}N){\downarrow}S)/CN, CN, PP \Rightarrow S} /L
\qquad CN \Rightarrow CN
$$

Montague (1973) (PTQ) presumably takes its title from its treatment of quantifiers and it is interesting to compare our treatment with his rule of term-insertion S14. Ignoring for the moment pronoun-binding aspects, S14 replaces by a noun phrase a syntactic variable in a nominal position in a sentence and semantically applies the noun phrase to the lambda abstraction of the sentence meaning over that of the nominal position. Our analysis splits such a step into two parts: conditionalization of the sentence over the nominal, semantically interpreted by functional abstraction over the nominal meaning, and infixing of the quantifier phrase into the conditionalized sentence, semantically interpreted by functional application of the infix to the circumfix.

Like that of Montague, our account allows quantifier phrases to take scope at the level of any embedding sentence, a feature which must eventually be constrained. However this successfully characterizes the de re/specific and de dicto/nonspecific ambiguity of (21).

(21)   Mary thinks someone left.

The de dicto reading, where the propositional attitude verb has wider scope than the existential quantifier (Mary does not necessarily have a particular person in mind), is generated by:

(22)
$$
\cfrac{
  \cfrac{
    \cfrac{N, N\backslash S \Rightarrow S}{[\,], N\backslash S \Rightarrow \sqrt[0]{S{\uparrow}N}, [\,], \sqrt[1]{S{\uparrow}N}} \uparrow R
    \qquad S \Rightarrow S
  }{(S{\uparrow}N){\downarrow}S, N\backslash S \Rightarrow S} \downarrow L
  \qquad N, N\backslash S \Rightarrow S
}{N, (N\backslash S)/S, (S{\uparrow}N){\downarrow}S, N\backslash S \Rightarrow S} /L
$$

The de re reading, where the existential quantifier has wider scope than the propositional attitude verb (Mary has a particular person in mind), is generated by:

(23)
$$\frac{N, (N\backslash S)/S, N, N\backslash S \Rightarrow S}{\dfrac{N, (N\backslash S)/S, [], N\backslash S \Rightarrow \sqrt[0]{S{\uparrow}N}, [], \sqrt[1]{S{\uparrow}N} \quad S \Rightarrow S}{N, (N\backslash S)/S, (S{\uparrow}N){\downarrow}S, N\backslash S \Rightarrow S}{\downarrow}L}{\uparrow}R$$

Also like the account of Montague, ours allows multiple quantifiers to scope in any order, another feature which must eventually be constrained (for example, *each* appears to always take wider scope). But this successfully characterizes the classical example of ambiguity:

(24) Everyone loves someone.

On the (dominant) subject wide scope reading, different people love, in general, different people (as in when we all love our respective mothers). On the (subordinate) object wide scope reading, different people love the same person (as in when we all love one and the same queen). The subject wide scope ($\forall\exists$) reading is generated by:

(25)
$$\frac{\dfrac{\dfrac{N, (N\backslash S)/N, N \Rightarrow S}{N, (N\backslash S)/N, [] \Rightarrow \sqrt[0]{S{\uparrow}N}, [], \sqrt[1]{S{\uparrow}N} \quad S \Rightarrow S}{\uparrow}R}{N, (N\backslash S)/N, (S{\uparrow}N){\downarrow}S \Rightarrow S}{\downarrow}L}{\dfrac{[], (N\backslash S)/N, (S{\uparrow}N){\downarrow}S \Rightarrow \sqrt[0]{S{\uparrow}N}, [], \sqrt[1]{S{\uparrow}N} \quad S \Rightarrow S}{(S{\uparrow}N){\downarrow}S, (N\backslash S)/N, (S{\uparrow}N){\downarrow}S \Rightarrow S}{\downarrow}L}{\uparrow}R$$

The object wide scope ($\exists\forall$) reading is generated by:

(26)
$$\frac{\dfrac{\dfrac{N, (N\backslash S)/N, N \Rightarrow S}{[], (N\backslash S)/N, N \Rightarrow \sqrt[0]{S{\uparrow}N}, [], \sqrt[1]{S{\uparrow}N} \quad S \Rightarrow S}{\uparrow}R}{(S{\uparrow}N){\downarrow}S, (N\backslash S)/N, N \Rightarrow S}{\downarrow}L}{\dfrac{(S{\uparrow}N){\downarrow}S, (N\backslash S)/N, [] \Rightarrow \sqrt[0]{S{\uparrow}N}, [], \sqrt[1]{S{\uparrow}N} \quad S \Rightarrow S}{(S{\uparrow}N){\downarrow}S, (N\backslash S)/N, (S{\uparrow}N){\downarrow}S \Rightarrow S}{\downarrow}L}{\uparrow}R$$

(The sooner processed, i.e. the nearer the root of the sequent proof, the wider the scope of the quantifier). Note that even assuming nondeterministic wrapping, in our account multiple quantifiers cannot get tangled up and bind each others' positions because the types driving the derivation ensure that the quantifier separator positions are only ever opened up and closed off one at a time, so that the only positions ever available are the unique correct ones.

In Chapter 4 we gave an account of left-to-right quantifier scope preference in terms of incremental complexity. Grammatically, we assumed continuous connectives and lexical ambiguity. Here we assume derivational ambiguity with discontinuous connectives and no lexical ambiguity. However, the same account of performance complexity carries over.

Exercise 6.1. Give the derivations for quantification with semantics in labelled natural deduction.

6.3.1.3 VP ellipsis VP ellipsis refers to a class of constructions in which a form of *do* (perhaps suffixed by *too*) takes its interpretation from a preceding verb phrase, for example:

(27) a. John slept before Mary did.
      b. John slept and Mary did too.

Let there be the following lexical type assignment to the auxiliary, where VP abbreviates N\S:

(28) **did** : $((VP{\uparrow}VP)/VP)\backslash(VP{\uparrow}VP)$: $\lambda x \lambda y(x \ y \ y)$

Then an example such as (27a) is derived as follows:

(29)

$$\cfrac{\cfrac{\cfrac{VP, (VP\backslash VP)/S, N, VP \Rightarrow VP}{[], (VP\backslash VP)/S, N, VP \Rightarrow \sqrt[9]{VP{\uparrow}VP}, [], \sqrt{VP{\uparrow}VP}} \ {\uparrow}R}{[], (VP\backslash VP)/S, N \Rightarrow \sqrt[9]{(VP \uparrow VP)/VP}, [], \sqrt{(VP \uparrow VP)/VP}} \ /R \qquad \cfrac{VP \Rightarrow VP \qquad N, VP \Rightarrow S}{N, \sqrt[9]{VP \uparrow VP}, VP, \sqrt{VP \uparrow VP} \Rightarrow S} \ {\uparrow}L}{N, VP, (VP\backslash VP)/S, N, ((VP \uparrow VP)/VP)\backslash(VP \uparrow VP) \Rightarrow S} \ \backslash L$$

VP ellipsis can also occur intersententially, so an account must eventually be set up at the level of discourse.

Exercise 6.2. Give the derivation for VP ellipsis with semantics in labelled natural deduction.

6.3.2 Linguistic applications of 1-DL

By 1-**DL** we mean **DL** with only ever a single separator, in which case the deterministic and nondeterministic connectives collapse into the same operators, which we notate ˇ, ˆ, ↓, ⊙, and ↑.

6.3.2.1 Medial extraction Extraction in which the gap is not at the periphery such as

(30) dog that Mary saw today

can be modelled as follows:

(31) **that** : $(CN\backslash CN)/\hat{\ }(S{\uparrow}N)$: $\lambda x\lambda y\lambda z[(x\ z)\wedge(y\ z)]$

Example (30) is derived thus in the hypersequent calculus:

(32)
$$\frac{\dfrac{\dfrac{N,(N\backslash S)/N,N,(N\backslash S)\backslash(N\backslash S)\Rightarrow S}{N,(N\backslash S)/N,[],(N\backslash S)\backslash(N\backslash S)\Rightarrow\sqrt[0]{S{\uparrow}N},[],\sqrt[1]{S{\uparrow}N}}\ {\uparrow}R}{N,(N\backslash S)/N,(N\backslash S)\backslash(N\backslash S)\Rightarrow\hat{\ }(S{\uparrow}N)}\ \hat{\ }R \qquad CN,CN\backslash CN\Rightarrow CN}{CN,(CN\backslash CN)/\hat{\ }(S{\uparrow}N),N,(N\backslash S)/N,(N\backslash S)\backslash(N\backslash S)\Rightarrow CN}\ /L$$

The derivation in labelled natural deduction is as shown in Fig. 6.9.[7]

6.3.2.2 Pied-piping

Pied-piping is the embedding of a filler such as a relative pronoun within accompanying material from the extraction site:

(33) mountain the painting of which by Cezanne John sold for $10,000,000

The depth of embedding is unbounded:

(34) thesis the height of the lettering on the first line of the second page of the third chapter of . . . of which is 0.5cm

Pied-piping can be treated by assignment as follows (cf. Morrill 1994, ch. 4; 1995):

(35) **which** : $(N{\uparrow}N){\downarrow}((CN\backslash CN)/\hat{\ }(S{\uparrow}N))$: $\lambda x\lambda y\lambda z\lambda w[(z\ w)\wedge(y\ (x\ w))]$

Then (33) is derived as shown in Fig. 6.10, where *PTV* abbreviates $(N\backslash S)/(N{\bullet}PP)$. Note that (35) can also generate relativization in which there is no pied-piping by deriving an empty pied-piping context as $N{\uparrow}N$ ($[]\Rightarrow N{\uparrow}N$ is a theorem): once the assignment (35) is included, that of Section 6.3.2.1 is no longer required: the assignment (31) is derivable from, and so subsumed by, (35).

Exercise 6.3. Give the derivation for pied-piping with semantics in labelled natural deduction.

---

[7] This treatment captures the long-distanceness of left extraction, but we believe something like the bracket modalities of Chapter 5 are needed to express island constraints and to generate parasitic gaps. We do not see an extension of discontinuity to parasiticy because the unboundedness of the number of parasitic gaps and of their depth of embedding within islands would seem to go against the idea of finitude of a single rule of inference. We propose to treat parasiticy (and mediality) as in Chapter 5. However we continue to use wrapping for left extraction in this chapter, to illustrate with the machinery at hand.

saw   today

$$\dfrac{\textbf{saw}:(N\backslash S)/N:see \qquad a:N:x^{i}}{\textbf{saw}+a:N\backslash S:(see\ x)}\ E/$$

$$\textbf{today}:(N\backslash S)\backslash(N\backslash S):today$$

$$\dfrac{\textbf{saw}+a+\textbf{today}:N\backslash S:(today\ (see\ x))}{}\ E\backslash$$

$$\textbf{Mary}:N:m$$

$$\dfrac{\textbf{Mary}+\textbf{saw}+a+\textbf{today}:S:(today\ (see\ x)\ m)}{}\ E\backslash$$

$$\dfrac{\textbf{Mary}+\textbf{saw}+1+\textbf{today}:S{\uparrow}N:\lambda x(today\ (see\ x)\ m)}{}\ I{\uparrow}^{i}$$

$$\dfrac{\textbf{Mary}+\textbf{saw}+\textbf{today}:{^\wedge}(S{\uparrow}N):\lambda x(today\ (see\ x)\ m)}{}\ I^{\wedge}$$

that

$$\textbf{that}:(CN\backslash CN)/{^\wedge}(S{\uparrow}N):\lambda x\lambda y\lambda z[(x\ z)\wedge(y\ z)]$$

$$\dfrac{\textbf{that}+\textbf{Mary}+\textbf{saw}+\textbf{today}:CN\backslash CN:\lambda y\lambda z[(today\ (see\ z)\ m)\wedge(y\ z)]}{}\ E/$$

dog

$$\textbf{dog}:CN:dog$$

$$\dfrac{\textbf{dog}+\textbf{that}+\textbf{Mary}+\textbf{saw}+\textbf{today}:CN:\lambda z[(today\ (see\ z)\ m)\wedge(dog\ z)]}{}\ E\backslash$$

FIGURE 6.9. Labelled natural deduction derivation of medial extraction (30)

$$N, PTV, N, PP \Rightarrow S$$

$$\frac{N, PTV, N, PP \Rightarrow S}{N, PTV, [], PP \Rightarrow \sqrt{S{\uparrow}N}, [], \sqrt{S{\uparrow}N}} \ {\uparrow}R$$

$$\frac{N, PTV, PP \Rightarrow {}^{\wedge}(S{\uparrow}N) \qquad CN, CN{\backslash}CN \Rightarrow CN}{CN, (CN{\backslash}CN)/{}^{\wedge}(S{\uparrow}N), N, PTV, PP \Rightarrow CN} \ {/}L$$

$$\frac{N/CN, CN/PP, PP/N, N, CN{\backslash}CN \Rightarrow N}{N/CN, CN/PP, PP/N, [], CN{\backslash}CN \Rightarrow \sqrt{N{\uparrow}N}, [], \sqrt{N{\uparrow}N}} \ {\uparrow}R$$

$$CN, N/CN, CN/PP, PP/N, (N{\uparrow}N){\downarrow}((CN{\backslash}CN)/{}^{\wedge}(S{\uparrow}N)), CN{\backslash}CN, N, PTV, PP \Rightarrow CN$$

FIGURE 6.10. Hypersequent derivation of pied-piping (33)

6.3.2.3 Appositive relativization   Appositive ('nonrestrictive') relativization is relativization in which the relative clause forms a lowered intonational phrase marked off by commas in writing, and modifies a noun phrase:

(36)   John, who jogs, sneezed.

Semantically, the predication of the body of the appositive relative clause to the noun phrase modified is conjoined with the semantics of the embedding sentence in which the noun phrase is (also) understood. This discontinuity can be treated by the following assignment:

(37)   **which** $:$ $(N\backslash((S{\uparrow}N){\downarrow}S))/{\char"02C6}(S{\uparrow}N)$ $:$ $\lambda x \lambda y \lambda z[(x\ y) \wedge (z\ y)]$

Our example (36) is derived as follows:

(38)

$$
\cfrac{
\cfrac{
\cfrac{
\cfrac{N, N\backslash S \Rightarrow S}{[], N\backslash S \Rightarrow \sqrt[0]{S{\uparrow}N},\ [],\ \sqrt{S{\uparrow}N}}{\uparrow}R
}{N\backslash S \Rightarrow {\char"02C6}(S{\uparrow}N)}{\char"02C6}R
\quad N \Rightarrow N
\quad
\cfrac{
\cfrac{N, N\backslash S \Rightarrow S}{[], N\backslash S \Rightarrow \sqrt[0]{S{\uparrow}N},\ [],\ \sqrt{S{\uparrow}N}}{\uparrow}R \quad S \Rightarrow S
}{(S{\uparrow}N){\downarrow}S, N\backslash S \Rightarrow S}{\downarrow}L
}{}
}{}
$$

In a full type-logical treatment, bracket operators would be used to project the lowered intonational phrase of an appositive relative clause, and the same means as for restrictive relativization would be used to allow pied-piping, so that the lexical assignment for an appositive relative pronoun would be:

(39)   **which** $:$ $(N{\uparrow}N){\downarrow}([l]^{-1}(N\backslash((S{\uparrow}N){\downarrow}S))/{\char"02C6}(S{\uparrow}N))$
          $:$ $\lambda w \lambda x \lambda y \lambda z[(x\ (w\ y)) \wedge (z\ y)]$

Exercise 6.4. Give the derivation for appositive relativization with semantics in labelled natural deduction.

6.3.2.4 Parentheticals   Parentheticals are adsentential modifiers such as *fortunately* which, to a very rough first approximation, can appear anywhere in the sentence they modify:[8]

(40)   a. Fortunately, John has perseverance.
          b. John, fortunately, has perseverance.
          c. John has, fortunately, perseverance.
          d. John has perseverance, fortunately.

---

[8]   Of course, parentheticals cannot really occur anywhere, e.g. *The, fortunately, man left. In the end there will have to be some kinds of domains which they cannot penetrate.

Such a distribution is captured by the following type assignment, as in Morrill and Merenciano (1996).

(41) **fortunately** : $\check{}S{\downarrow}S$: *fortunately*

For example, (40c) is derived as follows in the hypersequent calculus:

(42)
$$\cfrac{\cfrac{N,(N\backslash S)/N, N \Rightarrow S}{N,(N\backslash S)/N, [], N \Rightarrow \sqrt[0]{}S, [], \sqrt[1]{}S} \check{}R \qquad S \Rightarrow S}{N,(N\backslash S)/N, \check{}S{\downarrow}S, N \Rightarrow S} {\downarrow}L$$

In labelled natural deduction, example (40c) is derived as shown in Fig. 6.11.

6.3.2.5 Gapping Gapping is a coordinate construction in which, in English in the simplest case, a verb missing medially in the second conjunct shares its interpretation with one present in the first conjunct:

(43) John studies logic, and Charles, phonetics.

Coordinator types projecting such gapping were proposed in Solias (1992) and Morrill and Solias (1993). P. Hendriks (1995) proposed a like-type coordination assignment for gapping which we adapt as follows, where TV abbreviates $(N\backslash S)/N$.

(44) **and** : $((S{\uparrow}TV)\backslash(S{\uparrow}TV))/\hat{}(S{\uparrow}TV)$: $\lambda x\lambda y\lambda z[(y\ z) \wedge (x\ z)]$

That the coordination is (almost) like-type is attractive, since it narrows the distance between gapping and constituent coordination (cf. Steedman 1990). Example (43) is derived as shown in Fig. 6.12.

Exercise 6.5. Give the derivation for gapping with semantics in labelled natural deduction.

6.3.2.6 Comparative subdeletion Comparative subdeletion refers to comparisons in which the *than*-clause is missing a determiner:

(45) John ate more doughnuts than Mary bought bagels.

Type-logical analyses were given in P. Hendriks (1995), see also Morrill and Merenciano (1996). Here we assign separate types to the two comparative elements:

(46) **more** : $(S{\uparrow}(((S{\uparrow}N){\downarrow}S)/CN)){\downarrow}(S/(CP{\uparrow}\hat{}(((S{\uparrow}N){\downarrow}S)/CN)))$
$\quad\quad\quad$: $\lambda x\lambda y[|\lambda z(x\ \lambda p\lambda q[(p\ z) \wedge (q\ z)])| > |\lambda z(y\ \lambda p\lambda q[(p\ z) \wedge (q\ z)])|]$
$\quad\quad$ **than** : CP/S : $\lambda x x$

$$
\frac{\dfrac{\text{has}}{\text{\textbf{has}} : (N\backslash S)/N : \textit{have}} \quad \dfrac{\text{perseverance}}{\text{\textbf{perseverance}} : N : \textit{perseverance}}}{\text{\textbf{has+perseverance}} : N\backslash S : (\textit{have perseverance})} \; E\,/
$$

$$
\text{John} \quad \overline{\text{\textbf{John}} : N : j}
$$

$$
\frac{\text{\textbf{John+has+perseverance}} : S : (\textit{have perseverance j})}{\text{\textbf{John+has+1+perseverance}} : {}^{\smallsmile}S : (\textit{have perseverance j})} \; I^{\smallsmile}
$$

$$
\frac{\text{\textbf{John+has+1+perseverance}} : {}^{\smallsmile}S : (\textit{have perseverance j}) \qquad \dfrac{\text{fortunately}}{\text{\textbf{fortunately}} : {}^{\smallsmile}S{\downarrow}S : \textit{fortunately}}}{\text{\textbf{John+has+fortunately+perseverance}} : S : (\textit{fortunately} \, (\textit{have perseverance j}))} \; E{\downarrow}
$$

FIGURE 6.11. Labelled natural deduction derivation of parenthesization (40c)

$$
\cfrac{
  \cfrac{N, TV, N \Rightarrow S}{N, [], N \Rightarrow \sqrt{}S{\uparrow}TV, [], \sqrt{}S{\uparrow}TV} \; {\uparrow}R
}{N, N \Rightarrow {}^{\wedge}(S{\uparrow}TV)} \; {}^{\wedge}R
$$

$$
\cfrac{N, TV, N \Rightarrow S}{N, [], N \Rightarrow \sqrt{}S{\uparrow}TV, [], \sqrt{}S{\uparrow}TV} \; {\uparrow}R
$$

$$
\cfrac{
  \cfrac{TV \Rightarrow TV \qquad S \Rightarrow S}{\sqrt{}S{\uparrow}TV, TV, \sqrt{}S{\uparrow}TV \Rightarrow S} \; {\uparrow}L
}{} \; {\backslash}L
$$

$$
\cfrac{N, TV, N, (S{\uparrow}TV){\backslash}(S{\uparrow}TV) \Rightarrow S}{N, TV, N, ((S{\uparrow}TV){\backslash}(S{\uparrow}TV))/{}^{\wedge}(S{\uparrow}TV), N, N \Rightarrow S} \; /L
$$

FIGURE 6.12. Hypersequent derivation of gapping (43)

Then (45) is derived as shown in Fig. 6.13, where Q abbreviates $((S\uparrow N)\downarrow S)/CN$ and TV abbreviates $(N\backslash S)/N$.

Exercise 6.6. Give the derivation for comparative subdeletion with semantics in labelled natural deduction.

6.3.2.7 Null operators   Consider the following examples:

(47)   a. Dogs run.
       b. man Mary loves

In (47a) the subject consists of a bare plural common noun. The sentence has a reading synonymous with *Some dogs run*.[9] It is as if there is a null plural indefinite with the same semantics as (plural) *some*. In (47b) there is a that-less relative *Mary loves* synonymous with *that Mary loves*. It is as if there is a null relative pronoun.

    There are reasons to doubt the usual analysis of such examples in terms of null elements. For example, suppose we assumed a null plural indefinite of type $((S\uparrow Npl)\downarrow S)/CNpl$. Then we would generate (47a). Also, however, in exactly the same way that we generate *Most or some dogs run* with the overt indefinite, we would also generate the ungrammatical **Most or dogs run* with the covert indefinite. But in fact a recourse to null elements is not even an option for us here because we have assumed that the interpretation of functor types does not include the null element.

    Instead, we propose to treat apparent null operators uniformly by *unit assignment* wrapping assignments to the separator. Thus for (47) we assume the following:

(48) $1 : ((S\uparrow Npl)\downarrow S)\uparrow CNpl : \lambda x\lambda y\exists 2z[(x\ z)\wedge(y\ z)]$
      $1 : (CN\backslash CN)\uparrow(S/N) : \lambda x\lambda y\lambda z[(y\ z)\wedge(x\ z)]$

Thus, for example, (47b) is derived as shown in Fig. 6.14.

Exercise 6.7. Give the derivation for that-less relativization in hypersequent calculus.

Exercise 6.8. Give the derivations for (47a) in hypersequent calculus and labelled natural deduction.

Although the calculus itself of **DL** is decidable, the admission of assignments to the separator can challenge the decidability of recognition and parsing. For example, an assignment $1 : S\uparrow S : a$ loses the finite reading property since every sentence with meaning ϕ will also have meanings $a(\phi), a(a(\phi)), \ldots$.

     [9] There is also a generic reading, with which we do not concern ourselves here.

$$
\cfrac{
  \cfrac{
    \cfrac{CP/S, N, TV, Q, CN \Rightarrow CP}
          {CP/S, N, TV, [], CN \Rightarrow \sqrt{CP{\uparrow}Q}, [], \sqrt{CP{\uparrow}Q}} {\scriptstyle \uparrow R}
  }
  {CP/S, N, TV, CN \Rightarrow {}^{\wedge}(CP{\uparrow}Q)} {\scriptstyle \wedge R}
  \qquad S \Rightarrow S
}
{S/{}^{\wedge}(CP{\uparrow}Q), CP/S, N, TV, CN \Rightarrow S} {\scriptstyle /L}
$$

$$
\cfrac{
  \cfrac{
    \cfrac{N, TV, Q, CN \Rightarrow S}
          {N, TV, [], CN \Rightarrow \sqrt{S{\uparrow}Q}, [], \sqrt{S{\uparrow}Q}} {\scriptstyle \uparrow R}
  }{\ }
  \qquad S/{}^{\wedge}(CP{\uparrow}Q), CP/S, N, TV, CN \Rightarrow S
}
{N, TV, (S{\uparrow}Q){\downarrow}(S/{}^{\wedge}(CP{\uparrow}Q)), CN, CP/S, N, TV, CN \Rightarrow S} {\scriptstyle \downarrow L}
$$

FIGURE 6.13. Hypersequent derivation of comparative subdeletion (45)

loves

$$\dfrac{\mathbf{loves} : (N\backslash S)/N : love \qquad a : N : x^{i}}{\mathbf{loves+}a : N\backslash S : (love\ x)} \; E/$$

$$\dfrac{\mathrm{Mary} \quad}{\mathbf{Mary} : N : m}$$

$$\dfrac{\mathbf{Mary+loves+}a : S : (love\ x\ m)}{\mathbf{Mary+loves} : S/N : \lambda x(love\ x\ m)} \; I/^{i}$$

(right) $E/$; $E\backslash$; $E\uparrow$

$$\dfrac{\mathrm{man} \quad}{\mathbf{man} : CN : man}$$

$$\dfrac{1 : (CN\backslash CN)\uparrow(S/N) : \lambda x\lambda y\lambda z[(y\ z) \wedge (x\ z)]}{\mathbf{Mary+loves} : CN\backslash CN : \lambda y\lambda z[(y\ z) \wedge (love\ z\ m)]}$$

$$\dfrac{}{\mathbf{man+Mary+loves} : CN : \lambda z[(man\ z) \wedge (love\ z\ m)]} \; E\backslash$$

FIGURE 6.14. Labelled natural deduction derivation of that-less relativization (47b)

6.3.2.8 Right extraposition   In right extraposition an adnominal modifier appears clause-finally:

(49)   a. A man e_i sneezed [who jogs]$_i$
     b. Mary saw a man e_i today [from Brazil]$_i$

We propose to account for this by the following unit assignment:

(50) $1 : (\hat{}(S{\uparrow}(CN{\backslash}CN)){\backslash}S){\uparrow}(CN{\backslash}CN) : \lambda x \lambda y (y\ x)$

Exercise 6.9. Give the hypersequent and labelled natural deduction derivations of (49a).

Exercise 6.10. Give the hypersequent and labelled natural deduction derivations of (49b).

6.3.3 Linguistic applications of deterministic 2-DL

Here we consider deterministic discontinuity allowing two separators.

6.3.3.1 Reflexivization   Reflexive pronouns occupy nominal positions and take their interpretation from an antecedent noun phrase. This antecedent is usually clause-local (Principle A). The antecedent can be a subject as in (51a) or an object as in (51b):

(51)   a. John$_i$ sent himself$_i$ flowers.
     b. Dorothy bet [the straw man]$_i$ half of himself$_i$ that she would reach Emerald City first.

In for example Norwegian, subject-oriented and object-oriented reflexives have distinct forms; in English they are the same, but we treat them separately. For the subject-oriented case we assume the following assignment (cf. Moortgat 1991):

(52)   **himself** : $((N{\backslash}S){\uparrow}N){\downarrow}(N{\backslash}S) : \lambda x \lambda y (x\ y\ y)$

Then (51a) is derived as follows:

(53)
$$\cfrac{\cfrac{(N{\backslash}S)/(N{\bullet}N),\ N,\ N \Rightarrow N{\backslash}S}{(N{\backslash}S)/(N{\bullet}N),\ [],\ N \Rightarrow \sqrt[0]{(N{\backslash}S){\uparrow}N},\ [],\ \sqrt[1]{(N{\backslash}S){\uparrow}N}} {\uparrow}R \qquad N,\ N{\backslash}S \Rightarrow S}{N,\ (N{\backslash}S)/(N{\bullet}N),\ ((N{\backslash}S){\uparrow}N){\downarrow}(N{\backslash}S),\ N \Rightarrow S} {\downarrow}L$$

Exercise 6.11. Give the semantics of this derivation and check that this account of reflexivization interacts correctly with our account of quantification to create binding of a reflexive by a quantified antecedent, as in: *[Every man]$_i$ loves himself$_i$*.

On its own, however, this account overgenerates, allowing long-distance reflexivization in English:

(54)   *John$_i$ thinks Mary loves himself$_i$.

Chapter 8 modalizes categorial grammar so as to deliver intensional semantics in such a way that the locality of reflexivization can be captured by a modal type assignment suitably restricting the antecedent to lie within the local intensional/temporal domain, that is, the same tensed clause as the reflexive.

In English, an object-oriented reflexive must be preceded by its antecedent:

(55)   a. Mary talked to John$_i$ about himself$_i$.
       b. *Mary talked about himself$_i$ to John$_i$

Such a feature can be captured using second-position deterministic wrapping (VP abbreviates N\S):

(56)   **himself** : $\lambda x \lambda y(x \; y \; y)$: $((VP{\uparrow}N){\uparrow}_2 N){\downarrow}_2(VP{\uparrow}N)$

(The unsubscripted operators can be considered the first-position deterministic wrapping varieties, or equally the nondeterministic operators, since the sorting of the types ensures that the separator is always unique.) Then (51b) is derived as shown in Fig. 6.15.

Exercise 6.12. Give the derivation with semantics in labelled natural deduction.

We assume that clause-locality can again be ensured by intensionalization as before, but (56) additionally overgenerates in allowing an antecedent which does not c-command the reflexive as in:

(57)   *Mary talked to the friends of John$_i$ about himself$_i$.

On the other hand, a requirement that the antecedent always c-command a reflexive does not seem right either, since in (55a) the antecedent does not do so. Chomskyan syntax salvages c-command by claiming that in such an example, the preposition *to* is assimilated to the verb *talked* ('reanalysis'), but the issue remains a mystery to us. Likewise a mystery is the fact that a reflexive can sometimes precede a (non c-commanding) antecedent, or even apparently take its antecedent in another sentence:

(58)   That photofit poster of himself$_i$ hanging in every post office was really beginning to worry Clyde$_i$.

(59)   Clyde$_i$ was really beginning to get worried. That photofit poster of himself$_i$ in every post office was making it harder and harder to get around unnoticed.

$$(VP/CP)/(N\bullet N), N, N/N, N, N, CP \Rightarrow VP$$

$$\frac{}{(VP/CP)/(N\bullet N), [], N/N, N, N, CP \Rightarrow \sqrt[0]{}VP\uparrow\overline{N}, [], \sqrt{VP\uparrow N}}\uparrow R$$

$$N \Rightarrow N \qquad VP \Rightarrow VP$$

$$\frac{\sqrt[0]{}VP\uparrow\overline{N}, N, \sqrt{VP\uparrow N} \Rightarrow VP}{}\uparrow L$$

$$\frac{(VP/CP)/(N\bullet N), [], N/N, [], CP \Rightarrow \sqrt[0]{}(VP\uparrow N)\uparrow_2 N, [], \sqrt{(VP\uparrow N)\uparrow_2 N}, [], \sqrt[2]{}(VP\uparrow N)\uparrow_2 N}{}\uparrow_2 R$$

$$\frac{(VP/CP)/(N\bullet N), N, N/N, ((VP\uparrow N)\uparrow_2 N)\downarrow_2 (VP\uparrow N), CP \Rightarrow VP}{}\downarrow_2 L$$

FIGURE 6.15. Hypersequent derivation of VP medial object-oriented reflexivization (51b)

Pollard and Sag (1994) claim that such 'logophora' is possible just when the reflexive falls within the least 'oblique' complement of a verb. Note that an antecedent can occur in an adverbial phrase, and even be split:

(60)   When Bonnie met up with Clyde, they really began to get carried away with themselves.

Finally, note that a reflexive can also take a deictic antecedent:

(61)   Know yourself!

Our sketch of intrasentential reflexivization can only be a beginning.

6.3.3.2 Anaphora   Of course the possibility of intersentential dependencies is even more extensive with personal pronouns than with reflexive pronouns. In the end, a theory of sentential syntax must be integrated with a theory of discourse in this and other relations. But for the time-being we approximate intrasentential anaphora.

   Anaphora divides into backward anaphora or anaphora proper (antecedent precedes pronoun) and forward anaphora or cataphora (pronoun precedes 'antecedent'). At first blush it might seem that a single nondeterministic wrapping pronoun type $((S{\uparrow}N){\uparrow}N){\downarrow}(S{\uparrow}N)$ would conveniently allow both alternations, but reflection reveals that the very nondeterminism would make it impossible not to violate case restrictions when these are different between antecedent and pronoun positions:

(62)   a. *The friends of John$_i$ thought him$_i$ walked.
       b. *John$_i$ thought Mary liked he$_i$.

Therefore we propose to treat (intrasentential) backward anaphora in the same way that we did object-oriented reflexivization; cf. Morrill (2003). In that source an attempt was made to treat (configurational) case by type-lifting, but we now think that approach cannot be made to work;[10] here we assume features on N including case:

(63)   **him** : $((S{\uparrow}Nsg(3(m))C){\uparrow}_2 Nsg(3(m))acc){\downarrow}_2(S{\uparrow}Nsg(3(m))C)$
             : $\lambda x \lambda y (x\ y\ y)$

This interacts with our treatment of quantification to produce essentially the same characterization of quantification and bound anaphora that Montague's (1973) rule S14 of term-insertion gives in PTQ. But that rule is infinitary:

---

[10]   The lifting approach to case appears to flounder in the following respect. We would seem to want to say that an accusative noun phrase is $(VP{\uparrow}N){\downarrow}VP$. However *thinks e walks* has type $VP{\uparrow}N$ but misses a noun phrase which is nominative.

a term-inserted antecedent noun phrase looks to bind unboundedly many following pronouns in one go; in that respect the rule is not computational in the sense of being a finitary step. Our treatment is computationally finitary in that it is the responsibility of each pronoun to find in turn its single preceding antecedent, but unboundedly many pronouns can find the same antecedent, so the effect is basically the same as in PTQ.

As a result, our account suffers the same limitations as Montague's: it undergenerates in not producing any forward anaphora (cataphora), for example *Near him$_i$, [every cowboy]$_i$ kept a gun*, and it overgenerates with respect to Principle B (antilocality), for example *$^*John_i$ likes him$_i$.[11] Finally, the only reason why there are no Principle C violations is that the account generates no cataphora at all and English is right-branching. We could attempt to treat cataphora by, say:

(64) **he** : $((S{\uparrow}Nsg(3(m))nom){\uparrow}_2 Nsg(3(m))C){\downarrow}_1(S{\uparrow}Nsg(3(m))C)$
          : $\lambda x \lambda y (x\ y\ y)$

But then we would even overgenerate simultaneous Principle B and C violations like *$^*He_i$ likes John$_i$*.

Jacobson (1999) and Jäger (2001) both give accounts of anaphora invoking a new binary type constructor such that B^A (Jacobson's notation) or $B|A$ (Jäger's notation) is an expression of type B containing an unbound anaphor of type A; the meaning is the functional abstraction of the expression meaning over the anaphor meaning, that is, the semantic type is $T(A) \to T(B)$.

Although the introduction of new type-constructors is type-logical in spirit, Jacobson's account is couched in terms of combinatory categorial grammar, that is the characterization of derivability by a small number of axiomatic combinatory reduction schemata.[12]

The account of Jäger is type-logical in giving a sequent calculus, but we know of no straightforward syntactical interpretation of the type-constructor |. Like Jacobson's account, it has the attractive feature that a sentence with n free pronouns is simply of type $(\ldots (S|N^{(1)})\ldots)|N^{(n)}$ where the semantics is the functional abstraction of the sentence meaning over the

---

[11] Grodzinsky and Reinhart (1993) suggest that Principle B may be a pragmatic constraint rather than a syntactic one: that if the local interpretation was intended, the less ambiguous reflexive form would have been used. Morrill (2003) attempts to substantiate such an idea further by the principles on the incremental complexity of proof nets of Chapter 4.

[12] There is the following argument as to why combinatory categorial grammar is by definition incomplete. The product-free Lambek calculus is complete with respect to free semigroups, i.e. concatenation (Buszkowski, 1982), but it is not finitely axiomatizable (Zielonka, 1981). So combinatory categorial grammar qua a finite ('small') number of combinatory schemata cannot be complete with respect to concatenation. The essence of Zielonka's result is that the properties of recursively defined types cannot be fully captured without recursive rules, which is not really surprising.

meanings of the pronoun positions. This seems like a good point of departure to interface syntax with discourse, but as we say, syntactical interpretation is pending.

6.3.4 Linguistic applications of nondeterministic 2-DL

Here we consider nondeterministic discontinuity allowing two separators.

6.3.4.1 Complement alternation   By complement alternation we mean the free alternation in the order of the prepositional phrases in examples such as the following:[13]

(65) a. John talked to Mary about Bill.
       b. John talked about Bill to Mary.

The following single lexical assignment generates the alternation:

(66) **talked**+1+1 : $((N\backslash S){\uparrow}PP_{to}){\uparrow}PP_{about}$: *talk*

The hypersequent derivations of (65a, 65b) are as follows, where *VP* abbreviates $N\backslash S$.

(67)

$$\cfrac{PP_{about} \Rightarrow PP_{about} \qquad \cfrac{\cfrac{PP_{to} \Rightarrow PP_{to} \qquad VP \Rightarrow VP}{\sqrt[0]{VP \uparrow PP_{to}},\, PP_{to},\, \sqrt[1]{VP \uparrow PP_{to}} \Rightarrow VP}\;{\uparrow}L}{\sqrt[0]{VP \uparrow PP_{to}} \uparrow PP_{about},\, PP_{about},\, \sqrt[1]{VP \uparrow PP_{to}} \uparrow PP_{about},\, PP_{to},\, \sqrt[2]{(VP \uparrow PP_{to}) \uparrow PP_{about}} \Rightarrow VP}\;{\uparrow}L}{\sqrt[0]{(VP \uparrow PP_{to}) \uparrow PP_{about}},\, PP_{about},\, \sqrt[1]{(VP \uparrow PP_{to})} \uparrow PP_{about},\, PP_{to},\, \sqrt[2]{(VP \uparrow PP_{to}) \uparrow PP_{about}} \Rightarrow VP}$$

(68)

$$\cfrac{PP_{about} \Rightarrow PP_{about} \qquad \cfrac{\cfrac{PP_{to} \Rightarrow PP_{to} \qquad VP \Rightarrow VP}{\sqrt[0]{VP \uparrow PP_{to}},\, PP_{to},\, \sqrt[1]{VP \uparrow PP_{to}} \Rightarrow VP}\;{\uparrow}L}{\;}\;{\uparrow}L}{\sqrt[0]{(VP \uparrow PP_{to}) \uparrow PP_{about}},\, PP_{to},\, \sqrt[1]{(VP \uparrow PP_{about}) \uparrow PP_{to}},\, PP_{about},\, \sqrt[2]{(VP \uparrow PP_{to}) \uparrow PP_{about}} \Rightarrow VP}$$

Exercise 6.13. Give the semantically synonymous labelled natural deduction derivations of (65a, 65b).

6.3.4.2 Particle shift   Particle shift is the alternation in the order of a particle verb's object and its particle:[14]

---

[13] We have no explanation for the discrepancy: *John talked to Mary about herself/*John talked about Mary to herself*. Perhaps it has to do with an obliqueness ordering on the complement thematic roles and that a reflexive must have a less oblique antecedent (Pollard and Sag, 1994).

[14] We have no grammatical explanation of why the pronoun must be focused in *John called up HER*. or why *?John called the very heavy man up* is less acceptable. It seems that for the object to appear to the right it is necessary and sufficient for it to be 'informative'. This is the same issue as heavy noun phrase shift.

$$\dfrac{\dfrac{\text{called}\,(\dots)\,\text{up}\,(\dots)}{\text{called+1+up+1}:\,{}^{\vee}(N\backslash S)\!\uparrow\! N:phone} \quad \dfrac{\text{Mary}}{\text{Mary}:N:m}}{\dfrac{\text{called+1+up+Mary}:\,{}^{\vee}(N\backslash S):(phone\ m)}{\text{called+up+Mary}:N\backslash S:(phone\ m)}\ E^{\vee}}E\!\uparrow$$

$$\dfrac{\dfrac{\text{called}\,(\dots)\,\text{up}\,(\dots)}{\text{called+1+up+1}:\,{}^{\vee}(N\backslash S)\!\uparrow\! N:phone} \quad \dfrac{\text{Mary}}{\text{Mary}:N:m}}{\dfrac{\text{called+Mary+up+1}:\,{}^{\vee}(N\backslash S):(phone\ m)}{\text{called+Mary+up}:N\backslash S:(phone\ m)}\ E^{\vee}}E\!\uparrow$$

FIGURE 6.16. Labelled natural deduction derivations of particle shift (69a, 69b).

(69)   a. John called up Mary.
       b. John called Mary up.

The alternation is generated by the following single lexical assignment:

(70)   **called+1+up+1** : ${}^{\vee}(N\backslash S)\!\uparrow\! N$: *phone*

The labelled natural deduction derivations of (69a, 69b) are given in Fig. 6.16.

Exercise 6.14. Give hypersequent derivations of (69a, 69b).

7

Additive operators for polymorphism

Prepositional phrases can modify both nouns and verbs:

(1) a. man from Edinburgh
     b. walks from Edinburgh

In phrase structure grammar this is characterized as a syntactic ambiguity by classifying all prepositional phrases as *PP* and providing two rewrite rules:

(2) a. $CN \rightarrow CN\ PP$
     b. $VP \rightarrow VP\ PP$

But in categorial grammar as we have seen it up until now, the alternation must be reduced to a lexical ambiguity:

(3) a. **from** : $(CN\backslash CN)/N$
     b. **from** : $((N\backslash S)\backslash(N\backslash S))/N$

When a word or phrase can appear in more than one syntactic environment this may really be because of lexical ambiguity, but in at least some cases, such as prepositional phrases, we seem rather to want to be able to say that an element is syntactically *polymorphic*, that is, flexible with respect to and adaptive to different types in its environment, as opposed to lexically ambiguous. Categorial grammar restricted to *multiplicative* operators (in the terminology of linear logic) has to reduce polymorphism to lexical ambiguity. But in this chapter we see how *additive* operators (in the terminology of linear logic) enable us to express polymorphism and capture generalizations better in some cases, and in further cases enable coordination of unlike types which could not otherwise be captured at all.

$$\frac{}{A \Rightarrow A} \, id \qquad \frac{\Gamma \Rightarrow A \qquad \Delta(A) \Rightarrow B}{\Delta(\Gamma) \Rightarrow B} \, Cut$$

$$\frac{\Gamma \Rightarrow A \qquad \Delta(C) \Rightarrow D}{\Delta(\Gamma, A\backslash C) \Rightarrow D} \, \backslash L \qquad \frac{A, \Gamma \Rightarrow C}{\Gamma \Rightarrow A\backslash C} \, \backslash R$$

$$\frac{\Gamma \Rightarrow B \qquad \Delta(C) \Rightarrow D}{\Delta(C/B, \Gamma) \Rightarrow D} \, /L \qquad \frac{\Gamma, B \Rightarrow C}{\Gamma \Rightarrow C/B} \, /R$$

$$\frac{\Delta(A, B) \Rightarrow D}{\Delta(A{\bullet}B) \Rightarrow D} \, {\bullet}L \qquad \frac{\Gamma \Rightarrow A \qquad \Delta \Rightarrow B}{\Gamma, \Delta \Rightarrow A{\bullet}B} \, {\bullet}R$$

$$\frac{\Gamma(A) \Rightarrow C}{\Gamma(A\&B) \Rightarrow C} \, \&L_1 \qquad \frac{\Gamma(B) \Rightarrow C}{\Gamma(A\&B) \Rightarrow C} \, \&L_2$$

$$\frac{\Gamma \Rightarrow A \qquad \Gamma \Rightarrow B}{\Gamma \Rightarrow A\&B} \, \&R$$

$$\frac{\Gamma(A) \Rightarrow C \qquad \Gamma(B) \Rightarrow C}{\Gamma(A+B) \Rightarrow C} \, +L$$

$$\frac{\Gamma \Rightarrow A}{\Gamma \Rightarrow A+B} \, +R_1 \qquad \frac{\Gamma \Rightarrow B}{\Gamma \Rightarrow A+B} \, +R_2$$

FIGURE 7.1. The Lambek calculus with additives

Morrill (1990a) proposed to enrich Lambek categorial grammar with the additive conjunction & and disjunction + of linear logic. Then the set **F** of type formulas is defined as follows in terms of a set **P** of atomic type formulas:

(4) **F ::= P | F•F | F\F | F/F | F&F | F+F**

The Gentzen sequent calculus of the Lambek calculus with additives is as shown in Fig. 7.1.

As we shall see, this allows in the first place compression of some multiple lexical entries (lexical ambiguity) into single polymorphic lexical entries. For example, we will capture with a single polymorphic lexical entry the generalization that a preposition such as *from* can be both adnominal or adverbial. Similarly, we will capture with a single polymorphic lexical entry the generalization that the copula *is* can be either identificational (nominal complement) or predicational (e.g. with adjectival complement):

(5)   a.   Bond is 007/a spy.
      b.   Bond is teetotal.

Consider in the second place coordination of unlike types (Sag *et al.*, 1985) such as:

(6)   a.   007 is Bond and teetotal.
      b.   Bond is teetotal and a spy.

Our treatment of polymorphism predicts that such coordination is possible, assimilating it to like-type coordination (Morrill, 1990*a*; Johnson and Bayer, 1995; Bayer, 1996).

7.1 Curry–Howard semantic interpretation

For Curry–Howard semantic interpretation of the Lambek calculus with additives we need a Cartesian product for the additive conjunction (as for the multiplicative product) but also a disjoint union for the additive disjunction.

(7)   DEFINITION (*types*). The τ set of *types* is defined on the basis of a set δ of *basic types* as follows:

$$\tau ::= \delta \mid \tau \rightarrow \tau \mid \tau \& \tau \mid \tau + \tau$$

(8)   DEFINITION (*type domains*). The *type domain* D_τ of each type τ is defined on the basis of an assignment d of non-empty sets (*basic type domains*) to δ as follows:[1]

$$
\begin{aligned}
D_\tau &= d(\tau) & &\text{for } \tau \in \delta \\
D_{\tau_1 \rightarrow \tau_2} &= D_{\tau_2}{}^{D_{\tau_1}} & &\text{i.e. the set of all functions from } D_{\tau_1} \text{ to } D_{\tau_2} \\
D_{\tau_1 \& \tau_2} &= D_{\tau_1} \times D_{\tau_2} & &\text{i.e. } \{\langle m_1, m_2 \rangle \mid m_1 \in D_{\tau_1} \& m_2 \in D_{\tau_2}\} \\
D_{\tau_1 + \tau_2} &= D_{\tau_2} \uplus D_{\tau_1} & &\text{i.e. } (\{1\} \times D_{\tau_1}) \cup (\{2\} \times D_{\tau_2})
\end{aligned}
$$

Our typed terms now include, in addition to pairing and projection for Cartesian product types, a case statement $\phi \rightarrow x.\psi; y.\chi$ where ϕ is of disjoint union type. If ϕ is of the form $\iota_1 \phi'$ (first injection) this evaluates to $\psi\{\phi'/x\}$ and if ϕ is of the form $\iota_2 \phi'$ (second injection) it evaluates to $\chi\{\phi'/y\}$.

---

[1] Note incidentally that where $|\tau|$ signifies the cardinality of D_τ, the function $|\cdot|$ is a homomorphism from the algebra $(\mathbf{T}, +, \&, \rightarrow)$ of semantic types to the arithmetic algebra $(\mathbf{N}, +, \times, (\cdot)^{(\cdot)})$:

(i) $|\tau_1 + \tau_2| = |\tau_1| + |\tau_2|$
      $|\tau_1 \& \tau_2| = |\tau_1| \times |\tau_2|$
      $|\tau_1 \rightarrow \tau_2| = |\tau_2|^{|\tau_1|}$

(9) DEFINITION (*terms*). The sets Φ_τ of *terms* of type τ for each type τ are defined on the basis of a set C_τ of constants of type τ and an enumerably infinite set V_τ of variables of type τ for each type τ as follows:

$$\Phi_\tau ::= C_\tau \mid V_\tau$$
$$\mid (\Phi_{\tau'\to\tau}\,\Phi_{\tau'})$$
$$\mid \pi_1\Phi_{\tau\&\tau'} \mid \pi_2\Phi_{\tau'\&\tau}$$
$$\mid (\Phi_{\tau_1+\tau_2} \to V_{\tau_1}.\Phi_\tau;\ V_{\tau_2}.\Phi_\tau)$$
$$\Phi_{\tau\to\tau'} ::= \lambda V_\tau\Phi_{\tau'}$$
$$\Phi_{\tau\&\tau'} ::= (\Phi_\tau, \Phi_{\tau'})$$
$$\Phi_{\tau+\tau'} ::= \iota_1\Phi_\tau$$
$$\Phi_{\tau'+\tau} ::= \iota_2\Phi_\tau$$

Each term $\phi \in \Phi_\tau$ receives a semantic value $[\phi]^g \in D_\tau$ with respect to a valuation f which is a mapping sending each constant in C_τ to an element in D_τ, and an assignment g sending each variable in V_τ to an element in D_τ, as shown in Fig. 7.2.

An occurrence of a variable x in a term is called *free* iff it does not fall within any part of the term of the form $\lambda x\cdot$ or $x.\cdot$; otherwise it is *bound* (by the closest variable binding operator within the scope of which it falls). The result $\phi\{\psi/x\}$ of substituting term ψ (of type τ) for variable x (of type τ) in a term ϕ is the result of replacing by ψ every free occurrence of x in ϕ. We say that ψ is *free for x in ϕ* iff no variable in ψ becomes bound in $\phi\{\psi/x\}$. Manipulations can be pathological if substitution is not free. The laws of lambda conversion

$$[c]^g = f(c) \qquad\qquad \text{for } c \in C_\tau$$
$$[x]^g = g(x) \qquad\qquad \text{for } x \in V_\tau$$
$$[(\phi\,\psi)]^g = [\phi]^g([\psi]^g)$$
$$[\pi_1\phi]^g = \mathbf{fst}([\phi]^g)$$
$$[\pi_2\phi]^g = \mathbf{snd}([\phi]^g)$$
$$[\phi \to y.\psi; z.\chi]^g = \begin{cases} [\psi]^{(g-\{(y,g(y))\})\cup\{(y,d)\}} & \text{if } [\phi]^g = \langle 1, d\rangle \\ [\chi]^{(g-\{(z,g(z))\})\cup\{(z,d)\}} & \text{if } [\phi]^g = \langle 2, d\rangle \end{cases}$$
$$[\lambda x_\tau\phi]^g = D_\tau \ni d \mapsto [\phi]^{(g-\{(x,g(x))\})\cup\{(x,d)\}}$$
$$[(\phi, \psi)]^g = \langle [\phi]^g, [\psi]^g\rangle$$
$$[\iota_1\phi]^g = \langle 1, [\phi]^g\rangle$$
$$[\iota_2\phi]^g = \langle 2, [\phi]^g\rangle$$

FIGURE 7.2. Semantics of typed lambda calculus with Cartesian product and disjoint union

$$\lambda y \phi = \lambda x (\phi\{x/y\})$$
if x is not free in ϕ and x is free for y in ϕ
$$\phi \to y.\psi; z.\chi = \phi \to x.(\psi\{x/y\}); z.\chi$$
if x is not free in ψ and x is free for y in ψ
$$\phi \to y.\psi; z.\chi = \phi \to y.\psi; x.(\chi\{x/y\})$$
if x is not free in χ and x is free for z in χ

α-*conversion*

$$(\lambda x \phi\ \psi) = \phi\{\psi/x\}$$
if ψ is free for x in ϕ
$$\pi_1(\phi, \psi) = \phi$$
$$\pi_2(\phi, \psi) = \psi$$
$$\iota_1\phi \to y.\psi; z.\chi = \psi\{\phi/y\}$$
if ϕ is free for y in ψ
$$\iota_2\phi \to y.\psi; z.\chi = \chi\{\phi/z\}$$
if ϕ is free for z in χ

β-*conversion*

$$\lambda x(\phi\ x) = \phi$$
if x is not free in ϕ
$$(\pi_1\phi, \pi_2\phi) = \phi$$

η-*conversion*

FIGURE 7.3. Laws of lambda-conversion with Cartesian product and disjoint union

in Fig. 7.3 obtain (we omit the so-called commuting conversions for the case statement $\cdot \to x.\cdot; y.\cdot$).

The semantic readings of sequent derivations with additives are as shown in Fig. 7.4.

7.2 Polymorphism

To express the adnominal and adverbial polymorphism of prepositions and the identificational and predicational polymorphism of the copula we may have lexical entries such as the following:[2]

(10) a. **from** : $((CN\backslash CN)\&((N\backslash S)\backslash(N\backslash S)))/N$: $\lambda x((\textit{from}_{adn}\ x), (\textit{from}_{adv}\ x))$
      b. **is** : $(N\backslash S)/(N+(CN/CN))$: $\lambda x \lambda y x \to z.[y = z]; w.(w\ \lambda u[u = y]\ y)$

Note how the embedding of the additives in the types captures the generalizations that both adnominal and adverbial prepositions take objects and that both identificational and predicational copulas form verb phrases.

---

[2] The predicational part of the semantics of the copula is due to van Benthem (1991).

$$\left|\begin{array}{c} \vdots \\ \Gamma(A) \Rightarrow C \\ \hline \Gamma(A\&B) \Rightarrow C \end{array} \&L_1 \right|_{\mu(\phi)} = \left.\vert\; \begin{array}{c} \vdots \\ \Gamma(A) \Rightarrow C \end{array} \;\right\vert_{\mu(\pi_1\phi)}$$

$$\left|\begin{array}{c} \vdots \\ \Gamma(B) \Rightarrow C \\ \hline \Gamma(A\&B) \Rightarrow C \end{array} \&L_2 \right|_{\mu(\phi)} = \left.\vert\; \begin{array}{c} \vdots \\ \Gamma(B) \Rightarrow C \end{array} \;\right\vert_{\mu(\pi_2\phi)}$$

$$\left|\begin{array}{cc} \vdots & \vdots \\ \Gamma \Rightarrow A & \Gamma \Rightarrow B \\ \hline \multicolumn{2}{c}{\Gamma \Rightarrow A\&B} \end{array} \&R \right|_{\mu} = (\vert\; \Gamma \Rightarrow A \;\vert_{\mu}, \vert\; \Gamma \Rightarrow B \;\vert_{\mu})$$

$$\left|\begin{array}{cc} \vdots & \vdots \\ \Gamma(A) \Rightarrow C & \Gamma(B) \Rightarrow C \\ \hline \multicolumn{2}{c}{\Gamma(A+B) \Rightarrow C} \end{array} +L \right|_{\mu(\phi)} = \phi \to x.\vert\; \Gamma(A) \Rightarrow C \;\vert_{\mu(x)}; y.\vert\; \Gamma(B) \Rightarrow C \;\vert_{\mu(y)}$$

$$\left|\begin{array}{c} \vdots \\ \Gamma \Rightarrow A \\ \hline \Gamma \Rightarrow A+B \end{array} +R_1 \right|_{\mu} = \iota_1 \vert\; \Gamma \Rightarrow A \;\vert_{\mu}$$

$$\left|\begin{array}{c} \vdots \\ \Gamma \Rightarrow B \\ \hline \Gamma \Rightarrow A+B \end{array} +R_2 \right|_{\mu} = \iota_2 \vert\; \Gamma \Rightarrow B \;\vert_{\mu}$$

FIGURE 7.4. Semantic readings of sequent derivations with additives

In ordered natural deduction elimination of & and introduction of + are represented as follows:[3]

(11)

$$\begin{array}{c} \vdots \\ A\&B : \chi \\ \hline A : \pi_1\chi \end{array} E\&_1 \qquad \begin{array}{c} \vdots \\ A\&B : \chi \\ \hline B : \pi_2\chi \end{array} E\&_2$$

$$\begin{array}{c} \vdots \\ A : \phi \\ \hline A+B : \iota_1\phi \end{array} I+_1 \qquad \begin{array}{c} \vdots \\ B : \psi \\ \hline A+B : \iota_2\psi \end{array} I+_2$$

---

[3] It is not straightforward to represent the introduction of & and the elimination of + in ordered natural deduction, but these are not needed for our examples.

Then given the polymorphic preposition assignment (10a), *man from Edinburgh* and *walks from Edinburgh* have the following derivations in ordered natural deduction:

(12)

$$
\cfrac{
\cfrac{
\cfrac{
\cfrac{\text{from}}{((CN\backslash CN)\&((N\backslash S)\backslash(N\backslash S)))/N : \lambda x((\textit{from}_{adn}\ x), (\textit{from}_{adv}\ x))} \qquad \cfrac{\text{Edinburgh}}{N : e}
}{(CN\backslash CN)\&((N\backslash S)\backslash(N\backslash S)) : ((\textit{from}_{adn}\ e), (\textit{from}_{adv}\ e))} \ {\scriptstyle E/}
}{
\cfrac{\text{man}}{CN : man} \qquad \cfrac{CN\backslash CN : (\textit{from}_{adn}\ e)}{} \ {\scriptstyle E\&_1}
}{CN : (\textit{from}_{adn}\ e\ man)} \ {\scriptstyle E\backslash}
}
$$

(13)

$$
\cfrac{
\cfrac{
\cfrac{\text{walks}}{CN : walk} \qquad
\cfrac{
\cfrac{
\cfrac{\text{from}}{((CN\backslash CN)\&((N\backslash S)\backslash(N\backslash S)))/N : \lambda x((\textit{from}_{adn}\ x), (\textit{from}_{adv}\ x))} \qquad \cfrac{\text{Edinburgh}}{N : e}
}{(CN\backslash CN)\&((N\backslash S)\backslash(N\backslash S)) : ((\textit{from}_{adn}\ e), (\textit{from}_{adv}\ e))} \ {\scriptstyle E/}
}{(N\backslash S)\backslash(N\backslash S) : (\textit{from}_{adv}\ e)} \ {\scriptstyle E\&_2}
}{CN : (\textit{from}_{adv}\ e\ walks)} \ {\scriptstyle E\backslash}
}{}
$$

Using the polymorphic copula assignment (10b), the sentence *Tully is Cicero* is derived as follows:

(14)

$$
\cfrac{
\cfrac{\text{Tully}}{N : t} \qquad
\cfrac{
\cfrac{\text{is}}{(N\backslash S)/(N{+}(CN/CN)) : \lambda x\lambda y x \to z.[y = z]; w.(w\ \lambda u[u = y]\ y)} \qquad \cfrac{\cfrac{\text{Cicero}}{N : c}}{N{+}(CN/CN) : {}_{\iota_1} c} \ {\scriptstyle I+_1}
}{N\backslash S : \lambda y[y = c]} \ {\scriptstyle E/}
}{S : [t = c]} \ {\scriptstyle \backslash L}
$$

The same assignment allows us to correctly analyse *Cicero is a writer*; we do this in Fig. 7.5 using labelled natural deduction (since the indefinite uses discontinuous connectives). And the predicational *Cicero is humanist* is derived as shown in Fig. 7.6 (in ordered natural deduction again).

7.3 Coordination of unlike types

Assuming our additive-polymorphic type assignment to the copula $(N\backslash S)/(N{+}(CN/CN))$, with the like-type coordinator assignment schema we assumed in Chapter 3, the 'unlike type' coordination (15) is automatically predicted because each conjunct can assume the lift of $N{+}(CN/CN)$, as shown in Fig. 7.7, where $\frac{1}{A}$ abbreviates $(A\backslash A)/A$ and X abbreviates $(N\backslash S)/(N{+}(CN/CN))$.

Cicero

$$
\dfrac{i}{a : N : x}
$$

is

$$
\dfrac{\text{is} : (N\backslash S)/(N+(CN/CN)) : \lambda x \lambda y\, x \to z.[y = z]; w.(w\, \lambda u[u = y]\, y) \quad a : N+(CN/CN) : \iota_1 x}{\text{is}+a : N\backslash S : \lambda y[y = x]} \; E/
$$

Cicero : N : c

$$
\dfrac{\text{Cicero}+\text{is}+a : S : [c = x]}{\text{Cicero}+\text{is}+1 : S{\uparrow}N : \lambda x[c = x]} \; I{\uparrow}^i \qquad E\backslash
$$

a

$$
\dfrac{a : ((S{\uparrow}N){\downarrow}S)/CN : \lambda x \lambda y \exists z[(x\, z) \wedge (y\, z)] \quad \text{writer} : CN : writer}{\text{a}+\text{writer} : (S{\uparrow}N){\downarrow}S : \lambda y \exists z[(writer\, z) \wedge (y\, z)]} \; E/
$$

writer

$$
\text{Cicero}+\text{is}+a+\text{writer} : S : \exists z[(writer\, z) \wedge [c = z]] \qquad E{\downarrow}
$$

FIGURE 7.5. Derivation of *Cicero is a writer*

is **humanist**

$$\cfrac{CN/CN:\lambda x\lambda y[(x\,y)\wedge(humanist\,y)]}{N+(CN/CN):\iota_2\lambda x\lambda y[(x\,y)\wedge(humanist\,y)]}\;I+_2$$

Cicero $\quad\cfrac{(N\backslash S)/(N+(CN/CN)):\lambda x\lambda yx\to z.[y=z];w.(w\,\lambda u[u=y]\,y)\qquad N+(CN/CN):\iota_2\lambda x\lambda y[(x\,y)\wedge(humanist\,y)]}{\;}\;E/$

$N:c\quad\cfrac{N\backslash S:\lambda y[[y=y]\wedge(humanist\,y)]=\lambda y(humanist\,y)}{\;}$

$$\cfrac{}{S:(humanist\,c)}\;\backslash L$$

FIGURE 7.6. Derivation of *Cicero is humanist*

Cicero

$$\frac{N:c}{}$$

$$\frac{}{X:v}\,j \quad \frac{N:c}{N+(CN/CN):\iota_1 c}\,I+_1$$

$$\frac{N\backslash S:(v\ \iota_1 c)}{}\,E/$$

$$\frac{X\backslash(N\backslash S):\lambda v(v\ \iota_1 c)}{}\,I\backslash^j$$

humanist

$$\frac{CN/CN:\lambda x\lambda y[(x\ y)\wedge(\textit{humanist}\ y)]}{}$$

$$\frac{}{X:u}\,i \quad \frac{CN/CN:\lambda x\lambda y[(x\ y)\wedge(\textit{humanist}\ y)]}{N+(CN/CN):\iota_2\lambda x\lambda y[(x\ y)\wedge(\textit{humanist}\ y)]}\,I+_2$$

$$\frac{N\backslash S:(u\ \iota_2\lambda x\lambda y[(x\ y)\wedge(\textit{humanist}\ y)])}{}\,E/$$

$$\frac{X\backslash(N\backslash S):\lambda u(u\ \iota_2\lambda x\lambda y[(x\ y)\wedge(\textit{humanist}\ y)])}{}\,I\backslash^i$$

and

$$X:\lambda x\lambda y\lambda z\lambda w![(y\ z\ w)\wedge(x\ z\ w)]$$

$$\frac{1}{X\backslash(N\backslash S)}$$

$$\frac{(X\backslash(N\backslash S))\backslash(X\backslash(N\backslash S)):\lambda y\lambda z\lambda w![(y\ z\ w)\wedge(z\ \iota_2\lambda x\lambda y[(x\ y)\wedge(\textit{humanist}\ y)]\ w)]}{}\,E\backslash$$

$$\frac{X\backslash(N\backslash S):\lambda z\lambda w![(z\ \iota_1 c\ w)\wedge(z\ \iota_2\lambda x\lambda y[(x\ y)\wedge(\textit{humanist}\ y)]\ w)]}{}\,E\backslash$$

is

$$\textbf{Tully}\quad X:\lambda x\lambda y x\to z.[y=z];w.(w\ \lambda u[u=y]\ y)$$

$$\frac{}{N:t}$$

$$N\backslash S:\lambda w![w=c]\wedge[w=w]\wedge(\textit{humanist}\ w)] = \lambda w![w=c]\wedge(\textit{humanist}\ w)]$$

$$\frac{}{}\,E\backslash$$

$$S:[[t=c]\wedge(\textit{humanist}\ t)]$$

FIGURE 7.7. Derivation of unlike type coordination *Tully is Cicero and humanist*

(15) Tully is Cicero and humanist.

Exercise 7.1. Derive *Tully is Cicero and a writer* and *Tully is a writer and humanist*.

Observe that a verb may have two subcategorization frames which cannot coordinate:

(16) a. John wants to walk.
      b. John wants Mary to sing.
      c. *John wants [to walk and Mary to sing]

The non-coordinability is captured by assuming, instead of a single polymorphic lexical entry, two homomorphic lexical entries:

(17) a. **wants** : $(N \backslash S)/(N \backslash S)$: $\lambda x \lambda y (want\ (x\ y)\ y)$
      b. **wants** : $(N \backslash S)/(N \bullet (N \backslash S))$: $\lambda x \lambda y (want\ (\pi_2 x\ \pi_1 x)\ y)$

Neither non-polymorphic type assignment can generate the ungrammatical coordination.

Exercise 7.2. Test whether the verb *become* is ambiguous or polymorphic according to these criteria.

8

Modality for intensionality

> *'It was the best of times, it was the worst of times.'*
> Charles Dickens, A *Tale of Two Cities*: 1

Semantics, the study of the relation between language and the world, often assumes that an expression has a unique denotation, extension, or reference. But, in general, expressions have multiple references relative to different points which are variously considered or termed worlds, times, states, situations, contexts, or indices. We refer to this multiplicity as intensionality. Intensionality is a major challenge in semantics and the philosophy of language. We do not offer a new theory of intensional semantics here, but we give a technical refinement, a logical formalization, of Montague's treatment of intensionality. We give a type-driven intensional account in modal Lambek calculus, in the same way that unadorned Lambek calculus renders a type-driven extensional account.

So far, our semantic ontology has been based on entities and truth values. Possible worlds semantics (see e.g. Dowty *et al.* 1981) assumes in addition (possible) worlds. A Fregean sense (manner of referring) or intension is formalized as a function from possible worlds to its reference or extension in those worlds.

This is a rather declarative rendering of sense: manner of referring sounds like it should be more procedural. And it is well-known that possible worlds semantics does not afford a sufficiently fine-grained theory of intensions. For example, according to possible worlds semantics all contradictions have the same intension (the constant function from worlds to false) and all tautologies have the same intension (the constant function from worlds to true). Thus if one believes or knows one tautology, one believes or knows them all (logical omniscience). This omniscient competence is beyond human capacity, so we regard our possible worlds semantics as a theory of God's-eye idealized competence.[1]

Morrill (1990*b*) introduced modalities to categorial grammar, for intensionality; see also Morrill (1994, ch. 4, sect. 4, and ch. 5). Here we review this proposal.

8.1 Modal Lambek calculus

The set **F** of type formulas of our modal Lambek calculus is defined as follows in terms of a set **P** of atomic type formulas:

(1)   **F ::= P | F•F | F\F | F/F | □F**

Then the Gentzen sequent calculus rules for the modality are as follows, where $\Box\Gamma$ signifies a configuration Γ all the types of which have $\Box$ as the main connective:

(2) $$\frac{\Gamma(A) \Rightarrow B}{\Gamma(\Box A) \Rightarrow B}\Box L \qquad \frac{\Box\Gamma \Rightarrow A}{\Box\Gamma \Rightarrow \Box A}\Box R$$

These are the sequent calculus rules of the normal modal logic S4.

Exercise 8.1. Prove:

   a. $\Box A \Rightarrow A$ modal axiom T
   b. $\Box A \Rightarrow \Box\Box A$ modal axiom 4
   c. $\Box(A\backslash B) \Rightarrow \Box A\backslash\Box B$ distribution (modal normality)

8.2 Intensional lambda calculus

Just as Lambek calculus proofs have a semantic reading as terms of the lambda calculus, we define an intensional lambda calculus such that modal Lambek calculus proofs have a semantic reading as terms of the intensional lambda calculus.

(3)   DEFINITION (*types*). The set τ of *types* is defined on the basis of a set δ of *basic types* as follows:

$$\tau ::= \delta \mid \tau \rightarrow \tau \mid \tau \& \tau \mid L\tau$$

---

[1] For approaches to this problem see Fox and Lappin (2005) and Pollard (2008).

(4)   DEFINITION (*type domains*). The *type domain* D_τ of each type τ is defined on the basis of an assignment d of non-empty sets (*basic type domains*) to δ and a non-empty set W (of worlds) as follows:

$$
\begin{aligned}
D_\tau &= d(\tau) &&\text{for } \tau \in \delta \\
D_{\tau_1 \to \tau_2} &= D_{\tau_2}^{D_{\tau_1}} &&\text{functional exponentiation} \\
&&&\text{i.e. the set of all functions from } D_{\tau_1} \text{ to } D_{\tau_2} \\
D_{\tau_1 \& \tau_2} &= D_{\tau_1} \times D_{\tau_2} &&\text{Cartesian product} \\
&&&\text{i.e. } \{\langle m_1, m_2 \rangle \mid m_1 \in D_{\tau_1} \ \& \ m_2 \in D_{\tau_2}\} \\
D_{L\tau} &= D_\tau{}^W
\end{aligned}
$$

(5)   DEFINITION (*terms*). The sets Φ_τ of *terms* of type τ for each type τ are defined on the basis of a set C_τ of constants of type τ and a denumerably infinite set V_τ of variables of type τ for each type τ as follows:

$$
\begin{aligned}
\Phi_\tau &::= C_\tau \mid V_\tau \mid (\Phi_{\tau' \to \tau} \ \Phi_{\tau'}) \mid \pi_1 \Phi_{\tau \& \tau'} \mid \pi_2 \Phi_{\tau' \& \tau} \mid {}^\vee \Phi_{L\tau} \\
\Phi_{\tau \to \tau'} &::= \lambda V_\tau \Phi_{\tau'} \\
\Phi_{\tau \& \tau'} &::= (\Phi_\tau, \Phi_{\tau'}) \\
\Phi_{L\tau} &::= {}^\wedge \Phi_\tau
\end{aligned}
$$

Each term $\phi \in \Phi_\tau$ receives a semantic value $[\phi]^{g,i} \in D_\tau$ with respect to a valuation f which is a mapping sending each constant in C_τ to an element in D_τ, an assignment g which is a mapping sending each variable in V_τ to an element in D_τ, and a world $i \in W$ as shown in Fig. 8.1.

  As in the extensional lambda calculus, an occurrence of a variable x in a term is called *free* if and only if it does not fall within any part of the term of the form $\lambda x \cdot$; otherwise it is *bound* (by the closest λx within the scope of which it falls). The result $\phi\{\psi/x\}$ of substituting term ψ (of type τ) for variable x (of type τ) in a term ϕ is the result of replacing by ψ every free occurrence of x in

$$
\begin{aligned}
[c]^{g,i} &= f(c) &&\text{for } c \in C_\tau \\
[x]^{g,i} &= g(x) &&\text{for } x \in V_\tau \\
[(\phi\,\psi)]^{g,i} &= [\phi]^{g,i}([\psi]^{g,i}) &&\text{functional application} \\
[\pi_1\phi]^{g,i} &= \mathbf{fst}([\phi]^{g,i}) &&\text{first projection} \\
[\pi_2\phi]^{g,i} &= \mathbf{snd}([\phi]^{g,i}) &&\text{second projection} \\
[{}^\vee\phi]^{g,i} &= [\phi]^{g,i}(i) &&\text{extensionalization} \\
[\lambda x_\tau \phi]^{g,i} &= D_\tau \ni d \mapsto [\phi]^{(g-\{(x,g(x))\})\cup\{(x,d)\},i} &&\text{functional abstraction} \\
[(\phi,\psi)]^{g,i} &= \langle [\phi]^{g,i}, [\psi]^{g,i} \rangle &&\text{ordered pair formation} \\
[{}^\wedge\phi]^{g,i} &= W \ni j \mapsto [\phi]^{g,j} &&\text{intensionalization}
\end{aligned}
$$

FIGURE 8.1. Semantics of intensional lambda calculus

$$\lambda y \phi = \lambda x(\phi\{x/y\})$$

if x is not free in ϕ and x is free for y in ϕ

α-*conversion*

$$(\lambda x \phi \ \psi) = \phi\{\psi/x\}$$

if ψ is free for x in ϕ, and modally free for x in ϕ

$$\pi_1(\phi, \psi) = \phi$$
$$\pi_2(\phi, \psi) = \psi$$
$$^{\vee\wedge}\phi = \phi$$

β-*conversion*

$$\lambda x(\phi \ x) = \phi$$

if x is not free in ϕ

$$(\pi_1\phi, \pi_2\phi) = \phi$$
$$^{\wedge\vee}\phi = \phi$$

if ϕ is modally closed

η-*conversion*

FIGURE 8.2. Laws of intensional lambda-conversion

ϕ. We say that ψ is *free for x in ϕ* if and only if no variable in ψ becomes bound in $\phi\{\psi/x\}$.

Manipulations may be pathological if substitution is not free in this sense. But we need additional definitions in relation to intensionality (cf. Morrill, 1994: 139–40). We say that a term is *modally closed* if and only if every occurrence of $^{\vee}$ occurs within the scope of an $^{\wedge}$. A modally closed term is denotationally invariant across worlds. We say that a term ψ is *modally free for x in ϕ* if and only if either ψ is modally closed, or no free occurrence of x in ϕ is within the scope of an $^{\wedge}$. The laws of intensional lambda conversion in Fig. 8.2 obtain.

8.3 Curry–Howard semantic interpretation

The semantic readings of sequent derivations with the modality are as shown in Fig. 8.3. Natural deduction is as follows:

(6)

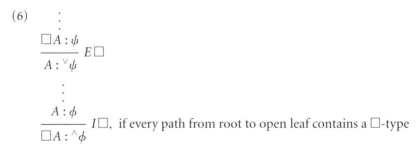

$$\left| \begin{array}{c} \vdots \\ \dfrac{\Gamma(A) \Rightarrow B}{\Gamma(\Box A) \Rightarrow B} \Box L \end{array} \right|_{\mu(\phi)} = \left| \begin{array}{c} \vdots \\ \Gamma(A) \Rightarrow B \end{array} \right|_{\mu(^{\vee}\phi)}$$

$$\left| \begin{array}{c} \vdots \\ \dfrac{\Box\Gamma \Rightarrow A}{\Box\Gamma \Rightarrow \Box A} \Box R \end{array} \right|_{\mu} = \; ^{\wedge} \left| \begin{array}{c} \vdots \\ \Box\Gamma \Rightarrow A \end{array} \right|_{\mu}$$

FIGURE 8.3. Semantic readings of sequent derivations with modality for intensionality

8.4 Example intensional fragment

Let there be the lexical entries of Fig. 8.4. Then *John walks* is analysed as follows:

(7)   John   walks

$$\dfrac{\dfrac{\Box N : {}^{\wedge}j}{N : j} E\Box \quad \dfrac{\dfrac{\Box(N\backslash S) : walk}{N\backslash S : {}^{\vee}walk} E\Box}{S : ({}^{\vee}walk\, j)} E\backslash}$$

Exercise 8.2. Analyse *John loves Mary*.

The sentence *Necessarily John is John* is analysed thus:

(8)

$$\dfrac{\begin{array}{c} necessarily \\ \hline \dfrac{\Box(S/\Box S) : {}^{\wedge}necessarily}{S/\Box S : necessarily} E\Box \end{array} \qquad \begin{array}{c} \dfrac{\begin{array}{c} \dfrac{John}{\dfrac{\Box N : {}^{\wedge}j}{N : j} E\Box} \quad \dfrac{\begin{array}{c} is \\ \hline \dfrac{\Box((N\backslash S)/N) : {}^{\wedge}\lambda x\lambda y[y=x]}{(N\backslash S)/N : \lambda x\lambda y[y=x]} E\Box \quad \dfrac{John}{\dfrac{\Box N : {}^{\wedge}j}{N : j} E\Box}}{N\backslash S : \lambda y[y=j]} E/ \end{array}}{S : [j=j]} E\backslash}{\dfrac{\Box S : {}^{\wedge}[j=j]}{}} I\Box \end{array}}{S : (necessarily\, {}^{\wedge}[j=j])} E/$$

Note how the $I\Box$ is allowed because all the lexical types are modalized.

alleged : $\Box(CN/\Box CN)$: *alleged*
> intensional adjective

believes : $\Box((N\backslash S)/\Box S)$: *believe*
> for subject extraction cf. Chapter 5

blind : $\Box(CN/CN)$: $^\wedge \lambda x \lambda y[(x\ y) \wedge (^\vee blind\ y)]$
> intersective adjective

everyone : $\Box((S\uparrow N)\downarrow S)$: $^\wedge \lambda x \forall y[(^\vee person\ y) \to (x\ y)]$

father : $\Box CN$: *father*

finds : $\Box((N\backslash S)/N)$: *find*
> extensional transitive verb

for : $\Box(PP/N)$: $^\wedge \lambda x x$

good : $\Box(CN/CN)$: $^\wedge \lambda x \lambda y[(x\ y) \wedge (^\vee good\ y\ x)]$
> non-intersective extensional adjective

himself : $\Box(((N\backslash S)\uparrow N)\downarrow(N\backslash S))$: $^\wedge \lambda x \lambda y(x\ y\ y)$

is : $\Box((N\backslash S)/N)$: $^\wedge \lambda x \lambda y[y = x]$
> for polymorphism cf. Chapter 7

John : $\Box N$: $^\wedge j$
> rigid designator

king : $\Box CN$: *king*

loves : $\Box((N\backslash S)/N)$: *love*
> extensional transitive verb

man : $\Box CN$: *man*

Mary : $\Box N$: $^\wedge m$
> rigid designator

necessarily : $\Box(S/\Box S)$: $^\wedge necessarily$

possibly : $\Box(S/\Box S)$: $^\wedge possibly$

prays : $\Box((N\backslash S)/PP)$: *pray_for*

seeks : $\Box((N\backslash S)/\Box(((N\backslash S)/N)\backslash(N\backslash S)))$: $^\wedge \lambda x \lambda y(^\vee try\ ^\wedge(^\vee x\ ^\vee find\ y)\ y)$
> intensional transitive verb

someone : $\Box((S\uparrow\Box N)\downarrow S)$: $^\wedge \lambda x \exists y[(^\vee person\ y) \wedge (x\ ^\wedge y)]$

son : $\Box CN$: *son*

the : $\Box(N/CN)$: $^\wedge \iota$

to : $\Box((N\backslash S)/(N\backslash S))$: $^\wedge \lambda x x$

tries : $\Box((N\backslash S)/\Box(N\backslash S))$: $^\wedge \lambda x \lambda y(^\vee try\ ^\wedge(^\vee x\ y)\ y)$
> equi control verb

walks : $\Box(N\backslash S)$: *walk*

who : $\Box((CN\backslash CN)/(N\backslash S))$: $^\wedge \lambda x \lambda y \lambda z[(y\ z) \wedge (x\ z)]$

who : $\Box((CN\backslash CN)/(S/\Box N))$: $^\wedge \lambda x \lambda y \lambda z[(y\ z) \wedge (x\ ^\wedge z)]$
> for extraction cf. Chapter 5

FIGURE 8.4. Intensional lexicon

The sentence *Everyone walks* is analysed as follows:

(9)

$$
\begin{array}{c}
\text{walks} \\
\hline
\text{walks} : \Box(N\backslash S) : walk
\end{array}
$$

$$
\cfrac{
  \cfrac{a : N : x}{}\ i
  \qquad
  \cfrac{\text{walks} : \Box(N\backslash S) : walk}{\text{walks} : N\backslash S : {}^{\vee}walk}\ E\Box
}{
  \cfrac{a{+}\text{walks} : S : ({}^{\vee}walk\ x)}{1{+}\text{walks} : S{\uparrow}N : \lambda x({}^{\vee}walk\ x)}\ I{\uparrow}^{i}
}\ E\backslash
$$

$$
\begin{array}{c}
\text{everyone} \\
\hline
\cfrac{\text{everyone} : \Box((S{\uparrow}N){\downarrow}S) : {}^{\wedge}\lambda x\forall y[({}^{\vee}person\ y) \to (x\ y)]}{\text{everyone} : (S{\uparrow}N){\downarrow}S : \lambda x\forall y[({}^{\vee}person\ y) \to (x\ y)]}\ E\Box
\end{array}
$$

$$
\text{everyone}{+}\text{walks} : S : \forall y[({}^{\vee}person\ y) \to ({}^{\vee}walk\ y)]\ \ E{\downarrow}
$$

The de re analysis of *John believes someone walks* is shown in Fig. 8.5. Note that the $I\Box$ is allowed because the hypothetical subtype of *someone* is modalized.

Exercise 8.3. Give the de dicto analysis of *John believes someone walks*.

Because the hypothetical subtype of *everyone* is not modalized, *John believes everyone walks* has only a narrow-scope analysis.

Exercise 8.4. Analyse:

a. An alleged king walks.
b. A good king walks.
c. A blind king walks.

Which of these entail that there is a king?

Exercise 8.5. Analyse:

a. father who loves the son
b. son who John believes the father loves

Note how the extraction from an intensional domain is licensed because the hypothetical subtype of the object relative pronoun *who* is modalized.

Exercise 8.6. Analyse:

a. John loves himself.
b. John prays for himself.
c. *John believes Mary loves himself.

Why is the long-distance reflexivization blocked?

walks

$$\dfrac{a : \Box N : x}{a : N : {}^{\vee}x}\ i \qquad \text{walks} : \Box(N\backslash S) : walk$$
$$E\Box \qquad\qquad \dfrac{}{\text{walks} : N\backslash S : {}^{\vee}walk}\ E\Box$$
$$\dfrac{a+\text{walks} : S : ({}^{\vee}walk\ {}^{\vee}x)}{}\ E\backslash$$

believes

$$\dfrac{\text{believes} : \Box((N\backslash S)/\Box S) : believe}{\text{believes} : (N\backslash S)/\Box S : {}^{\vee}believe}\ E\Box$$
$$\dfrac{a+\text{walks} : S : ({}^{\vee}walk\ {}^{\vee}x)}{a+\text{walks} : \Box S : {}^{\wedge}({}^{\vee}walk\ {}^{\vee}x)}\ I\Box$$
$$\dfrac{\text{believes}+a+\text{walks} : N\backslash S : ({}^{\vee}believe\ {}^{\wedge}({}^{\vee}walk\ {}^{\vee}x))}{}\ E/$$

John

$$\dfrac{\Box N : {}^{\wedge}j}{N : j}\ E\Box$$

$$\dfrac{\text{John}+\text{believes}+a+\text{walks} : S : ({}^{\vee}believe\ {}^{\wedge}({}^{\vee}walk\ {}^{\vee}x)\ j)}{}\ E\backslash$$
$$\dfrac{\text{John}+\text{believes}+1+\text{walks} : S\uparrow\Box N : \lambda x({}^{\vee}believe\ {}^{\wedge}({}^{\vee}walk\ {}^{\vee}x)\ j)}{}\ I\uparrow^{i}$$

someone

$$\dfrac{\text{someone} : \Box((S\uparrow\Box N)\downarrow S) : {}^{\wedge}\lambda x\exists y[({}^{\vee}person\ y)\wedge(x\ {}^{\wedge}y)]}{\text{someone} : (S\uparrow\Box N)\downarrow S : \lambda x\exists y[({}^{\vee}person\ y)\wedge(x\ {}^{\wedge}y)]}\ E\Box$$

$$\dfrac{\text{John}+\text{believes}+\text{someone}+\text{walks} : S : \exists y[({}^{\vee}person\ y)\wedge({}^{\vee}believe\ {}^{\wedge}({}^{\vee}walk\ y)\ j)]}{}\ E\downarrow$$

FIGURE 8.5. De re analysis of John believes someone walks

Exercise 8.7. Analyse:

a. John tries to find Mary.
b. John seeks Mary.
c. John tries to find himself.
d. John seeks himself.
e. John tries to find someone.
f. John seeks someone.

Note the synonymy of each sentence pair, even extending to the shared specific/non-specific ambiguity of the last sentence pair.

Just as we have used one modality for worlds, we may introduce another modality for times. Then we would have a bimodal Lambek calculus (Morrill, 1994: 147–8), or, in general for multiple indices, polymodal Lambek calculi. Such a tense modality can be used to define a tensed S locality constraint on reflexivization by reference to temporal domains.

Part III
Further Processing Issues

In this part we expand and develop on the application of proof nets to language processing. In Chapter 9 we apply the processing theory of Chapter 4 to aphasic comprehension. So far we have considered how syntax may be represented as proof nets; in Chapter 10 we consider how semantics may also be represented as proof nets. In Chapter 11 we describe a method for chart parsing with proof nets. We conclude in Chapter 12.

9

Aphasic comprehension

In this chapter we broaden the range of empirical application of categorial grammar by considering aphasia.[1] We add to the arguments for proof net syntactic structures with a statistically significant account of aphasic comprehension in terms of the proof net complexity metric. We address the issue as to whether aphasia is due to grammatical or processing impairment. A comparison is made of complexity as measured by the categorial complexity metric of Chapter 4 with the aphasic performance observed in a large study carried out by Caplan and his colleagues. We find a significant negative linear correlation, suggesting that notwithstanding other possible grammatical and/or performance factors, aphasics suffer a deficit of working memory capacity in the incremental comprehension of language.

Haarmann *et al.* (1997) describes a computational model of aphasic sentence comprehension based on the premise that all aphasics share a common deficit in the activation resources of working memory. They simulate the data from Caplan *et al.* (1985) (see Caplan and Hildecrandt, 1988) of aphasic patients from all major syndrome types. In their system 'As each word comes in, the model attempts to incorporate it as much as possible into the evolving syntactic and semantic representation. First, the word is perceptually encoded. Then, lexical access makes available its meaning and syntactic class and, in the case of verbs, also its argument structure. Based on its word class and a grammar, the word is integrated into a parse tree representation. The thematic role mapping component computes thematic-role bindings.' (Haarmann *et al.*, 1997: 88). 'The hypothesized resource reduction in aphasia was then induced by decreasing the model's working memory capacity considerably, reducing it by half to a level of fifteen activation units, to optimize the fit

---

[1] This chapter is a reworking of Morrill and Gavarró (2004).

with the Caplan et al. data.' (Haarmann *et al.*, 1997: 96). Our result echoes that of Haarmann *et al.* (1997) but with the logical categorial grammar architecture.

We focus on experiment 2 reported in chapter 4 of Caplan and Hildecrandt (1988). In this experiment the subjects were thirty-seven native English speaker aphasics. The experimenter read a sentence with normal nonemphatic intonation and the subjects were required to perform an object-manipulation task using toys to demonstrate semantic features of the sentence. The types of sentences used were as follows:

(1) Active   A   The rat hit the dog.
     Dative   D   The rat gave the dog to the cow.
     Conjoined   C   The rat hit the dog and kissed the cow.
     Passive   P   The rat was hit by the dog.
     Dative Passive   DP   The rat was given to the dog by the cow.
     Object–Subject relative   OS   The rat hit the dog that kissed the cow.
     Subject–Object relative   SO   The rat that the dog hit kissed the cow.
     Cleft-Subject   CS   It was the rat that hit the dog.
     Cleft-Object   CO   It was the rat that the dog hit.

The sentences are all unambiguous except the Object–Subject relative (OS) type, which has a right extraposed reading in which the relative clause modifies the subject. This is presumably an unintended defect in experimental design since apparent aphasic error could be the consequence of interference from the grammatical extraposition reading. (Indeed, in only this case is the error which is attributed much higher than that predicted by our model.)

9.1 Grammar of the experiment sentence types

Let there be the following basic types and type map and the lexicon in Fig. 9.1.

(2)

Atomic syntactic type	P	$T(P)$
count noun	CN	$e \rightarrow t$
proper name	N	e
expletive pronoun	$NPit$	$t \rightarrow t$
prepositional phrase	PP	e
declarative sentence	S	t
abstract passive sentence	$S-$	t

Then the experiment sentence types are generated as shown in Fig. 9.2.

9.2 Sentences

In the following subsections we give the nets and semantics for each of the sentence types. We also give the complexity profiles, these being a plot of the

and : $((N\backslash S)\backslash (N\backslash S))/(N\backslash S) : \lambda x\lambda y\lambda z(\wedge (y\ z)\ (x\ z))$
by : $((N\backslash S-)\backslash (N\backslash S-))/N : \lambda x\lambda y\lambda z(\wedge (y\ z)\ (= x\ z))$
cow : $CN : cow$
dog : $CN : dog$
gave : $((N\backslash S)/PP)/N : give$
given : $((CN\backslash CN)/(N\backslash (N\backslash S-)))\bullet (N\backslash ((N\backslash S-)/PP)) : (\lambda x\lambda y\lambda z(\wedge (y\ z)\ (\exists (x\ z))), give)$
hit : $(N\backslash S)/N : hit$
hit : $(((CN\backslash CN)/(N\backslash (N\backslash S-)))\bullet (N\backslash (N\backslash S-)) : (\lambda x\lambda y\lambda z(\wedge (y\ z)\ (\exists (x\ z))), hit)$
it : $NPit : \lambda x x$
kissed : $(N\backslash S)/N : kiss$
rat : $CN : rat$
that : $(CN\backslash CN)/(N\backslash S) : \lambda x\lambda y\lambda z(\wedge (y\ z)\ (x\ z))$
that : $(CN\backslash CN)/(S/N) : \lambda x\lambda y\lambda z(\wedge (y\ z)\ (x\ z))$
the : $N/CN : \iota$
to : $PP/N : \lambda x x$
was : $(N\backslash S)/(CN\backslash CN) : \lambda x\lambda y(x\ (= y)\ y)$
was : $((NPit\backslash S)/(CN\backslash CN))/N : \lambda x\lambda y\lambda z(z\ (y\ (= x)\ x))$

FIGURE 9.1. Type logical lexicon for the experiment sentence types

number of unresolved dependencies (overarching identity links) at each word boundary. Following Johnson (1998) we refer to this number as the 'cut' and we note maximal cuts and average cuts.

9.2.1 Active (A)

The net for a sentence of this type is given in Fig. 9.3. The result of the semantic trip is the following:

(3) $(hit\ (\iota\ dog)\ (\iota\ rat))$

The complexity profile is thus:

(4)
```
3  |            a
2  |                    a
1  | a                      a    a
0  |                               a
   |_____
   | The    rat   hit   the   dog.
```

The maximal cut is 3; the average cut is 1.33.

9.2.2 Dative (D)

The net for a sentence of this type is given in Fig. 9.4. The result of the semantic trip is (5a) which normalizes to (5b).

(5)   a. $(give\ (\iota\ dog)\ (\lambda x x\ (\iota\ cow)\ (\iota\ rat)))$
       b. $(give\ (\iota\ dog)\ (\iota\ cow)\ (\iota\ rat))$

A   the+rat+hit+the+dog : S : $(hit\ (\iota\ dog)\ (\iota\ rat))$

D   the+rat+gave+the+dog+to+the+cow : S : $(give\ (\iota\ dog)\ (\iota\ cow)\ (\iota\ rat))$

C   the+rat+hit+the+dog+and+kissed+the+cow : S : $(\wedge\ (hit\ (\iota\ dog)\ (\iota\ rat))\ (kiss\ (\iota\ cow)\ (\iota\ rat)))$

P   the+rat+was+hit+by+the+dog : S : $(hit\ (\iota\ rat)\ (\iota\ dog))$

DP   the+rat+was+given+to+the+dog+by+the+cow : S : $(give\ (\iota\ rat)\ (\iota\ dog)\ (\iota\ cow))$

OS   the+rat+hit+the+dog+that+kissed+the+cow : S : $(hit\ (\iota\ \lambda z(\wedge\ (dog\ z)\ (kiss\ (\iota\ cow)\ z)))\ (\iota\ rat))$

SO   the+rat+that+the+dog+hit+kissed+the+cow : S : $(kiss\ (\iota\ cow)\ (\iota\ \lambda z(\wedge\ (rat\ z)\ (hit\ z\ (\iota\ dog)))))$

CS   it+was+the+rat+that+hit+the+dog : S : $(hit\ (\iota\ dog)\ (\iota\ rat))$

CO   it+was+the+rat+that+the+dog+hit : S : $(hit\ (\iota\ rat)\ (\iota\ dog))$

FIGURE 9.2. Experiment sentence types generated

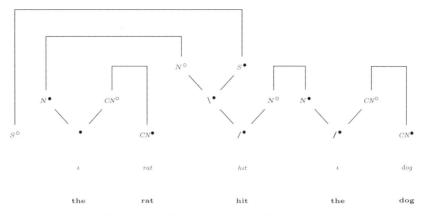

FIGURE 9.3. Net for an Active (A) sentence

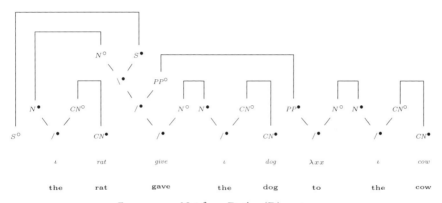

FIGURE 9.4. Net for a Dative (D) sentence

The complexity profile is as follows:

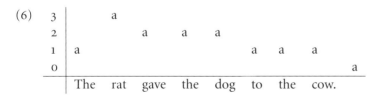

The maximal cut is 3; the average cut is 1.44.

9.2.3 Conjoined (C)

The net for a sentence of this type is given in Fig. 9.5. The normalized semantics is as follows.

(7) $(\wedge \; (hit \; (\iota \; dog) \; (\iota \; rat)) \; (kiss \; (\iota \; cow) \; (\iota \; rat)))$

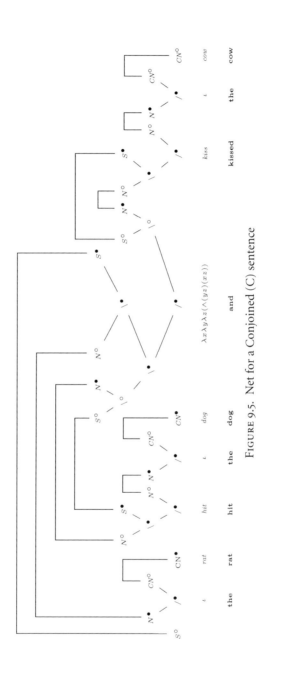

FIGURE 9.5. Net for a Conjoined (C) sentence

The complexity profile is thus:

```
(8)  5                    a     a
     4                          a
     3          a
     2                a                a
     1    a                                a     a
     0                                                a
         ─────────────────────────────────────────────
         The   rat   hit   the   dog   and   kissed   the   cow.
```

The maximal cut is 5; the average cut is 2.40.

9.2.4 Passive (P)

The net for a sentence of this type is given in Fig. 9.6; the analysis of passive is that of Morrill (2000). The normalized semantics is (9a) which is logically equivalent to (9b).

(9)   a. $(\wedge (= (\iota\, rat)\, (\iota\, rat))\, (\exists\, \lambda z(\wedge\, (hit\, (\iota\, rat)\, z)\, (= (\iota\, dog)\, z))))$
       b. $(hit\, (\iota\, rat)\, (\iota\, dog))$

The complexity profile is as follows:

```
(10)  4                          a
      3          a
      2                a     a
      1    a                       a     a
      0                                      a
         ───────────────────────────────────────
         The   rat   was   hit   by   the   dog.
```

The maximal cut is 4; the average cut is 1.75.

9.2.5 Dative passive (DP)

The net for a sentence of this type is given in Fig. 9.7; the analysis of dative passive is a generalization of that of passive from Morrill (2000). The normalized semantics is (11a) which is logically equivalent to (11b).

(11)   a. $(\wedge (= (\iota\, rat)\, (\iota\, rat))\, (\exists\, \lambda z(\wedge\, (give\, (\iota\, rat)\, (\iota\, dog)\, z)\, (= (\iota\, cow)\, z))))$
       b. $(give\, (\iota\, rat)\, (\iota\, dog)\, (\iota\, cow))$

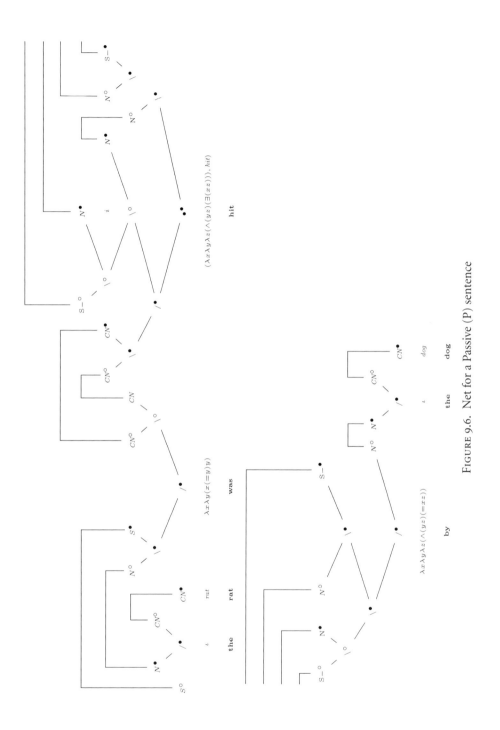

FIGURE 9.6. Net for a Passive (P) sentence

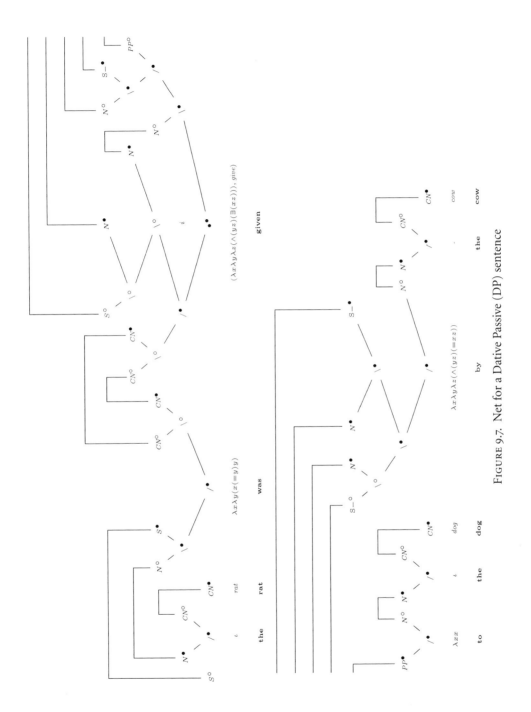

FIGURE 9.7. Net for a Dative Passive (DP) sentence

The complexity profile is as follows:

(12)

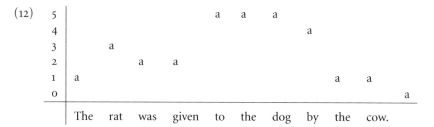

| | The | rat | was | given | to | the | dog | by | the | cow. |

The maximal cut is 5; the average cut is 2.64.

9.2.6 Object–subject relative (OS)

The net for a sentence of this type is given in Fig. 9.8. The normalized semantics is as follows:

(13) $(hit\ (\iota\ \lambda z(\wedge\ (dog\ z)\ (kiss\ (\iota\ cow)\ z)))\ (\iota\ rat))$

The complexity profile is thus:

(14)   3 | a
       2 | a   a   a
       1 | a   a   a   a   a
       0 | a

| | The | rat | hit | the | dog | that | kissed | the | cow. |

The maximal cut is 3; the average cut is 1.40.

9.2.7 Subject–object relative (SO)

The net for a sentence of this type is given in Fig. 9.9. The normalized semantics is as follows:

(15) $(kiss\ (\iota\ cow)\ (\iota\ \lambda z(\wedge\ (rat\ z)\ (hit\ z\ (\iota\ dog)))))$

The complexity profile is thus:

(16)   6 | a
       5 | a
       4 | a   a
       3 | a
       2 | a
       1 | a   a   a
       0 | a

| | The | rat | that | the | dog | hit | kissed | the | cow. |

The maximal cut is 6; the average cut is 2.70.

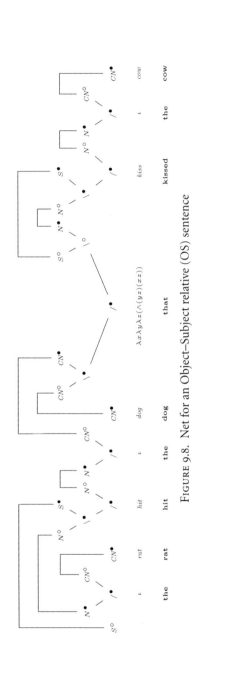

FIGURE 9.8. Net for an Object–Subject relative (OS) sentence

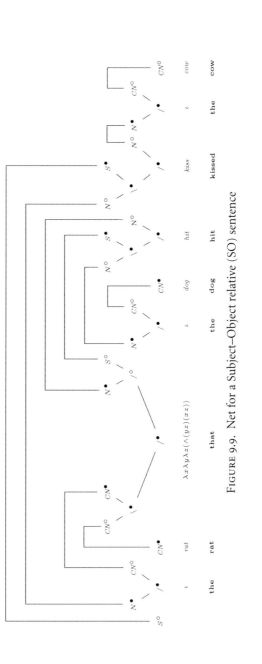

FIGURE 9.9. Net for a Subject–Object relative (SO) sentence

9.2.8 Cleft-subject (CS)

The net for a sentence of this type is given in Fig. 9.10. Observe how our analysis of the expletive subject of cleft constructions involves assigning the identity function to the expletive, and lexically lifting the copula over it. This avoids a treatment involving both vacuous abstraction and a dummy expletive semantics. The normalized semantics is (17a) which is logically equivalent to (17b).

(17) a. $(\wedge\ (=\ (\iota\ rat)\ (\iota\ rat))\ (hit\ (\iota\ dog)\ (\iota\ rat)))$
   b. $(hit\ (\iota\ dog)\ (\iota\ rat))$

The complexity profile is as follows:

(18)

3			a	a					
2		a			a	a			
1	a						a	a	
0									a
	It	was	the	rat	that	hit	the	dog.	

The maximal cut is 3; the average cut is 1.67.

9.2.9 Cleft-object (CO)

The net for a sentence of this type is given in Fig. 9.11. The normalized semantics is (19a) which is logically equivalent to (19b).

(19) a. $(\wedge\ (=\ (\iota\ rat)\ (\iota\ rat))\ (hit\ (\iota\ dog)\ (\iota\ rat)))$
   b. $(hit\ (\iota\ dog)\ (\iota\ rat))$

The complexity profile is as follows:

(20)

4							a		
3			a	a			a		
2		a			a	a			
1	a								
0								a	
	It	was	the	rat	that	the	dog	hit.	

The maximal cut is 4; the average cut is 2.22.

9.3 Results

The mean comprehension results on a scale of 0 (worst) to 5 (best) were as follows (Caplan and Hildecrandt, 1988: 105), compared to the maximal cut and average cut of the proof net analyses:

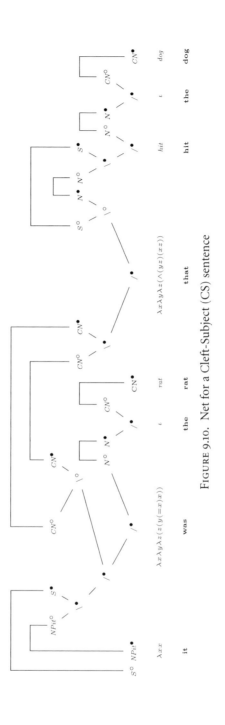

FIGURE 9.10. Net for a Cleft-Subject (CS) sentence

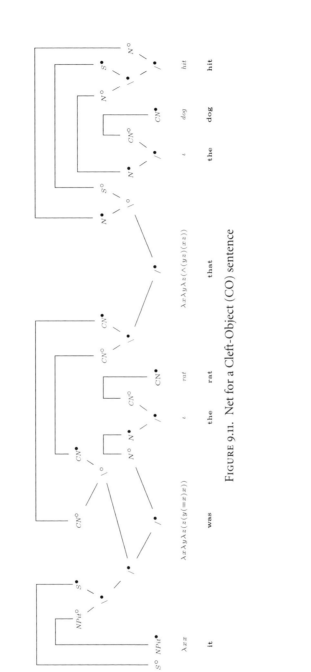

FIGURE 9.11. Net for a Cleft-Object (CO) sentence

(21)	Sentence type	mean comprehension	maximal cut	average cut
	A	4.4	3	1.33
	CS	4.2	3	1.67
	D	3.2	3	1.44
	P	2.9	4	1.75
	C	2.7	5	2.40
	CO	2.6	4	2.22
	OS	2.3	3	1.40
	DP	2.0	5	2.64
	SO	1.3	6	2.70

The maximal cut and average cut appear to correlate quite well with the mean comprehension with the exception of the OS sentence type for which comprehension is lower than would be expected from the proof net complexity. As we noted in the introduction, this sentence type is ambiguous, allowing a right extraposed reading, so that the existence of this reading would be expected to detract from the prescribed interpretation. Otherwise, in particular, the A sentence type has the best comprehension and the lowest cut complexity and the SO sentence type has the worst comprehension and the highest cut complexity.

Statistically, even including the detractive data point, the Spearman correlation coefficient shows a significant negative correlation between mean comprehension and both maximal cut ($r = -0.720$, p-value < 0.05) and average cut ($r = -0.717$, p-value < 0.05).

We observe that the aphasic comprehension of the sentence types of the Caplan *et al.* experiment has a negative linear correlation with the proof net complexity of these sentence types, suggesting that aphasics suffer impairment of the capacity of working memory for unresolved dependencies.

10

Lexico-syntactic interaction

Partial proof structures which can be extended into proof nets are called *modules*.[1] Lecomte and Retoré (1996) introduce the slogan 'words as modules' for the idea that what is associated with a word need not be seen as just a type, but may be a partial proof net, or module. In de Groote and Retoré (1996) it is shown how semantics as well as syntax can be represented in the formalism of proof nets. They consider the following points: (i) the semantic reading of proof nets (cf. Chapter 4), (ii) that lexical semantics may also be represented by an (intuitionistic) proof net, (iii) that the substitution of lexical semantics into derivational semantics corresponds to connecting, with a Cut link, the output conclusion of the lexical semantics proof net, on the one hand, to the root of the polar type tree of the lexical type, on the other, and (iv) that semantic evaluation corresponds to elimination of Cuts from the resulting proof net. By (geometry of) *interaction*, Girard (1989) means the geometry of Cut-elimination, particularly as represented by graph-transformation in proof nets.

Taking inspiration from these ideas, Morrill (1999a) proposes to preevaluate lexical and syntactic interaction by eliminating Cuts, so far as possible, from lexical modules built by step (iii) above. This precompilation of the categorial lexicon allows partial execution of some, though not all, lexico-syntactic interaction. Section 10.1 discusses the relevant notions of proof nets and illustrates the lexical preevaluation. Section 10.2 illustrates lexical words as modules and Section 10.3 illustrates with some sentence analyses according to this method.

---

[1] This chapter is a reworking of Morrill (2005) Copyright © 2005 CSLI Publications; material reused by kind permission.

10.1 Nets

The following subsections define respectively syntactic, semantic, and lexico-syntactic proof nets for Lambek categorial grammar. We illustrate with reference to the following lexical assignments:

(1) **bag+end** : $N : b$
     frodo : $N : f$
     in : $(S \backslash S)/N : in$
     inhabits : $(N \backslash S)/N : \lambda x \lambda y ((in\ x)\ (live\ y))$
     lives : $N \backslash S : live$

These define the following synonymy:

(2) a. **frodo+lives+in+bag+end** : $S : ((in\ b)\ (live\ f\,))$
     b. **frodo+inhabits+bag+end** : $S : ((in\ b)\ (live\ f\,))$

10.1.1 Syntactic nets

We recall from Chapter 4 the definitions of (Cut-free) proof nets for the Lambek calculus **L**, but here we label links slightly differently. A *polar type* is a syntactic type together with a polarity input ($\bullet$) or output ($\circ$). Where p is a polarity, $\bar{p}$ is the opposite polarity. Labels A^p and $A^{\bar{p}}$ are *complementary*. A *literal* is a polar type the type of which is atomic.

A *link* has a list of *premise* labels (above) and a list of *conclusion* labels (below) with some edges between them. An *identity link* is of the form:

(3)

P^p $P^{\bar{p}}$

A *logical link* is one of the local trees given in Fig. 10.1. A *syntactic polar type tree* is a tree the leaves of which are literals and each local tree of which is a logical link. Each polar type is the root of a unique syntactic polar type tree, which is the result of unfolding the label upwards according to the logical links. For example, the syntactic polar type tree for $(CN \backslash CN)/(S/N)^\bullet$ is:

(4)

A *syntactic frame* is a cyclic list of polar type trees exactly one of which has an output root. For example, the following (read as a cyclic list) is a syntactic frame:

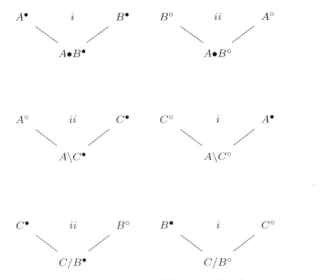

FIGURE 10.1. Logical links of the Lambek calculus

(5)

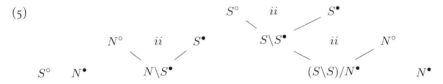

A *syntactic net* is the result of connecting by an identity link every leaf in a syntactic frame with a unique complementary leaf such that:

(6) • (*Acyclicity*). Every cycle crosses both edges of some i-link.
   • (*Planarity*). The identity links are planar in the cyclic ordering.
   • (*No subtending*). No identity link connects the leftmost and rightmost descendent leaves of an output division node.

For example, the following is a syntactic net:

(7)

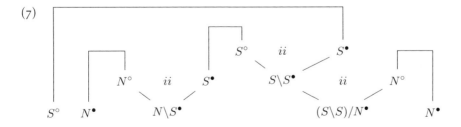

10.1.2 Semantic nets

By semantic nets we mean proof nets which represent not syntactic structure but lexical semantics. Lexical semantics are (closed) typed lambda terms, that is intuitionistic proofs, so we want proof nets which relax order (planarity) and which allow multiple binding. We define partial proof structures for the Lambek calculus with Permutation and Contraction with Cut (**LPC+Cut**). A *contraction link* is of the form:

(8)

We define i- and ¡-links as 1-links. A *Cut link* is of the form:

(9)

A *semantic polar type tree* is a tree the leaves of which are literals and each local tree of which is a logical link or a contraction link. Note that syntactic polar type trees are semantic polar type trees—without contraction links. A *semantic frame* is a bag of semantic polar type trees. Note that syntactic frames are semantic frames where we forget about the cyclic order. A *semantic module* is the result of (i) connecting, in a semantic frame, some leaves with unique complementary leaves by an identity link, and some roots with unique complementary roots by a Cut link, and (ii) associating semantic constants to every open input root, such that:

(10) • (*Orientation*). There is a unique open output root.
      • (*Acyclicity*). Every cycle crosses both edges of some 1-link.

A *semantic net* is a semantic module with no open leaves. For example, the following is a semantic net:

(11)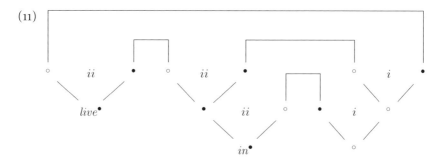

The *semantic trip* of a semantic net with each $\backslash^\circ$ and $/^\circ$ logical link assigned a distinct semantic variable is the trip which starts upwards at the unique open output root and generates a textual form proceeding as follows and bouncing with the associated semantic form at input roots:

(12)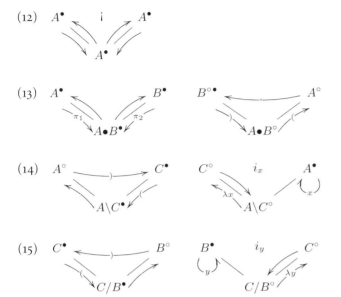

(13)

(14)

(15)

The semantic trip ends when it returns to the unique open output root. The *reading* of a semantic net is the textual form generated by its semantic trip. For example, the semantic reading of (11) is

(16) $\lambda x \lambda y ((in\ x)\ (live\ y))$

The following conversions on semantic nets preserve equivalence of readings (see de Groote and Retoré, 1996):

(17)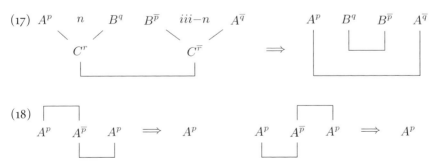

(18)

10.1.3 Lexico-syntactic nets

Let us define a *lexico-syntactic module* as a semantic module with only input roots and with a strict ordering on its open leaves. We define a *lexico-syntactic frame* as a cyclic list of lexico-syntactic modules and exactly one output syntactic polar type tree. And we define a *lexico-syntactic net* as the result of connecting by an identity link every leaf in a lexico-syntactic frame with a unique complementary leaf such that:

(19) (*Acyclicity*). Every cycle crosses both edges of some 1-link.
       (*Planarity*). The identity links added are planar in the cyclic ordering.

Let an *initial lexico-syntactic module* for a lexical assignment $a : A : \phi$ be a lexico-syntactic module which results from connecting by a Cut link the syntactic polar type tree of $A^\bullet$ with a semantic net the reading of which is ϕ. A *final lexico-syntactic module* for a lexical assignment $a : A : \phi$ is a result of normalizing according to (17) and (18) an initial lexico-syntactic module for $a : A : \phi$, with the reduction (18) required to preserve the order on open leaves.

For example, for **Frodo** $: N : f$ we have the initial lexico-syntactic module:

$$
(20) \qquad
\begin{array}{ccc}
\ulcorner & & \\
f^\bullet & \circ & N^\bullet \\
\llcorner & & \\
\end{array}
$$

Which simplifies to the final lexico-syntactic module:

$$
(21) \qquad N^\bullet_{\,f}
$$

Similarly, for **bag+end** $: N : b$ we obtain the final lexico-syntactic module:

$$
(22) \qquad N^\bullet_{\,b}
$$

For **lives** $: N \backslash S : live$ we have the initial lexico-syntactic module, preevaluation and final lexico-syntactic module:

(23)   a.

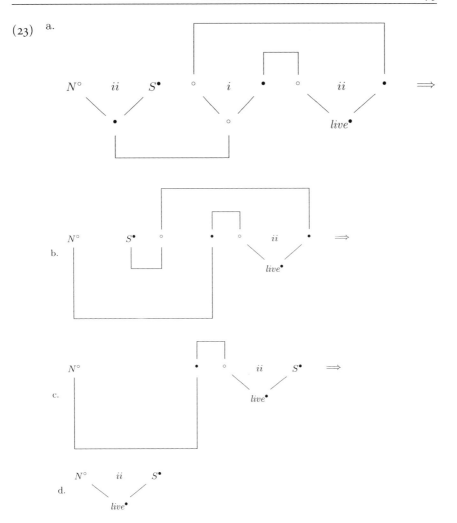

Similarly, for **in** : $(S\backslash S)/N$: *in* we obtain the final lexico-syntactic module:

(24)

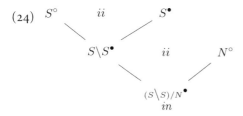

For **inhabits** : $(N\backslash S)/N$: $\lambda x\lambda y((in\ x)\ (live\ y))$ we have the initial lexico-syntactic module in Fig. 10.2a, preevaluation in Figs. 10.2 and 10.3, and final

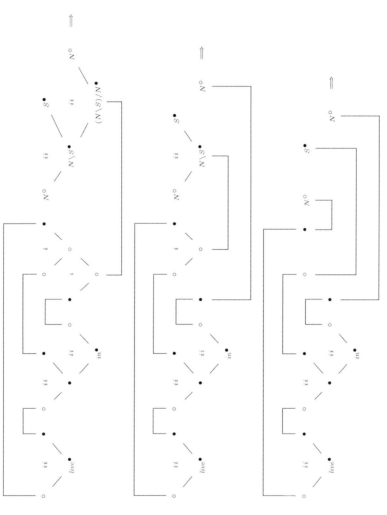

FIGURE 10.2. Preevaluation for inhabits : $(N \backslash S)/N : \lambda x \lambda y ((in \; x) \; (live \; y))$, Part I

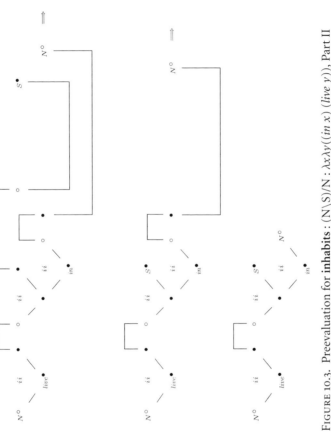

FIGURE 10.3. Preevaluation for **inhabits** : $(N \backslash S)/N : \lambda x \lambda y ((in\ x)\ (live\ y))$, Part II

lexico-syntactic module in Fig. 10.3f. So, for example, from the final lexico-syntactic modules we have for the sentence *Frodo lives in Bag End* the lexico-syntactic frame:

(25)

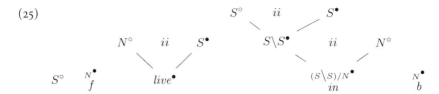

And the lexico-syntactic net:

(26)

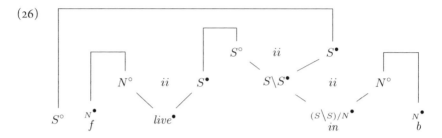

And for *Frodo inhabits Bag End* from the final lexico-syntactic modules we have the lexico-syntactic frame (27) and hence the same lexico-syntactic net (26). The semantic reading of (26) is $((in\ b)\ (live\ f))$, which is consistent with the synonymy.

(27)

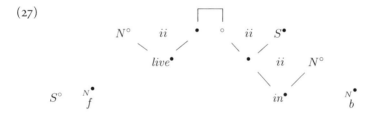

10.2 Words

In this section we illustrate final lexico-syntactic modules for sample lexical assignments. The motivation is to give an idea of the kinds of form the integrated representations take. It will be noted that the relation between the compiled modules and the lexical assignments which are their source is not necessarily transparent to the eye, that is, over and above notational variation, the work of Cut-elimination is performing significant computation.

10.2.1 $a : ((S/N)\backslash S)/CN : \lambda x \lambda y (\exists \lambda z (\wedge (x\ z)\ (y\ z)))$

Indefinite article in subject.

(28)

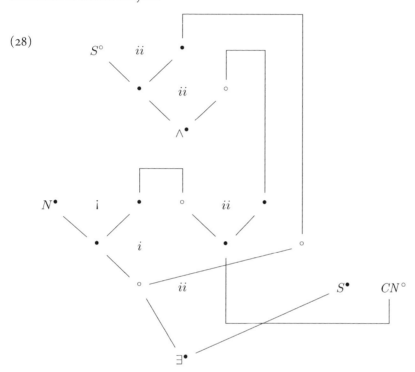

10.2.2 $alleged : CN/CN : alleged$

Intensional adjective.

(29)

10.2.3 $bachelor : CN : \lambda x (\wedge (\neg (married\ x))\ (man\ x))$

Count noun with built-in meaning postulate.

(30)

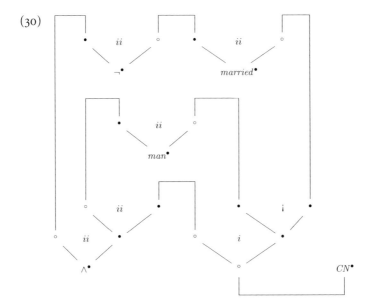

10.2.4   *consider* : $((N\backslash S)/(CN/CN))/N$: $\lambda x \lambda y(consider\ (y\ (=x)\ x))$
Small-clause verb.

(31)

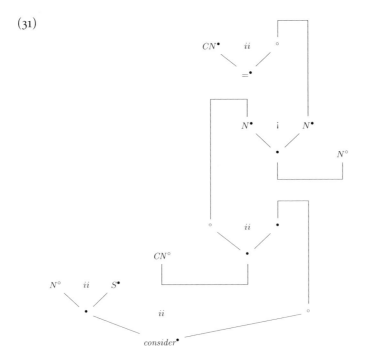

10.2.5 every : $(S/(N\backslash S))/CN : \lambda x \lambda y(\forall \lambda z(\rightarrow (x\ z)\ (y\ z)))$
Universal quantifier in object.

(32)

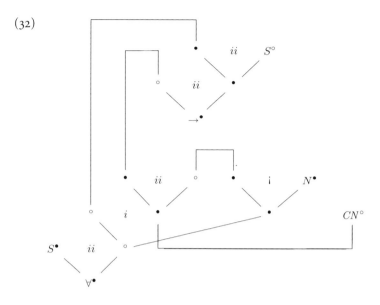

10.2.6 everything : $S/(N\backslash S) : \lambda x(\forall \lambda y(\rightarrow (thing\ y)\ (x\ y)))$
Universal quantifier phrase as subject.

(33)

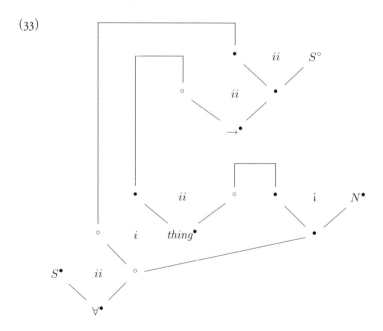

10.2.7 gives : $((N\backslash S)/N)/N$: give

Dative shifted ditransitive verb.

(34)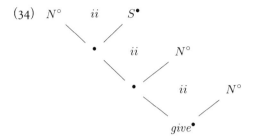

10.2.8 gives : $((N\backslash S)/PP)/N$: $\lambda x \lambda y (give\ y\ x)$

Ditransitive verb.

(35)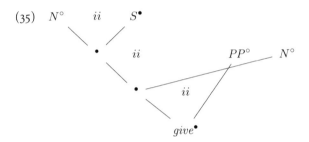

10.2.9 himself : $((N\backslash S)/N)\backslash(N\backslash S)$: $\lambda x \lambda y (x\ y\ y)$

Reflexive pronoun.

(36)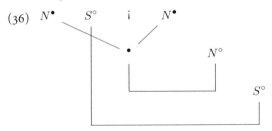

10.2.10 is : $(N\backslash S)/N$: =

Copula of identification.

(37)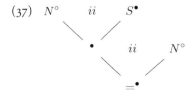

10.2.11 is : $(N\backslash S)/(CN/CN) : \lambda x \lambda y (x (= y) \, y)$

Copula of predication.

(38)

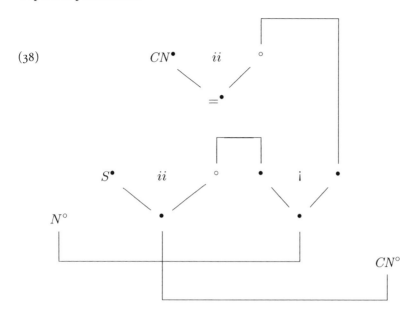

10.2.12 loves : $(N\backslash S)/N$: love

Transitive verb.

(39)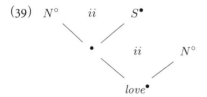

10.2.13 man : CN : man

Count noun.

(40) $CN^{\bullet}_{man}$

*10.2.14 **mortal** : CN/CN : $\lambda x \lambda y (\wedge \, (mortal \, y) \, (x \, y))$*

Intersective adjective.

(41)

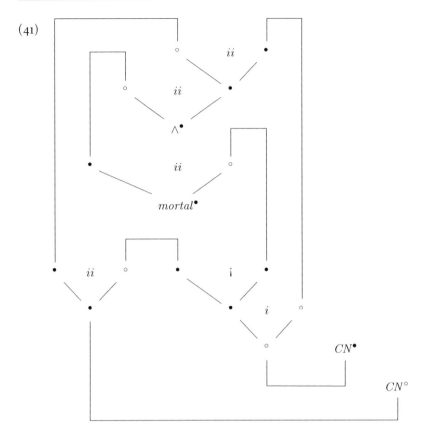

10.2.15 $no : S : \Box$

Disaffirmative particle as logical falsehood.

(42)

10.2.16 $runs : N \backslash S : run$

Intransitive verb.

(43) $N°$ ii $S^\bullet$

$run^\bullet$

10.2.17 seems : (N\S)/(N\S) : λxλy(seem (x y))

Subject raising verb.

(44)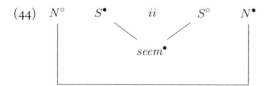

10.2.18 socrates : N : s

Proper name.

(45) $N_s^\bullet$

10.2.19 something : S/(N\S) : λx(∃ λy(∧ (thing y) (x y)))

Existential quantifier phrase as subject.

(46)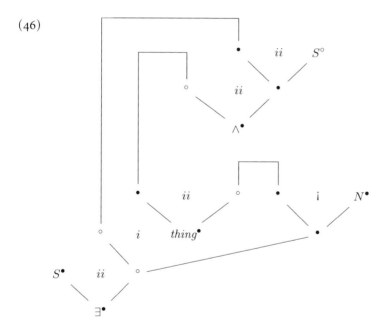

10.2.20 tries : (N\S)/(N\S) : λxλy(try (x y) y)

Subject equi verb.

(47)

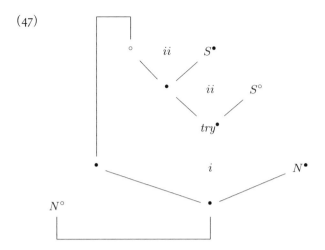

10.2.21 *yes* : S : ∎

Affirmative particle as logical truth.

(48) $\overset{S^{\bullet}}{∎}$

10.3 Sentences

In this section we illustrate complete proof net derivations over lexico-syntactic modules. We analyse the sentences of the classical syllogism: *Socrates is a man, Every man is mortal / Socrates is mortal.*

10.3.1 *Socrates is a man*

The lexico-syntactic net is that given in Fig. 10.4. The semantic reading is:

$$(49) \quad (\exists\, \lambda x((\wedge\, (man\; x))\, ((=x)\; s)))) $$
$$= $$
$$(man\; s) $$

10.3.2 *Every man is mortal*

The lexico-syntactic net is shown in Figs. 10.5 and 10.6. The semantic reading is:

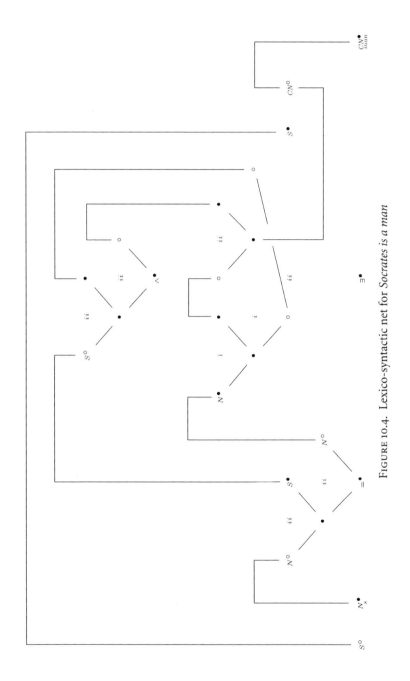

FIGURE 10.4. Lexico-syntactic net for *Socrates is a man*

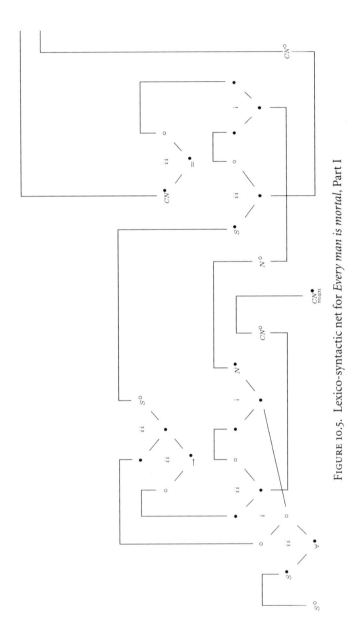

FIGURE 10.5. Lexico-syntactic net for *Every man is mortal*, Part I

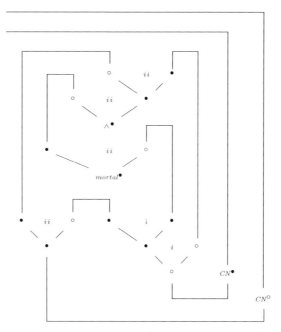

FIGURE 10.6. Lexico-syntactic net for *Every man is mortal*, Part II

(50) $(\forall\ \lambda x((\rightarrow (man\ x))\ ((\wedge\ (mortal\ x))\ ((= x)\ x)))))$

$=$

$(\forall\ \lambda x(\rightarrow (man\ x)\ (mortal\ x)))$

10.3.3 Socrates is mortal

The lexico-syntactic net is as shown in Fig. 10.7. The semantic reading is:

(51) $(\lambda x((\wedge\ (mortal\ x))\ ((= s)\ x))\ s)$

$=$

$(mortal\ s)$

Indeed, according to our analyses the premises of the syllogism entail its conclusion.

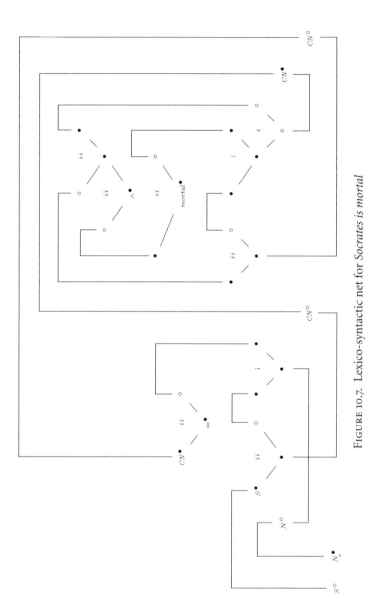

FIGURE 10.7. Lexico-syntactic net for *Socrates is mortal*

11

Memoizing Lambek theorem-proving

Efficient (n^3) parsing algorithms for context-free grammar employ memoization of partial analyses in a chart, as in Early chart parsing or CYK chart parsing. The chart is a data structure recording all the grammatical categories of each substring of the string analysed, these being computed from smallest to largest. Efficiency is gained by compacting in a single category for a given span all the analyses under that category of the corresponding substring.

In Lambek categorial grammar grammaticality is equated with provability, and hence parsing is theorem-proving. The problem of determining Lambek theoremhood is NP-complete (Pentus 2006) even in the product-free case (Savateev 2009), so we cannot expect worst-case polynomial-time algorithms for Lambek categorial grammar parsing/theorem-proving. However, it is still interesting to consider whether a memoization strategy can lead to improved efficiency in some cases.

It is not straightforward to adapt chart parsing methods to Lambek sequent calculus because we need to take into account the shifting of premises under hypothetical reasoning; see, for example, König (1994) and Hepple (1992).

In an alternative approach, Morrill (1996) proposes CYK memoization of proof nets for Lambek calculus. This avoids the problem of shifting premises because all types are fixed in the global and unchanging proof frame; however it is necessary to control for the correctness of (partial) proof nets. In that paper a unification criterion was suggested in which chart cell entries are most general unifiers of the corresponding span, but the graph-theoretical framework of proof nets invites a purer geometrical approach. In this chapter we provide such an approach in which the chart cell entries are simply the planar axiom linkings (well-bracketings) of the corresponding span.

In Section 11.1 we repeat a version of the relevant technical background of proof nets. In Section 11.2 we give the algorithm.

11.1 Background

The following theory of proof nets for the calculus of Lambek (1958) is repeated from earlier chapters; see principally Roorda (1991).

Given a set **A** of *atomic types*, we define the set **F** of *types* by:

(1) **F ::= A | F•F | F\F | F/F**

A *polar type* A^p comprises a type A together with a *polarity* $p = \bullet$ (input) or $\circ$ (output). The *polar type tree* $|A^p|$ of a polar type A^p is the ordered tree defined by:

(2) $|P^p| = P^p$ if P is atomic

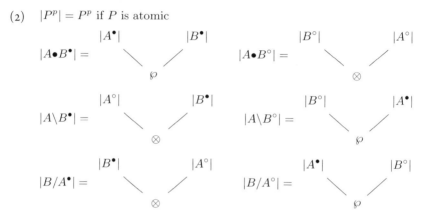

A *sequent* $A_0, \ldots, A_n \Rightarrow A$ comprises a finite non-empty sequence $A_0, \ldots, A_n$ of *antecedent* types and a *succedent* type A. The *(proof) frame* of a sequent $A_0, \ldots, A_n \Rightarrow A$ is the sequence:

(3) $\langle |A^\circ|, |A_0{}^\bullet|, \ldots, |A_n{}^\bullet| \rangle$

For example, the proof frame for the sequent (4) is given in Fig. 11.1, where we have numbered the leaves.

(4) $S/(N\backslash S), (N\backslash S)/N, (S/N)\backslash S \Rightarrow S$

We define the *complement* $\overline{X}$ of a polar type X by $\overline{A^\bullet} = A^\circ$ and $\overline{A^\circ} = A^\bullet$. Two polar types are *complementary* if and only if they are the complements of each

FIGURE 11.1. Proof frame for $S/(N\backslash S), (N\backslash S)/N, (S/N)\backslash S \Rightarrow S$

other. An *axiom link* on a proof frame is a pair of complementary leaves. An *axiom linking* for a proof frame is a set of axiom links with at most one axiom link per leaf and which is *planar*, that is there are no two axiom links (i, k) and (j, l) such that $i < j < k < l$. That an axiom linking is planar means that it can be drawn in the half-plane without crossing lines. A *partial proof structure* (PPS) is a frame together with an axiom linking. A *proof structure* is a frame together with an axiom linking that links every leaf.

A *switching* of a PPS is a graph that results from removing one of the immediate descendent edges of each $\wp$-node. A *proof net* is a proof structure in which (i) every switching is a connected and acyclic graph (Danos–Regnier acylicity and connectedness); see Danos and Regnier (1989), and (ii) no axiom link connects the leftmost and rightmost descendent leaves of the node resulting from the unfolding of an output division (we call this Retoré no subtending); see de Groote and Retoré (2003). No subtending prohibits empty antecedents.

(5)   THEOREM (*Correctness of proof nets*).
       A sequent is a theorem of the Lambek calculus if and only if there
       is an axiom linking which forms a proof net on its frame.

Fadda and Morrill (2005) show that in view of the intuitionistic nature of Lambek sequents (that there is exactly one root of output polarity), every proof structure which satisfies Danos–Regnier (DR) acyclicity also satisfies DR connectedness. Therefore we need only check for DR acyclicity (and no subtending). We call a partial proof structure *correct* if and only if it satisfies DR acyclicity and no subtending.

(6)   COROLLARY (*Correctness of proof nets*).
       A sequent is a theorem of the Lambek calculus if and only if there
       is an axiom linking which forms a correct proof structure on its frame.

Therefore we can carry out Lambek theorem-proving by building up proof nets incrementally, checking for correctness (DR acyclicity and Retoré no subtending) at each step. We have a Lambek theorem if and only if we succeed in linking all the leaves while satisfying these criteria.

11.2 Chart theorem-proving

Our algorithm is based on the observation in Morrill (1996) that the planar linking of non-commutative proof nets is context-free, and so can be memoized, for example as in CYK chart parsing (Cocke and Schwartz, 1970; Younger, 1967; Kasami, 1965).

Planar linking is a Dyck language. Its grammar can be given as follows:

(7) $S \rightarrow A\,\overline{A} \mid A\,S\,\overline{A} \mid S\,S$

We memoize continuous planar linkings, where a continuous planar linking is a set of axiom links connecting contiguous leaves. The *span* of a continuous planar linking is identified with the pair comprising the positions of the start of its first axiom link and the end of its last axiom link. A CYK chart is a triangular matrix with a cell for each span. These cells are filled bottom-up, that is from smallest to largest, and from left to right. For our Dyck language continuous planar linkings are always of even length. Hence, for a proof frame of ten literals (as in Fig. 11.1), the cells of a checked triangular matrix are filled in the order shown as follows:

(8)

	2	3	4	5	6	7	8	9	10
9									9
8								8	
7							7		16
6						6		15	
5					5		14		21
4				4		13		20	
3			3		12		19		24
2		2		11		18		23	
1	1		10		17		22		25

We will notate a continuous planar linking as a well-parenthesized string of brackets encoding textually the planar axiom linking over the span.

For a frame to be a candidate at all for a proof net it must contain an even number of leaves; indeed, it must contain the same number of positive and negative literals of each atomic type (van Benthem 1991), in order that they may be matched by axiom links. So there may be a preprocessing filter on this basis.

Given a frame with $n = 2$ leaves $L_1, \ldots, L_n$ there is the CYK chart theorem-proving algorithm defined in Fig. 11.2.

The first **for**-loop is for placing axiom links on adjacent complementary literals (i.e. spans of length 2) by the production $S \rightarrow A\,\overline{A}$. By DR acyclicity, for an axiom link to be placed between two such literals they must not be the descendents of a common $\otimes$-link (for then there would be a cycle in switchings). Nor, by no subtending, can they be the premises of an output

```
for i := 1 to n − 1 do
    if L_i = \overline{L_{i+1}} and [] with span (i, i + 1) is a correct linking
        then C(i, i + 1) := {[]}
        else C(i, i + 1) := ∅;
for l := 4 to n in steps of 2 do
    for i := 1 to n + 1 − l do
        begin
        k := i + l − 1;
        C(i, k) := ∅;
        if L_i = \overline{L_k}
            then for each K ∈ C(i + 1, k − 1) do
                if [K] with span (i, k) is a correct linking
                    then C(i, k) := C(i, k) ∪ {[K]};
            for j := i + 2 to k − 1 in steps of 2 do
                for each K_1 ∈ C(i, j − 1) and K_2 ∈ C(j, k) do
                    if K_1 K_2 with span (i, k) is a correct linking
                        then C(i, k) := C(i, k) ∪ {K_1 K_2}
        end;
if C(0, n) ≠ ∅
    then print "theorem"
    else print "non-theorem".
```

FIGURE 11.2. Lambek chart theorem-proving algorithm

division node (for then the node would be subtended). Therefore, a PPS built by $S \rightarrow A\,\overline{A}$ is a correct linking if and only if the complementary literals do not share any $\otimes$-ancestor and are not the premises of an output division.

The second **for**-loop is for building continuous planar linkings on spans of length 4, 6, … by means of the remaining productions.

First, we consider extending continuous planar linkings between $i + 1$ and $k − 1$ by placing an axiom link between L_i and $L_k = \overline{L_i}$ with $S \rightarrow A\,S\,\overline{A}$. By DR acyclicity, for the axiom link to be placed, every path from L_i to L_k must cross both premises of some $\wp$-link (otherwise there would be a switching with a cycle going through the new axiom link). By no subtending, L_i and L_k must not be the leftmost and rightmost descendent leaves of an output division. If these two conditions are satisfied, the resulting PPS is correct.

Let us consider in more detail the acyclicity check. Call a $\wp$-*free path* in a PPS any path which does not cross the two premise edges of any $\wp$-link. Thus $\wp$-free paths are extended by connecting the extremities of any link except for the two premises of a $\wp$-link. Therefore a PPS built by $S \rightarrow A\,S\,\overline{A}$ is a correct linking if and only if before the new link is placed there is no $\wp$-free path between the complementary literals, and they are not the leftmost and rightmost descendent leaves of an output division.

Second, we consider joining continuous planar linkings between i and $j − 1$, and j and k with $S \rightarrow S\,S$. This time, no new links are added so there is no need for any no subtending check. But the combined PPS might violate DR acyclicity. Cycles always pass through some axiom link. Therefore a PPS built by $S \rightarrow S\,S$ is a correct linking if and only if in the resulting PPS, every pair of literals connected by an axiom link are connected by no $\wp$-free path other than their direct axiom link itself.

Let us consider the chart computed for the frame in Fig. 11.1.

At the very first step we entertain the possibility of placing an axiom link between $S°_1$ and $S•_2$. The literals are complementary and do not share any descendent, therefore the axiom link can be placed and the chart becomes:

(9)

9									
8									
7									
6									
5									
4									
3									
2									
1 {[]}									
	2	3	4	5	6	7	8	9	10

Next, we consider placing an axiom link between $S•_2$ and $S°_3$. The literals are complementary but they share a $\otimes$-ancestor, therefore when a switching conserves the edge between $S°_3$ and its mother there would be a cycle going through the new axiom link. So the axiom link cannot be placed and the chart becomes:

(10)

9									
8									
7									
6									
5									
4									
3									
2	Ø								
1 {[]}									
	2	3	4	5	6	7	8	9	10

An axiom link cannot be placed between $S°_3$ and $N•_3$ (they are not complementary), and so on. The completed first diagonal of the chart is as follows:

(11)

	2	3	4	5	6	7	8	9	10
9									Ø
8								Ø	
7							{[]}		
6						Ø			
5					Ø				
4				{[]}					
3			Ø						
2		Ø							
1	{[]}								

Continuing on the next even diagonal, cell $C(1, 4)$ cannot be filled by $S \rightarrow A\ S\ \bar{A}$ because $C(2, 3)$ is empty (and S°_1 and $N^\bullet_4$ are not complementary), and it cannot be filled by $S \rightarrow S\ S$ because $C(3, 4)$ is empty. Cell $C(2, 5)$ cannot be filled by $S \rightarrow A\ S\ \bar{A}$, nor can it be filled by $S \rightarrow S\ S$ because $C(2, 3)$ is empty. But cell $C(3, 6)$ can be filled by $S \rightarrow A\ S\ \bar{A}$:

(12)

	2	3	4	5	6	7	8	9	10
9									Ø
8								Ø	
7							{[]}		
6						Ø			
5					Ø				
4				{[]}					
3			Ø		{[[]]}				
2		Ø	Ø						
1	{[]}	Ø							

	2	3	4	5	6	7	8	9	10
9									Ø
8								Ø	
7							{[]}		Ø
6						Ø		{[[]]}	
5					Ø		Ø		Ø
4				{[]}		Ø		{[[]]}	
3			Ø		{[[]]}		{[[]][]}		{[[[]]]}
2		Ø		Ø		Ø		{[[[]][]]}	
1	{[]}		Ø		{[][]}		{[[]][]}		{[[[]][]]], [][[][]]}

FIGURE 11.3. Completed chart for the proof frame of Figure 11.1

Exercise 11.1. Compute the completion of the chart.

At the very last step, two linkings are obtained: from $C(2, 9)$ and an axiom link from beginning to end by $S \rightarrow A\ S\ \overline{A}$, and from $C(1, 2)$ and $C(3, 10)$ by $S \rightarrow S\ S$. The full chart is given in Fig. 11.3.

12

Conclusion

Symbolic grammar and formal semantics may not be quite the main fashion in computational linguistics, but it does not seem that anyone has shown that their methods are flawed or that the problems they address are any less real. Rather, it is as if we have found them to be hard and slow, and have been seduced by new methods that seem easier and quicker. This book is an attempt to bring an old school of categorial grammar to its logical conclusion. It remains to be seen where it can be taken from here.

Our categorial grammar is purely lexicalist. A grammar is just a lexicon: an assignment of types (and lexical semantics) to basic expressions. The type calculus is universal and contains all the logical theorems and no non-logical axioms. The formalism is non-commutative intuitionistic linear logic. In Part II we considered four kinds of connective with which the basic calculus, the Lambek calculus, can be extended. The implicit eventual goal, extremely ambitious and long-term, is to integrate these and whatever other connectives may be appropriate and necessary into a single logic capable of expressing the syntax and semantics of all possible human languages.

12.1 Grammar

Our rendering of grammar as logic entails that syntactic structures are proofs. But what is a proof? Proofs can be presented informally, semiformally, or formally, and in many different formats. What is the essence of a proof? With what structure could we identify it? Of what could we say that it is the actual structure of a proof? In the case of categorial proofs there seems to be no better answer to this question than to say that the proofs are proof nets. A major thesis here is that syntactic structures are not just trees, but proof nets, which are more complex graphical structures, and more sophisticated ones because

identity	$\overline{Q^p \quad Q^{\bar{p}}}$
	where Q is atomic or a bracket

product	$\dfrac{A^\bullet \quad B^\bullet}{A\bullet B^\bullet}$ i	$\dfrac{B^\circ \quad A^\circ}{A\bullet B^\circ}$ ii
under	$\dfrac{A^\circ \quad C^\bullet}{A\backslash C^\bullet}$ ii	$\dfrac{C^\circ \quad A^\bullet}{A\backslash C^\circ}$ i
over	$\dfrac{C^\bullet \quad B^\circ}{C/B^\bullet}$ ii	$\dfrac{B^\bullet \quad C^\circ}{C/B^\circ}$ i
bracket	$\dfrac{[^\bullet \quad A^\bullet \quad]^\bullet}{[\,]A^\bullet}$ i	$\dfrac{]^\circ \quad A^\circ \quad [^\circ}{[\,]A^\circ}$ ii
antibracket	$\dfrac{[^\circ \quad B^\bullet \quad]^\circ}{[\,]^{-1}B^\bullet}$ ii	$\dfrac{]^\bullet \quad B^\circ \quad [^\bullet}{[\,]^{-1}B^\circ}$ i

FIGURE 12.1. Links for the Lambek calculus with brackets

they are not just static hierarchical structures, but dynamical processes which tell a story.

As we have seen, proof nets for the Lambek calculus are well-understood. But proof nets for the extensions in Part II are more topics for current research, on which we now remark.

For proof nets for bracket operators (Chapter 5), see Fadda and Morrill (2005). That article proposes unfolding bracketed and antibracketed types into logical links containing polar bracket atoms as shown in Fig. 12.1.

It is an open question how to represent in proof nets bracket operators with structural properties such as commutativity and so forth.

For attempts to formulate proof nets for discontinuity operators (Chapter 6) see Morrill (1999b) and Morrill and Fadda (2008), although 'theorem' (25) has a counterexample when empty antecedents are allowed (Fadda 2010). These advocate channel proof nets in which a discontinuous type of sort n will have $2(n + 1)$ incident edges, representing the starting points and end points of its $n + 1$ segments. When we consider the translation of discontinuous types into (commutative) first-order intuitionistic logic (Moot and Piazza, 2001), some edges correspond to positions bound by universal quantifiers and some edges correspond to positions bound by existential quantifiers. These edges are represented by continuous lines and dashed lines respectively in Figs. 12.2 and 12.3, which give the channel logical links for the continuous connectives and the basic discontinuous connectives. In channel proof nets, edges come in pairs (segment start/end) thus, for example, an axiom link is as follows where P is an atomic type of sort 0:

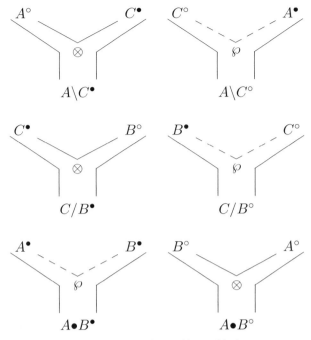

FIGURE 12.2. L channel logical links

(1)

Naturally, in the future it would be appropriate to define proof nets for the additives of Chapter 7 and the normal modalities of Chapter 8 as well as for whatever other new connectives may be introduced.

12.2 Processing

There is a dogma that natural language grammar formalisms should be polynomial-time processable. On the one hand, people in general quickly find the correct interpretations in the context of utterances: in most cases a hearer has correctly comprehended a speaker by the time the speech stream has ended. On the other hand, on the *computational metaphor* the mind, or at least the language faculty, is considered to be (like) a computer. Thus the standard position is that unless a formalism is polynomial-time recognizable, it fails as a psychological model of real-time human language processing. But logical categorial grammar is NP-hard, and there are three objections we would like to raise against this standard position.

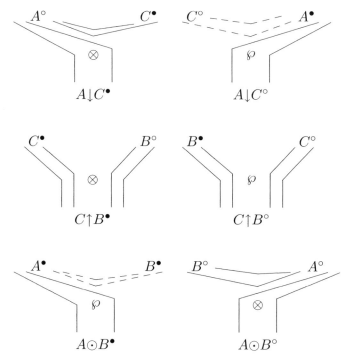

FIGURE 12.3. **BDLC** channel discontinuous logical links

First, what would polynomial-time processability of a formalism prove unless the formalism had been shown to be able to express an adequate ('all and only') and elegant (descriptively satisfactory) account of natural language(s)? For example, how does a formalism stand by linguistic criteria if it invokes massive lexical ambiguity? Surely the first scientific priority is to capture generalizations elegantly. Indeed, how can we even enquire as to how efficient processing may be possible before we have a deep insight into the structure of language, the object of computation?

Second, when we say polynomial-time, do we mean for the fixed language recognition (FLR) problem or for the universal language recognition (ULR) problem (Barton *et al.*, 1987)? That is, are we talking about an upper bound on time as a function of string-length for a language defined (FLR problem) or as a function of both string-length and grammar size for each string and each grammar expressible in the formalism (ULR problem)? For example, deciding whether sequents of the Lambek calculus are theorems is an NP-complete problem (Pentus, 2006), but Lambek categorial grammar is equivalent in weak generative capacity to context-free grammar (Pentus, 1992), so the FLR problem for Lambek categorial grammar is n^3.

Third, Gödel's incompleteness theorem showed that even elementary arithmetic is not semidecidable. He interpreted this result as showing that either mathematics exists outside of the mind, or that the mind is not a machine. There is a fact of the matter as to whether an arithmetic statement is true or not but this fact of the matter is not attributable to mind as machine. Thus either way, according to Gödel's view, there is more to the world of mathematics than the mind as mechanism.

Nobody asks of putative laws of physical science that they be such that nature would be able to compute her behaviour fast. Gödel's theorem already refutes the computational metaphor of mind as machine embodying mathematics. In a similar spirit, we would like to defend the position that although language processing is automatic, the mind may be only *like* a computer under the Church–Turing thesis, that is that the computational metaphor in relation to the language faculty may indeed be just a metaphor: that there is more to the world of language than mind as mechanism.

12.3 Open problems

To conclude, we list here a number of open research problems in type logical categorial grammar.

- Logical categorial grammar as here operates within the traditional paradigm of sentential grammar whereby the meaning assigned to a sentence is represented by a closed logical formula. But phenomena such as anaphora and VP ellipsis include intersentential binding. Can the type logical categorial architecture be adjusted to accommodate discourse binding?
- How can we formulate proof nets for bracket operators including structural properties? And how can we carry out the associated processing? In particular, if we assume that the inputs to the parsing process are unbracketed strings, how can parsing/theorem-proving discover the existence of appropriate bracketings?
- How can we give proof nets for the discontinuous Lambek calculus in general? Cf. Fadda (2010).
- How can we give give proof nets for the Lambek calculus with additives? Cf. e.g. Hughes and van Glabbeck (2005). Can this account be improved upon and/or simplified in the present context?
- Can we give simple proof nets for the Lambek calculus with normal modalities? Cf. Restall (2007).
- For all accounts of proof nets for logical categorial grammar extending those for Lambek categorial grammar, can we adapt and extend the

shift-reduce parsing model of Chapter 4 to include them? In that model correctness is maintained incrementally by only reducing (i.e. placing an axiom link) once it has been checked that this would maintain well-formedness: it is checked that a certain kind of path (a $\wp$-free path) does not exist between the two literals to be connected. Can more general proof net shift-reduce parsing models also operate on the basis of such negative path constraints?

- How can we integrate bracket operators and discontinuity operators in a single calculus? Would we allow wrapping into bracketed domains under certain circumstances, and how would this be controlled, for example in relation to sorting?

- Can the memoization of Lambek theorem-proving of Chapter 11 be developed so as to accommodate lexical ambiguity in a single chart? Can it be extended to other logical categorial grammar proof nets? How can Early deduction be formulated for categorial proof nets?

- How can categorial generation as opposed to parsing be formulated, in relation to proof nets (cf. Merenciano and Morrill, 1997; Pogodalla, 2000).

Appendix A
Mathematical background

A.1 Naturals

The *natural numbers* are $0, 1, 2, \ldots$. There are the arithmetic operations of addition ($+$), multiplication ($\times$), and exponentiation ($(\cdot)^{\cdot}$). These obey the laws shown in Fig. A.1.

Consider the course of growth of n^3 and 2^n:

(1)

n	0	1	2	3	4	5	6	7	8	9	10
n^3	0	1	8	27	64	125	216	343	512	729	1000
2^n	1	2	4	8	16	32	64	128	256	512	1024

We see that $n^3 < 2^n$ for $n < 2$, then that $n^3 > 2^n$ for $2 \le n \le 9$, and then that $n^3 < 2^n$ for $n = 10$ (and above). When we compare the rate of growth of functions it is the way the pattern eventually settles that we take into account. We call this comparison 'in the limit'. In the limit, 2^n grows faster than n^3.

$$
\begin{array}{llll}
x + (y + z) & = & (x + y) + z & \text{associativity} \\
x \times (y \times z) & = & (x \times y) \times z & \\[4pt]
x + y & = & y + x & \text{commutativity} \\
x \times y & = & y \times x & \\[4pt]
0 + x = \; x & = & x + 0 & \text{0 is an identity for } + \\
1 \times x = \; x & = & x \times 1 & \text{1 is an identity for } \times \\[4pt]
x \times (y + z) & = & (x \times y) + (x \times z) & \text{distributivity}
\end{array}
$$

FIGURE A.1. Some arithmetic laws

Indeed, in the limit, all exponential functions grow faster than all polynomial functions.

A.2 Sets

A *set* is a collection of distinct objects which are called the *members* or *elements* of that set. For example, there is the set containing the natural numbers one, two, and three, which we may write $\{1, 2, 3\}$. This is a finite set. The set $\mathbf{N} = \{0, 1, 2, \ldots\}$ of all natural numbers is an infinite set.

To say that an element a belongs to a set A, we write $a \in A$. For example, $1 \in \{1, 2, 3\}$. To say that an element a does not belong to a set A, we write $a \notin A$. For example, $0 \notin \{1, 2, 3\}$. The *empty set* $\{\}$ is the set which contains no elements; we sometimes write it $\emptyset$.

Where A is a set, the *cardinality* of A, $|A|$, is the number of elements it contains. For example, $|\{1, 2, 3\}| = 3$. We name the cardinality of the set $\mathbf{N}$ of natural numbers ω (or aleph zero).

Apart from defining sets by listing their members, a set may be defined by stating a property necessary and sufficient for an element to qualify as a member. For example:

(2)   a. $\{x \in \mathbf{N}| 1 \le x \le 3\} = \{1, 2, 3\}$
      b. $\{x \in \mathbf{N}| x \bmod 2 = 0\} = \{0, 2, 4, \ldots\}$

A set X is a *subset* of a set Y, $X \subseteq Y$, if and only if (iff) every member of X is also a member of Y. For example, $\{1, 2\} \subseteq \{1, 2, 3\}$. Note that every set X is a subset of itself, $X \subseteq X$, and that for all sets X, Y, and Z, if $X \subseteq Y$ and $Y \subseteq Z$ then $X \subseteq Z$. The empty set is a subset of every set.

The *power set* $\mathbf{P}(X)$ of a set X is the set of all subsets of X:

(3) $\mathbf{P}(X) =_{df} \{Y| Y \subseteq X\}$

The *intersection* $X \cap Y$ of two sets X and Y is the set of elements that belong to both X and Y:

(4) $X \cap Y =_{df} \{x| x \in X \text{ and } x \in Y\}$

The *union* of two sets X and Y is the set of elements that belong to either X or Y (or both):

(5) $X \cup Y =_{df} \{x| x \in X \text{ or } x \in Y\}$

The *difference* $X - Y$ between a set X and a set Y is the set of elements of X which are not elements of Y:

(6) $X - Y =_{df} \{x| x \in X \text{ and } x \notin Y\}$

$$X \cap (Y \cap Z) = (X \cap Y) \cap Z \qquad \text{associativity}$$
$$X \cup (Y \cup Z) = (X \cup Y) \cup Z$$

$$X \cap Y = Y \cap X \qquad \text{commutativity}$$
$$X \cup Y = Y \cup X$$

$$X \cap X = X \qquad \text{idempotency}$$
$$X \cup X = X$$

$$\overline{\overline{X}} = X \qquad \text{involution}$$

$$X \cap (Y \cup Z) = (X \cap Y) \cup (X \cap Z) \quad \text{distribution}$$
$$X \cup (Y \cap Z) = (X \cup Y) \cap (X \cup Z)$$

$$\emptyset \cap X = \emptyset \qquad \text{identity laws}$$
$$\emptyset \cup X = X$$
$$U \cap X = X$$
$$U \cup X = U$$

$$\overline{X \cap Y} = \overline{X} \cup \overline{Y} \qquad \text{de Morgan laws}$$
$$\overline{X \cup Y} = \overline{X} \cap \overline{Y}$$

FIGURE A.2. Set-theoretic laws

For example, $\{1, 2, 3\} - \{0, 1\} = \{2, 3\}$. In the context of a *universal set* U from which all elements are drawn, the *complement* $\overline{X}^{U}$ (or $\overline{X}$ if U is understood) is the difference between U and X:

(7) $\overline{X} =_{df} \{x \mid x \in U \text{ and } x \notin X\}$

The set-theoretic operations obey the laws shown in Fig. A.2.

A.3 Mappings

An *ordered pair* (x, y) comprises a first element x and a second element y. We define the *first projection* $\mathrm{fst}((x, y)) =_{df} x$ and the *second projection* $\mathrm{snd}((x, y)) =_{df} y$. A *mapping* is a set A of ordered pairs such that for each x there is at most one y such that $(x, y) \in A$; in the case that there is such a y we say that the mapping A is *defined* for x and that the *value* of A for the *argument* x is y: $A(x) = y$; otherwise we say that A is *undefined* for x.

The *domain* of a mapping A is the set of arguments for which it is defined, i.e. $\{x \mid (x, y) \in A \text{ for some } y\}$. The *codomain* or *range* of a mapping A is the set of its values, i.e. $\{y \mid (x, y) \in A \text{ for some } x\}$. If a mapping has as domain a subset of a set X and as range a subset of a set Y, we say that the mapping is a *partial function from X to Y*; if the domain is exactly X we say that the mapping is a *total function from X to Y*.

A.4 More operations on sets

Given sets X and Y, the *functional exponentiation* X^Y is the set of all total functions from Y to X.

Exercise A.1. Show that $|X^Y| = |X|^{|Y|}$.

The *Cartesian product* $X \times Y$ is the set of all ordered pairs of elements from X (first) and Y (second):

(8) $X \times Y =_{df} \{(x, y)|\ x \in X \text{ and } y \in Y\}$

Exercise A.2. Show that $|X \times Y| = |X| \times |Y|$.

The *disjoint union* $X \uplus Y$ is defined as follows:

(9) $X \uplus Y =_{df} (\{1\} \times X) \cup (\{2\} \times Y)$

Exercise A.3. Show that $|X \uplus Y| = |X| + |Y|$.

A.5 Data structures and formal languages

Given a universal set U from which all elements are drawn, there is associated with a set X a unique total function f from U to $\{0, 1\}$ such that $f(a) = 1$ if $a \in X$ and $f(a) = 0$ if $a \notin X$; this f is called the *characteristic function* of the set X.

We define a *multiset* or *bag* as a total function from U into the set **N** of natural numbers. Thus whereas all elements of a set are distinct, elements of a multiset have a multiplicity of occurrence. But a multiset, like a set, is unordered.

We define a (finite) *sequence* or *list* as a function from $\{1, 2, \ldots, n\}$ to U for some natural n. Unlike the elements of sets and multisets (or bags) the elements of sequences (or lists) are ordered. In sequence notation we write the successive values in successive positions within angle brackets, for example $\langle a, b, a \rangle$. In list notation we write the successive values in successive positions with square brackets, for example $[a, b, a]$. We call n the *length* $l(\sigma)$ of the sequence or list σ. The length of the empty sequence $\langle \rangle$ or list $[]$ is zero.

An *alphabet* is a finite non-empty set the members of which are called *symbols*. Given an alphabet, a *string* is a finite sequence of symbols from the alphabet. We write, for example, aba. In string notation the empty sequence $\langle \rangle$ is written ϵ. Where Σ is an alphabet, Σ^* is the set of all strings over Σ. We define a (formal) *language* as a set of strings, i.e. a subset of Σ^*.

A.6 Relations

Where n is a natural, the *nth power* of a set X, X^n, is the set of all sequences of length n of elements of X. An *n-ary relation* on X is a set of sequences of length n of elements of X, i.e. a subset of the nth power X^n of X. Where R is a binary relation, we may abbreviate $\langle x, y \rangle \in R$ as xRy.

A binary relation R on a set D is *reflexive* iff for all $x \in D$, xRx. It is *irreflexive* iff for all $x \in D$, it is not the case that xRx. It is *nonreflexive* iff it is neither reflexive nor irreflexive.

A binary relation R on a set D is *symmetric* iff for all x and $y \in D$, if xRy then yRx. It is *asymmetric* iff for all $x \in D$, if xRy then it is not the case that yRx. It is *nonsymmetric* iff it is neither symmetric nor asymmetric.

A binary relation R on a set D is *transitive* iff for all x, y, and $z \in D$, if xRy and yRz then xRz. It is *intransitive* iff for all x, y and $z \in D$, if xRy and yRz then it is not the case that xRz. It is *nontransitive* iff it is neither transitive nor intransitive.

Note that every binary relation is exclusively reflexive, irreflexive, or nonreflexive, symmetric, asymmetric, or nonsymmetric, and transitive, intransitive, or non-transitive.

A binary relation R on a set D is *antisymmetric* iff for all x and $y \in D$, if xRy and yRx then $x = y$.

For example, we have already seen that the subset relation $\subseteq$ is reflexive and transitive. It is also nonsymmetric, and antisymmetric. The arithmetic relation $<$ is irreflexive, asymmetric (and, vacuously, antisymmetric), and transitive. The arithmetic relation $\leq$ (like $\subseteq$) is reflexive, nonsymmetric (and antisymmetric), and transitive. The arithmetic relation $= \bmod 4$ is reflexive, symmetric (but not antisymmetric), and transitive. The arithmetic relation $=$ is reflexive, symmetric (and antisymmetric), and transitive.

A.7 Operations

Where n is a natural, an *n-ary operation* on a set D is a mapping from D^n to D.

A binary operation $\cdot$ on a set D is *associative* iff for all x, y, and $z \in D$,

(10) $x \cdot (y \cdot z) = (x \cdot y) \cdot z$

It is *commutative* iff for all x and $y \in D$,

(11) $x \cdot y = y \cdot x$

It is *idempotent* iff for all $x \in D$,

(12) $x \cdot x = x$

Two binary operations $\smile$ and $\frown$ on a set D have the property of *absorption* iff for all x and $y \in D$,

(13) $x \smile (y \frown x) = x = (x \smile y) \frown x$

We say that $\smile$ *distributes* over $\frown$ iff

(14) $x \smile (y \frown z) = (x \smile y) \frown (x \smile z)$

We say that $\frown$ *distributes* over $\smile$ iff

(15) $x \frown (y \smile z) = (x \frown y) \smile (x \frown z)$

We say that a unary operation $-$ on a set D *distributes* over a binary operation $\cdot$ over the same set iff for all x and $y \in D$,

(16) $-(x \cdot y) = (-x) \cdot (-y)$

A unary operation $-$ on a set D is *involutive* iff for all $x \in D$,

(17) $- - x = x$

An element $1 \in D$ is a *left identity* for a binary operation $\cdot$ on D iff for all $x \in D$,

(18) $1 \cdot x = x$

It is a *right identity* iff for all $x \in D$,

(19) $x \cdot 1 = x$

A.8 Algebras

We say that a set D is *closed* under an operation $\circ$ of arity m iff for all $x_1, \ldots, x_m \in D$, $o(x_1, \ldots, x_m) \in D$. An *algebra* $(D, \circ_1, \ldots, \circ_n)$ comprises a set (*domain*) D together with some operations $\circ_1, \ldots, \circ_n$ on this set. Since we define the operations to be on the domain, an algebra is always closed under its operations. By way of example, $(\mathbf{N}, +, \times, (\cdot)')$ is an (arithmetic) algebra. Where the operations $\circ_1, \ldots, \circ_n$ have arities $m_1, \ldots, m_n$ we say that the *algebra has arity* $(m_1, \ldots, m_n)$.

We can classify algebras according to the properties of their operations.

- A *semigroup* is an algebra $(D, \cdot)$ of arity (2) where $\cdot$ is associative.
- A *monoid* is an algebra $(D, \cdot, 1)$ of arity $(2, 0)$ where $(D, \cdot)$ is a semigroup and 1 is a (left and right) identity for $\cdot$.
- A *lattice* is an algebra $(D, \smile, \frown)$ of arity $(2, 2)$ where $(D, \smile)$ and $(D, \frown)$ are semigroups and where in addition $\smile$ and $\frown$ are commutative and idempotent, and have the property of absorption.

- A *Boolean algebra* is an algebra $(D, \smile, \frown, ', \perp, \top)$ of arity $(2, 2, 1, 0, 0)$ where $(D, \smile, \frown)$ is a lattice, $\smile$ and $\frown$ are distributive, $\perp$ is an identity for $\smile$ and for all $x \in D \perp \frown x = \perp$ and $\top$ is an identity for $\frown$ and for all $x \in D \top \smile x = \top$, and (*complementarity*):

(20) $x' \smile x = \top$ and $x' \frown x = \perp$

For example, where Σ is an alphabet and $\oplus$ is the operation of string concatenation, $(\Sigma^*, \oplus, \epsilon)$ is a monoid. And where U is a set, $(\mathbf{P}(U), \cup, \cap, \bar{\ }, \emptyset, U)$ is a Boolean algebra.

A.9 Structures

Structures are like algebras, but contain in addition relations. A *structure* $(D, \circ_1, \ldots, \circ_i; R_1, \ldots, R_j)$ comprises a set (domain) D, some operations $\circ_1, \ldots, \circ_i$ on D and some relations $R_1, \ldots, R_j$ on D. Where the arities of $\circ_1, \ldots, \circ_i$ and $R_1, \ldots, R_j$ are $m_1, \ldots, m_i$ and $n_1, \ldots, n_j$ respectively, we say that the *structure has arity* $(m_1, \ldots, m_i; n_1, \ldots, n_j)$.

We can classify structures according to their properties. We start with some structures without any operations.

- A *strict order* is a structure $(D; <)$ of arity (2) where $<$ is irreflexive, asymmetric, and transitive.
- A *preorder* is a structure $(D; \sqsubseteq)$ of arity (2) where $\sqsubseteq$ is reflexive and transitive.
- A *partial order* is a preorder $(D; \leq)$ where $\leq$ is antisymmetric.
- An *equivalence* is a preorder $(D; \equiv)$ where $\equiv$ is symmetric.

For example, $(\mathbf{N}; <)$ is a strict order; $(\mathbf{N}; \leq)$ is a partial order and, where U is any set, so is $(\mathbf{P}(U), \subseteq)$; and $(\mathbf{N}; = mod\ 4)$ is an equivalence but not a partial order, and $(\mathbf{N}; =)$ is an equivalence and a partial order (as is the identity relation $\{\langle d, d \rangle | d \in D\}$ on any set $\mathbf{D}$).

Including now operations, a *residuated pair* is a structure $(D, \Diamond, \Box^{\downarrow}; \sqsubseteq)$ of arity $(1, 1; 2)$ where $(D; \sqsubseteq)$ is a preorder, and for all x and $y \in D$ $((unary)$ *residuation*$)$:

(21) $\Diamond x \sqsubseteq y$ iff $x \sqsubseteq \Box^{\downarrow} y$

A *residuated triple* is a structure $(D, \rightarrow, \cdot, \leftarrow; \sqsubseteq)$ of arity $(2, 2, 2; 2)$ where $(D; \sqsubseteq)$ is a preorder, and for all x, y, and $z \in D$ $((binary)$ *residuation*$)$:

(22) $x \sqsubseteq z \leftarrow y$ iff $x \cdot y \sqsubseteq z$ iff $y \sqsubseteq x \rightarrow z$

A *preordered/partially ordered semigroup* is a structure $(D, \cdot; \sqsubseteq)$ of arity $(2; 2)$ where $(D, \cdot)$ is a semigroup, $(D; \sqsubseteq)$ is a preorder/partial order, and for all x, y, and $z \in D$ *(compatibility of $\cdot$ with $\sqsubseteq$)*:

(23)   if $x \sqsubseteq y$ then $x \cdot z \sqsubseteq y \cdot z$ and $z \cdot x \sqsubseteq z \cdot y$

A *residuated semigroup* is a residuated triple $(D, \rightarrow, \cdot, \leftarrow; \sqsubseteq)$ where $(D, \cdot; \sqsubseteq)$ is a preordered semigroup.

A.10 Homomorphisms

Where $(D_1, \circ_1, \ldots, \circ_m)$ and $(D_2, \bullet_1, \ldots, \bullet_n)$ are algebras, a mapping h from D_1 to D_2 and from $\{\circ_1, \ldots, \circ_m\}$ to $\{\bullet_1, \ldots, \bullet_n\}$ preserving arity is a *homomorphism* iff for all i, $1 \leq i \leq m$, $\circ_i$ of arity j, for all $x_1, \ldots, x_j \in D_1$,

(24) $h(\circ_i(x_1, \ldots, x_j)) = h(\circ_i)(h(x_1), \ldots, h(x_j))$

For example, where $(\Sigma^*, \oplus, \epsilon)$ is the monoid of strings over an alphabet Σ, the function l of length is a homomorphism from the monoid of strings $(\Sigma^*, \oplus, \epsilon)$ to the additive monoid $(\mathbf{N}, +, 0)$ since for all x and $y \in \Sigma^*$,

(25) $l(x \oplus y) = l(x) + l(y)$
       and $l(\epsilon) = 0$

Again, let F be a set of sets which is closed under disjoint union, Cartesian product, and functional exponentiation. Then $(F, \uplus, \times, (\cdot)^{\cdot})$ is an algebra. The function $|\cdot|$ of cardinality is a homomorphism from $(F, \uplus, \times, (\cdot)^{\cdot})$ to the arithmetic algebra $(\mathbf{N}, +, \times, (\cdot)^{\cdot})$ since for all X, Y, and $Z \in F$:

(26) $|X \uplus Y| = |X| + |Y|$
       $|X \times Y| = |X| \times |Y|$
       $|X^Y| = |X|^{|Y|}$

Two structures are *isomorphic* iff there is a homomorphism from each to the other.

A.11 Decidability

The Turing machine (TM) is a model of computation due to Turing (1936). The workspace of a TM is a tape divided into cells which is infinite to the left and to the right (there is no first cell or last cell). Each cell contains a symbol from an alphabet Γ including a special blank symbol b. (It turns out that a TM tape only ever has a finite number of non-blank cells.) At any one time, the processor of a TM is in one of a finite set Q of states including an initial state q_0 and an acceptor state q_F. The functioning of a TM is governed by a *transition function* δ which is a partial function from $Q \times \Gamma$ to $Q \times \Gamma \times \{-, +\}$; the transition function is such that $\delta(q_F, a)$ is undefined for all $a \in \Gamma$. The TM has a head which at any given moment is over one cell. Thus at each point in a computation a TM has a current state $q \in Q$ and a current symbol $a \in \Gamma$ in the cell it is reading. If $\delta(q, a)$ is undefined, the TM halts, but otherwise where its value is (q', a', m) it changes state to q', writes a' in the current cell, and moves its head one cell to the left or to the right according as m is $-$ or $+$.

Let $\Sigma =_{df} \Gamma - \{b\}$. The input for a TM is a string $w \in \Sigma^*$. The *initial configuration* for input w has the tape blank everywhere except for the string w starting at the TM head. The execution of a TM for a given input w either continues forever or else halts (when the transition function is undefined) after a finite number of steps. A TM may be interpreted in two ways. It may be interpreted as defining a language, the language it recognizes, and it may be interpreted as defining a function, the function it computes. We consider these in turn.

If a TM halts for a given input, it either halts in the acceptor state q_F or in another state. We say that a TM *accepts* a string $w \in \Sigma^*$ iff the execution of the TM starting from the initial configuration for w halts in q_F. (If it halts in another state, or does not halt, it does not accept w.) We call the set of strings accepted by the TM the language *recognized* by the TM. We call a language *recursively enumerable* iff it is recognized by some TM. We call a TM *terminating* iff it halts on all inputs. We call a language *recursive* iff it is recognized by some terminating TM.

When we want to consider a TM as computing a function, we define its output, for the initial configuration for $w \in \Sigma^*$, when it halts, as the string over Σ compressed between the TM head and the first blank to its right. Thus a TM computes a partial function from Σ^* to Σ^*. The function is undefined for inputs on which the TM does not halt. A terminating TM computes a total function from Σ^* to Σ^*.

The Church–Turing thesis is that the functions computed by TMs are exactly the functions computable by mechanical means. This claim could be falsified (if we found a mechanical procedure for computing a function that cannot be implemented on a TM), but it cannot be verified (because we cannot guarantee that there is no such counterexample). However, there are grounds for confidence in the thesis because for decades alternative models of computation consistently turn out to be equivalent to TMs.

We say that a language is *decidable* iff there exists a mechanical procedure for determining whether or not a string belongs to the language (a *decision procedure*). In view of the Church–Turing thesis, we equate a language being decidable with the language being *recursive*, that is recognized by a terminating

TM. A terminating TM that recognizes the language provides such a decision procedure.

We say that a language is *semidecidable* iff there exists a mechanical procedure which verifies that a string belongs to the language in the case that it does (a *semidecision procedure*). Note that on a string that does not belong to the language, a semidecision procedure may halt and report this, but it may also simply fail to halt. In view of the Church–Turing thesis, we equate a language being semidecidable with the language being *recursively enumerable*, that is, recognized by a not necessarily terminating TM. A TM that recognizes the language provides such a semidecision procedure.

A.12 Computational time complexity

Given a terminating TM M, we define the time of computation for input w, as the number of steps until M halts on input w. We say that a language is polynomially decidable (in class **P**) iff it is recognized by a terminating TM the time of computation of which is bounded from above by some polynomial function of the length of the input.

There is also a nondeterministic variant of Turing machines in which the range of the transition function is not $Q \times \Gamma \times \{-, +\}$ but $P(Q \times \Gamma \times \{-, +\})$ so that a configuration can have multiple successor configurations. We say that a language is nondeterministically polynomially decidable (in class **NP**) iff it is decided by a nondeterministic TM, the time of computation of which is bounded from above by some polynomial function of the length of the input.

It is almost certain that $P \neq NP$, but proving this is the biggest open problem in theoretical computer science.

Appendix B
Prolog implementation

B.1 Program listing 213   B.2 Session log 217

Here we present a Prolog implementation of the shift-reduce parsing algorithm for the Lambek categorial grammar of Chapter 4.

B.1 Program listing

```
:- dynamic(count/1).
:- dynamic(loglnk/4).
:- dynamic(axlnk/2).
:- dynamic(rootsem/2).

:- op(400, xfx, *).
:- op(400, xfx, \).
:- op(400, xfx, /).
```

t(?I) tests string I.

```
t(I) :- str(I, Str, A), clean,
        nl, nl, write(I), write(' '), write(Str), write(' '), write(A),
        unfold(out(A), 0, Fringe, []),
        prs(Fringe, [], Str),
        sem_trip_up(0, Phi),
        eval(Phi, Phi2),
        nl, nl, pp(Phi2),
        fail.

t(_).
```

clean removes from dynamic memory the results of previous processing.

```
clean :- retractall(count(_)),
         retractall(loglnk(_, _, _, _)),
         retractall(axlnk(_, _)),
         retractall(rootsem(_, _)),
         assert(count(0)).
```

unfold(+PolA, +N, -Lits, -Lts) unfolds polar type PolA labelling
nodes starting from N and means that the fringe of the resulting polar type
tree is represented by the difference list Lits-Lts.

```
unfold(PolA, N, Lits, Lts) :-
        unfold2(PolA, D1, M, D2), !,
        gensymb(N1),
```

```
        gensymb(N2),
        unfold(D1, N1, Lits, Lts2),
        unfold(D2, N2, Lts2, Lts),
        add(loglnk(M, N1, N, N2)).

unfold(inp(P), N, [inp(P, N)|Lts], Lts) :- !.
unfold(out(P), N, [out(P, N)|Lts], Lts).
```

unfold2(+PolA, -D1, -M, -D2) means that polar type PolA unfolds in
its logical link to left daughter D1 and right daughter D2, and that the link is
of type M.

```
unfold2(inp(A\C), out(A), inp_under, inp(C)) :- !.
unfold2(inp(C/B), inp(C), inp_over, out(B)) :- !.
unfold2(inp(A*B), inp(A), i(inp_prod), inp(B)) :- !.
unfold2(out(A\C), out(C), i(out_div(under)), inp(A)) :- !.
unfold2(out(C/B), inp(B), i(out_div(over)), out(C)) :- !.
unfold2(out(A*B), out(B), out_prod, out(A)).

gensymb(N1) :- retract(count(N)), !,
        N1 is N+1,
        assert(count(N1)).

add(C) :- assert(C).

add(C) :- retract(C), fail.
```

prs(+LS, +GS, +Str) parses buffer Str starting from local stack LS and
global stack GS.

```
prs([], [], Str) :- !, Str=[].

prs([], GS, [Word|Str]) :- !, lex(Word, A, Sem),
        gensymb(N),
        add(rootsem(N, Sem)),
        unfold(inp(A), N, Fringe, []),
        prs(Fringe, GS, Str).

prs([L2|LS], [L1|GS], Str) :- compl(L1, L2, N1, N2),
        \+i_free_dn(N1, N2, []),
        \+subtend(N1, N2),
        add(axlnk(N1, N2)),
        prs(LS, GS, Str).

prs([Lit|LS], GS, Str) :-
        prs(LS, [Lit|GS], Str).
```

compl(+L1, +L2, -N1, -N2) means that literals L1 and L2 are complementary and that they are numbered N1 and N2 respectively.

```
compl(inp(P, N1), out(P, N2), N1, N2) :- !.
compl(out(P, N1), inp(P, N2), N1, N2).
```

i_free_up(+N, +L, +V) means that there is a i-free path to L starting by
travelling upwards from N without visiting the nodes in V. i_free_dn(+N,
+L, +V) means that there is a i-free path to L starting by travelling downwards from N without visiting the nodes in V.

```
i_free_up(N, N, _).

i_free_up(N, L, V) :- loglnk(Kind, D1, N, D2), !,
        i_free_up2(Kind, D1, N, D2, L, V).

i_free_up(N, L, V) :- (axlnk(N, M); axlnk(M, N)), !,
        i_free_dn(M, L, V).

i_free_dn(N, L, V) :- (loglnk(Kind, N, M, D); loglnk(Kind, D, M, N)), !,
        i_free_dn2(Kind, M, D, L, V).

i_free_up2(i(_), D1, N, D2, L, V) :- !, not_visited(V, N),
        (i_free_up(D1, L, [N|V]); i_free_up(D2, L, [N|V])).

i_free_up2(_, D1, _, D2, L, V) :- i_free_up(D1, L, V); i_free_up(D2, L, V).

i_free_dn2(i(_), M, _, L, V) :- !, not_visited(V, M),
        i_free_dn(M, L, [M|V]).

i_free_dn2(_, M, D, L, V) :- i_free_dn(M, L, V); i_free_up(D, L, V).

not_visited([], _).

not_visited([H|T], N) :- \+H=N,
        not_visited(T, N).
```

subtend(+N, +L) means that N and L are the leftmost and rightmost descendent leaves of an output division node.

```
subtend(N, L) :- loglnk(i(out_div(_)), N, _, D),
        subtend2(D, L).

subtend(N, L) :- loglnk(_, N, M, _), !,
        subtend(M, L).

subtend2(L, L) :- !.

subtend2(N, L) :- loglnk(_, _, N, D), !,
        subtend2(D, L).
```

sem_trip_up(+N, -Phi) means that Phi is the semantic reading that results from taking the semantic trip starting upwards on node N. sem_trip_dn(+N, -Phi) means that Phi is the semantic reading that results from taking the semantic trip starting downwards on node N.

```
sem_trip_up(N, Phi) :- (axlnk(N, M); axlnk(M, N)), !,
        sem_trip_dn(M, Phi).

sem_trip_up(N, [lmd, N, Phi]) :-
        (loglnk(i(out_div(under)), D, N, _); loglnk(i(out_div(over)), _, N, D)), !,
        sem_trip_up(D, Phi).

sem_trip_up(N, [pair, Phi, Psi]) :- loglnk(prodout, D1, N, D2), !,
        sem_trip_up(D1, Phi),
        sem_trip_up(D2, Psi).

sem_trip_dn(N, Phi) :- rootsem(N, Phi), !.

sem_trip_dn(D, [app, Chi, Phi]) :-
        (loglnk(inp_under, Arg, M, D); loglnk(inp_over, D, M, Arg)), !,
```

```
        sem_trip_dn(M, Chi),
        sem_trip_up(Arg, Phi).

sem_trip_dn(D, N) :-
        (loglnk(i(out_div(under))), _, N, D); loglnk(i(out_div(over)), D, N, _)), !.

sem_trip_dn(D, [pi1, Chi]) :- loglnk(i(inp_prod), D, M, _), !,
        sem_trip_dn(M, Chi).

sem_trip_dn(D, [pi2, Chi]) :- loglnk(i(inp_prod), _, M, D), !,
        sem_trip_dn(M, Chi).
```

eval(+Phi, -NF) means that lambda term Phi normalizes to NF.

```
eval(Phi, NF) :- !, numbervars(Phi, 0, _),
        eval2(Phi, NF).

eval2(Phi, NF) :- contract(Phi, Phi2), !,
        eval2(Phi2, NF).

eval2(Phi, Phi).
```

contract(+Phi, -Phi2) means that lambda term Phi contracts in one step to Phi2.

```
contract([app, [lmd, X, Phi], Psi], Chi) :- !, subst(Phi, X, Psi, Chi).

contract([pi1, [pair, Phi, _]], Phi) :- !.
contract([pi2, [pair, _, Psi]], Psi) :- !.

contract([H|T], [H1|T]) :- contract(H, H1), !.
contract([H|T], [H|T1]) :- contract(T, T1).

contract([app, [app, eq, Phi], Phi], true).

contract([app, [app, and, true], Phi], Phi).

contract([app, [app, and, Phi], true], Phi).
```

subst(+Phi, +X, +Psi, -Chi) means that Chi is the result of substituting Phi for X in Psi.

```
subst(X, X, Phi, Phi) :- !.

subst([H|T], X, Phi, [H1|T1]) :- !, subst(H, X, Phi, H1),
        subst(T, X, Phi, T1).

subst(X, _, _, X).
```

pp(+Phi) pretty prints lambda term Phi.

```
pp([lmd, X, Phi]) :- !, write('L'), write(X), pp(Phi).
pp([app, Phi, Psi]) :- !, write('('), pp(Phi), write(' '), pp(Psi), write(')').
pp([pair, Phi, Psi]) :- !, write('('), pp(Phi), write(', '), pp(Psi), write(')').
pp([pi1, Phi]) :- !, write(pi1), pp(Phi).
pp([pi2, Phi]) :- !, write(pi2), pp(Phi).

pp(X) :- write(X).
```

member(+X, +L) means that X belongs to list L.

```
member(X, [X|_]).

member(X, [_|T]) :-
        member(X, T).
```

lex(+W, -A, -Phi) means that word W has lexical type A with semantics
Phi.

```
lex(and, ((((n\s)/n)\(n\s))\(((n\s)/n)\(n\s)))/(((n\s)/n)\(n\s)),
[lmd, X, [lmd, Y, [lmd, Z, [lmd, W, [app, [app, and, [app, [app, Y, Z], W]], [app,
        [app, X, Z], W]]]]]]).
lex(beginning, cn, beginning).
lex(created, (n\s)/n, created).
lex(earth, cn, earth).
lex('God', n, 'God').
lex(heavens, cn, heavens).
lex(in, (s/s)/n, in).
lex(the, n/cn, the).
```

str(?I, -Str, -A) means that I labels string Str to be analysed as type A.

```
str(gen(1, 1), [in, the, beginning, 'God', created, the, heavens, and, the, earth], s).
```

B.2 Session log

```
Script started on Tue Apr 14 13:27:22 2009
[entropia] ~/SSR/Bible > sicstus

SICStus 2.1 #9: Thu Jun 19 13:03:29 MET DST 1997
| ?- [cgprs090414].
{consulting /usr/usuaris/ia/morrill/SSR/Bible/cgprs090414.pl...}
{/usr/usuaris/ia/morrill/SSR/Bible/cgprs090414.pl consulted, 50 msec 25024 bytes}

yes
| ?- t(_).


gen(1,1) [in,the,beginning,God,created,the,heavens,and,the,earth] s

((in (the beginning)) ((and ((created (the heavens)) God)) ((created (the earth)) God)))
yes
| ?- ^D
[entropia] ~/SSR/Bible > ^Dexit

script done on Tue Apr 14 13:28:04 2009
```

References

Ajdukiewicz, K. (1935). Die syntaktische Konnexität. *Studia Philosphica*, **1**, 1–27. Translated in Storrs McCall (ed.), 1967, *Polish Logic: 1920–1939*, Oxford University Press, Oxford, 207–31.

Avron, A. (1987). A constructive analysis of **RM**. *Journal of Symbolic Logic*, 52(4), 993–51.

Bar-Hillel, Y. (1950). On syntactical categories. *Journal of Symbolic Logic*, **15**, 1–16.

——(1953). A quasi-arithmetical notation for syntactic description. *Language*, **29**, 47–58.

——, Gaifman, C., and Shamir, E. (1960). On categorial and phrase structure grammars. *Bulletin of the Research Council of Israel*, **9F**, 1–16. Also in Yehoshua Bar-Hillel (1964) *Language and Information: Selected Essays on their Theory and Application*, Addison-Wesley Publishing Company, Reading, MA, ch. 8, 99–115.

Barry, G., Hepple, M., Leslie, N., and Morrill, G. (1991). Proof Figures and Structural Operators for Categorial Grammar. In *Proceedings of the Fifth Conference of the European Chapter of the Association for Computational Linguistics*, Berlin.

Barton, G. E., Berwick, R. C., and Ristad, E. S. (1987). *Computational Complexity and Natural Language*. Computational Models of Cognition and Perception. The MIT Press, Cambridge, MA.

Bayer, S. (1996). The coordination of unlike categories. *Language*, **72**(3), 579–616.

Bernardi, R. and Moortgat, M. (2007). Continuation semantics for symmetric categorial grammar. In D. Leivant and R. de Queiros (eds), *Proceedings of the 14th Workshop on Logic, Language, Information and Computation (WoLLIC07)* Number 4576 in LNCS. Springer, New York.

Bever, T. (1970). The cognitive basis for linguistic structures. In J. R. Hayes (ed.), *Cognition and the Growth of Language*, Wiley, New York.

Bresnan, J. W. (1972). *Theory of complementation in English syntax*. Ph. D. thesis, MIT.

Buszkowski, W. (1982). Compatibility of categorial grammar with an associated category system. *Zeitschrift für mathematische Logik und Grundlagen der Mathematik*, **28**, 539–48.

——(1986). Completeness results for Lambek syntactic calculus. *Zeitschrift für mathematische Logik und Grundlagen der Mathematik*, **32**, 13–28.

Cann, R., Kempson, R., and Gregoromichelaki, E. (2009). *Semantics: An Introduction to Meaning in Language*. Cambridge University Press, Cambridge.

Caplan, D., Baker, C., and Dehaut, F. (1985). Syntactic determinants of sentence comprehension in aphasia. *Cognition*, **21**, 117–75.

——and Hildecrandt, N. (1988). *Disorders of Syntactic Comprehension*. The MIT Press, Cambridge, MA.

Carpenter, Bob (1996). *Type-Logical Semantics*. MIT Press, Cambridge, MA.

Chomsky, N. (1955). *The Logical Structure of Linguistic Theory*. Ph. D. thesis, Harvard University. Excerpt from 1956 revision published by Plenum, New York, 1975, and University of Chicago Press, Chicago, 1985.

—— (1957). *Syntactic Structures*. Mouton, The Hague.

—— (1965). *Aspects of the Theory of Syntax*. MIT Press, Cambridge, MA.

—— (1973). Conditions on transformations. In S. Anderson and P. Kiparsky (eds), *A Festschrift for Morris Halle*. Holt, Rinehart and Winston, New York.

—— and Lasnik, H. (1977). Filters and control. *Linguistic Inquiry*, **8**, 425–504.

Church, Alonzo (1940). A formulation of the simple theory of types. *Journal of Symbolic Logic*, **5**, 56–68.

Clark, H. H. and Clark, E. V. (1977). *Psychology and Language: An Introduction to Psycholinguistics*. Harcourt Brace Jovanovich, New York.

Cocke, J. and Schwartz, J. T. (1970). Programming languages and their compilers: Preliminary notes. Technical report, Courant Institute of Mathematical Sciences, New York University.

Danos, V. and Regnier, L. (1989). The structure of multiplicatives. *Archive for Mathematical Logic*, **28**, 181–203.

de Groote, P. (2001). Towards abstract categorial grammars. In *Proceedings of the 39th Annual Meeting of the Association for Computational Linguistics (ACL)*, Toulouse.

—— and Retoré, Ch. (1996). On the semantic readings of proof nets. In G.-J. M. Kruijff, G. Morrill, and R. T. Oehrle (eds), *Proceedings of Formal Grammar*. Prague, pp. 57–70.

—— and —— (2003). *Proof-theoretic methods in computational linguistics*. Lecture Notes of the 15th European Summer School in Logic, Language, and Information.

Došen, K. (1985). A completeness theorem for the Lambek calculus of syntactic categories. *Zeitschrift für mathematische Logik und Grundlagen der Mathematik*, **31**, 235–41.

Dowty, D. (1988). Type Raising, Functional Composition, and Non-Constituent Conjunction. In R. T. Oehrle, E. Bach, and D. Wheeler (eds), *Categorial Grammars and Natural Language Structures*, Volume 32 of *Studies in Linguistics and Philosophy*, pp. 153–97. D. Reidel, Dordrecht.

——, Wall, R. E., and Peters, S. (1981). *Introduction to Montague Semantics*, Volume 11 of *Synthese Language Library*. D. Reidel, Dordrecht.

Engdahl, E. (1983). Parasitic gaps. *Linguistics and Philosophy*, **6**, 5–34.

Fadda, M. (2010). *Geometry of Grammar: Exercises in Lambek Style*. Ph.D. thesis, Universitat Politècnica de Catalunya.

Fadda, M. and Morrill, G. (2005). The Lambek Calculus with Brackets. In C. Casadio, P. Scott, and R. Seely (eds), *Language and Grammar: Studies in Mathematical Linguistics and Natural Language*, Number 168 in CSLI Lecture Notes, pp. 113–28. CSLI Publications, Stanford.

Fox, C. and Lappin, S. (2005). *Foundations of Intensional Semantics*. Blackwell, Oxford.

Gentzen, G. (1934). Untersuchungen über das logische Schliessen. *Mathematische Zeitschrift*, **39**, 176–210 and 405–431. Translated in M. E. Szabo (ed.), 1969, *The Collected Papers of Gerhard Gentzen*, North-Holland, Amsterdam, 68–131.

Gibson, E. (1998). Linguistic complexity: locality of syntactic dependencies. *Cognition*, **68**, 1–76.

Girard, J.-Y. (1987). Linear logic. *Theoretical Computer Science*, **50**, 1–102.

—— (1989). Towards a geometry of interaction. In *Contemporary Mathematics*, 92, 69–108. American Mathematical Society.

——, Taylor, P., and Lafont, Y. (1989). *Proofs and Types*, Volume 7. Cambridge Tracts in Theoretical Computer Science, Cambridge University Press, Cambridge.

Grodzinsky, Y. (2000). The neurology of syntax: Language use without broca's area. *Behavioural and Brain Sciences*, **23**, 1–71.

—— and Reinhart, T. (1993). The innateness of binding and coreference. *Linguistic Inquiry*, **24**(1), 69–101.

Haarmann, H. J., Just, M. A., and Carpenter, P. A. (1997). Aphasic sentence comprehension as a resource deficit: A computational approach. *Brain and Language*, **59**, 76–100.

Hendriks, H. (1993). *Studied flexibility. Categories and types in syntax and semantics.* Ph. D. thesis, Universiteit van Amsterdam, ILLC, Amsterdam.

Hendriks, P. (1995). *Comparatives and Categorial Grammar.* Ph. D. thesis, Rijksuniversiteit Groningen, Groningen.

Hepple, M. (1990). Normal form theorem proving for the Lambek calculus. In H. Karlgren (ed.), *Proceedings of COLING* Stockholm.

—— (1992). Chart parsing Lambek grammars: Modal extensions and incrementality. In *Proceedings of the 14th conference on Computational Linguistics (COLING92)*, Nantes, France, pp. 134–40.

Hughes, D. J. D. and van Glabbeck, R. J. (2005). Proof nets for unit-free multiplicative-additive linear logic. *ACM Transactions on Computacional Logic (TOCL)*, **6**(4), 784–842.

Jacobson, P. (1999). Towards a variable-free semantics. *Linguistics and Philosophy*, **22**(2), 117–84.

Jäger, G. (2001). Anaphora and quantification in categorial grammar. In M. Moortgat (ed.), *Logical Aspects of Computational Linguistics*, Number 2014 in Lecture Notes in Artificial Intelligence, Berlin, Springer, pp. 70–89.

Johnson, M. E. (1998). Proof nets and the complexity of processing center-embedded constructions. *Journal of Logic, Language, and Information*, **4**(7), 433–47.

Johnson, M. and Bayer, S. (1995). Features and Agreement in Lambek Categorial Grammar. In G. Morrill and R. Oehrle (eds), *Proceedings of the 1995 Conference on Formal Grammar*, Barcelona. ESSLLI.

Kasami, T. (1965). An efficient recognition and syntax-analysis algorithm for context-free languages. Scientific report AFCRL-65-758, Air Force Cambridge Research Lab, Bedford, MA.

Katre, S. M. (1987). *Astadhyayi of Panini* (1st edn). University of Texas Press, Austin. Translation of the Sanskrit.

Kimball, J. (1973). Seven principles of surface structure parsing in natural language. *Cognition*, **2**, 15–47.

König, E. (1989). Parsing and natural deduction. In *Proceedings of the Annual Meeting of the Association for Computational Linguistics*, Vancouver.

König, Esther (1994). A hypothetical reasoning algorithm for linguistic analysis. *Journal of Logic and Computation*, **4**, 1–19.

Kurtonina, N. (1995). *Frames and labels. A modal analysis of categorial inference*. Ph. D. thesis, Universiteit Utrecht, ILLC, Amsterdam.

Lambek, J. (1958). The mathematics of sentence structure. *American Mathematical Monthly*, **65**, 154–70. Reprinted in Buszkowski, Wojciech, Wojciech Marciszewski, and Johan van Benthem (ed.), 1988, *Categorial Grammar*, Linguistic & Literary Studies in Eastern Europe volume 25, John Benjamins, Amsterdam, 153–72.

—— (1961). On the calculus of syntactic types. In R. Jakobson (ed.), *Structure of Language and its Mathematical Aspects, Proceedings of the Symposia in Applied Mathematics XII*. American Mathematical Society, Providence, RI, pp. 166–78.

—— (1999). Type grammars revisited. In A. Lecomte, F. Lamarche, and G. Perrier (eds), *Logical Aspects of Computational Linguistics: Selected Papers from the Second International Conference, LACL '97*, Number 1582 in Lecture Notes in Artificial Intelligence. Springer, New York, pp. 1–27.

—— (2008). *From Word to Sentence. A Computational Algebraic Approach to Grammar*. Monza, Italy Polimetrica.

Lecomte, A. and Retoré, Ch. (1996). Words as modules and modules as partial proof-nets. In V. Abrusci and C. Casadio (eds), *Proofs and Linguistic categories— Applications of Logic to the Analysis and Implementation of Natural Language*. Bologna. CLUEB.

Merenciano, J. M. and Morrill, G. (1997). Generation as deduction on labelled proof nets. In C. Retoré (ed.), *Logical Aspects of Computational Linguistics: Proceedings of LACL'96*, Number 1328 in Lecture Notes in Artificial Intelligence. Springer-Verlag, Berlin, pp. 310–28.

Montague, R. (1973). The proper treatment of quantification in ordinary English. In J. Hintikka, J. Moravcsik, and P. Suppes (eds), *Approaches to Natural Language: Proceedings of the 1970 Stanford Workshop on Grammar and Semantics*. D. Reidel, Dordrecht, pp. 189–224. Reprinted in R. H. Thomason (ed.), 1974, *Formal Philosophy: Selected Papers of Richard Montague*, Yale University Press, New Haven, 247–70.

Moortgat, M. (1988). *Categorial Investigations: Logical and Linguistic Aspects of the Lambek Calculus*. Foris, Dordrecht. PhD thesis, Universiteit van Amsterdam.

—— (1991). Generalized Quantification and Discontinuous Type Constructors. Manuscript, Universiteit Utrecht. Published in H. Bunt (ed.), 1996, *Discontinuous Constituency*, De Gruyter, Berlin.

Moortgat, Michael (1995). Multimodal linguistic inference. *Journal of Logic, Language and Information*, **5**, 349–85. Also in *Bulletin of the IGPL*, 1995, 3(2,3), 371–401.

—— (1997). Categorial type logics. In J. van Benthem and A. ter Meulen (eds), *Handbook of Logic and Language*. Elsevier Science B.V. and The MIT Press, Amsterdam and Cambridge, MA, pp. 93–177.

Moortgat, Michael (1999). Constants of grammatical reasoning. In G. Bouma, E. Hinrichs, G.-J. Kruijff, and R. Oehrle (eds), *Constraints and Resources in Natural Language Syntax and Semantics*. CSLI Publications, Stanford, pp. 195–219.

Moot, R. and Piazza, M. (2001). Linguistic applications of first order intuitionistic linear logic. *Journal of Logic, Language and Information*, **10**, 211–32.

Morrill, G. (1990*a*). Grammar and Logical Types. In M. Stockhof and L. Torenvliet (eds), *Proceedings of the Seventh Amsterdam Colloquium*, pp. 429–50. Also in G. Barry and G. Morrill (ed.), 1990, *Studies in Categorial Grammar*, Edinburgh Working Papers in Cognitive Science, Volume 5, pp. 127–48. Revised version published as Grammar and Logic, *Theoria*, 1996, LXII, 3, 260–93.

——(1990*b*). Intensionality and Boundedness. *Linguistics and Philosophy*, **13**(6), 699–726.

——(1992). Categorial Formalisation of Relativisation: Pied Piping, Islands, and Extraction Sites. Technical Report LSI-92-23-R, Departament de Llenguatges i Sistemes Informàtics, Universitat Politècnica de Catalunya.

——(1994). *Type Logical Grammar: Categorial Logic of Signs*. Kluwer Academic Press, Dordrecht.

——(1995). Discontinuity in categorial grammar. *Linguistics and Philosophy*, **18**(2), 175–219.

——(1996). Memoisation of categorial proof nets: Parallelism in categorial processing. In V. M. Abrusci and C. Casadio (eds), *Proofs and Linguistic Categories, Proceedings 1996 Roma Workshop*, pp. 157–69.

——(1997). Proof syntax of discontinuity. In P. Dekker, M. Stokhof, and Y. Venema (eds), *Proceedings of the 11th Amsterdam Colloquium*. Universiteit van Amsterdam, Institute for Logic, Language and Computation, ILLC, pp. 235–40.

——(1999*a*). Geometry of lexico-syntactic interaction. In *Proceedings of the Ninth European Chapter of the Association for Computational Linguistics*, Bergen, pp. 61–70.

——(1999*b*). Relational interpretation and geometrical form. In V. M. Abrusci and C. Casadio (eds), *Dynamic Perspectives in Logic and Linguistics*. Bulzoni, pp. 145–82.

——(2000). Incremental processing and acceptability. *Computational Linguistics*, **26**(3), 319–338.

——(2002*a*). Islands, coordination and parasitic gaps. In V. Abrusci and C. Casadio (eds), *New Perspectives in Logic and Formal Linguistics, Proceedings Vth Roma Workshop*. Bulzoni Editore, Roma. Also Report de Recerca LSI–02–16–R, Departament de Llenguatges i Sistemes Informàtics, Universitat Politècnica de Catalunya.

——(2002*b*). Towards generalised discontinuity. In G. Jäger, P. Monachesi, G. Penn, and S. Wintner (eds), *Proceedings of the 7th Conference on Formal Grammar*. Trento, ESSLLI, pp. 103–11.

——(2003). On bound anaphora in type logical grammar. In G.-J. M. Kruijff and R. T. Oehrle (eds), *Resource-Sensitivity, Binding and Anaphora*. Volume 80 of *Studies in Linguistics and Philosophy*. Kluwer Academic Press, Dordrecht, pp. 159–77.

—— (2005). Geometry of language and linguistic circuitry. In C. Casadio, P. Scott, and R. Seely (eds), *Language and Grammar: Studies in Mathematical Linguistics and Natural Language* Number 168 in CSLI Lecture Notes. CSLI Publications, Stanford, pp. 237–64.

—— and Fadda, Mario (2008). Proof nets for basic discontinuous Lambek calculus. *Logic and Computation*, **18**(2), 239–56.

——, —— and Valentín, O. (2007). Nondeterministic Discontinuous Lambek Calculus. In J. Geertzen, E. Thijsse, H. Bunt, and A. Schiffrin (eds), *Proceedings of the Seventh International Workshop on Computational Semantics, IWCS-7.* Tilburg University. pp. 129–41.

—— and Gavarró, A. (2004). On aphasic comprehension and working memory load. In *Categorial Grammars. An Efficient Tool for Natural Language Processing*, Montpellier.

—— and Merenciano, J.-M. (1996). Generalising discontinuity. *traitement automatique des langues*, **37**(2), 119–43.

—— and Solias, M. T. (1993). Tuples, discontinuity and gapping in categorial frammar. In *Proceedings of the European Chapter of the Association for Computational Linguistics, EACL93*, Utrecht, pp. 287–97.

——,Valentín, O., and Fadda, M. (2008). Discontinuous Lambek Calculus. *Journal of Logic, Language and Information*, forthcoming.

——, ——, and —— (2009). Dutch grammar and processing: A case study in TLG. In P. Bosch, D. Gabelaia, and J. Lang (eds), *Logic, Language, and Computation: 7th International Tbilisi Symposium, Revised Selected Papers*, Number 5422 in Lecture Notes in Artificial Intelligence. Berlin, Springer, pp. 272–86.

Muskens, R. (2001). Lambda grammars and the syntax–semantics interface. In R. van Rooy and M. Stokhof (eds), *Proceedings of the Thirteenth Amsterdam Colloquium* Amsterdam, pp. 150–5.

Oehrle, R. T. (1999). Multi-modal type-logical grammar. In R. D. Borsley and K. Börjars (eds), *Nontransformational Syntax: A Guide to Current Models*. Oxford: Blackwell. To appear.

Ojeda, A. (2006). Discontinuous dependencies. In K. Brown (ed.), *Encyclopedia of Language & Linguistics*, 2nd edn. Elsevier, Amsterdam, Volume 3, pp. 624–30.

Partee, B., ter Meulen, A., and Wall, R. (1990). *Mathematical Methods in Linguistics*. Kluwer Academic Publishers, Dordrecht.

Pentus, M. (1992). Lambek grammars are context-free. Technical report, Dept. Math. Logic, Steklov Math. Institute, Moskow. Also published as ILLC Report, University of Amsterdam, 1993, and in *Proceedings Eighth Annual IEEE Symposium on Logic in Computer Science*, Montreal, 1993.

Pentus, M. (1995). Models for the Lambek calculus. *Annals of Pure and Applied Logic*, **75**(1–2), 179–213.

—— (2006). Lambek calculus is NP-complete. *Theoretical Computer Science*, **357**(1), 186–201.

Pogodalla, Sylvain (2000). Generation, Lambek calculus, Montague's semantics and semantic proof nets. In *Proceedings of the 18th conference on Computational Linguistics*, Volume 2, Saarbrücken, Germany, pp. 628–34.

Pollard, Carl (2008). Hyperintensions. *Logic and Computation*, **18**(2), 257–82.

——and Sag, Ivan A. (1987). *Information-based Syntax and Semantics*. Number 13 in CSLI Lecture Notes. CSLI, Stanford, CA.

——and ——(1994). *Head-Driven Phrase Structure Grammar*. The University of Chicago Press, Chicago.

Postal, Paul M. (1993). Parasitic Gaps and the Across-the-Board Phenomenon. *Linguistic Inquiry*, **24**(4), 735–54.

Prawitz, Dag (1965). *Natural Deduction*. Almqvist & Wiksell, Stockholm.

Reape, M. (1993). *A Formal Theory of Word Order: A Case Study in West Germanic*. Ph. D. thesis, University of Edinburgh.

Restall, Greg (2000). *An Introduction to Substructural Logics*. Routledge.

——(2007). Proofnets for S5: Sequents and circuits for modal logic. In C. Dimitracopoulos, L. Newelski, and D. Norman (eds), *Logic Colloquium 2005*. Number 28 in Lecture Notes in Logic, pp. 151–72. Cambridge University Press, Cambridge.

Roorda, Dirk (1991). *Resource Logics: Proof-Theoretical Investigations*. Ph. D. thesis, Universiteit van Amsterdam.

Ross, J. R. (1967). *Constraints on variables in syntax*. Ph. D. thesis, MIT.

Sag, I. A. (1983). On parasitic gaps. *Linguistics and Philosophy*, **6**, 35–45.

——Gazdar, G., Wasow, T., and Weisler, S. (1985). Coordination and how to distinguish categories. *Natural Language and Linguistic Theory*, **3**, 117–71.

Saussure, F. de (1915). *Cours de linguistique générale*. English translation published in 1959 by McGraw Hill, New York.

Savateev, Y. (2009). Product-free Lambek Calculus is NP-complete. In LFCS '09: *Proceedings of the 2009 International Symposium on Logical Foundations of Computer Science*, pp. 380–394, Berlin, Heidelberg. Springer-Verlag.

Solias, M. Teresa (1992). *Gramatiques Categoriales, Coordinacion Generalizada y Elision*. Ph. D. thesis, Universidad Autónoma de Madrid. Revised version published as *Gramática categorial: Modelos y aplicaciones*, Editorial Sintesis, Madrid, 1996.

Steedman, Mark (1985). Dependency and coordination in the grammar of Dutch and English. *Language*, **61**, 523–68.

——(1987). Combinatory grammars and parasitic gaps. *Natural Language and Linguistic Theory*, **5**, 403–39.

——(1990). Gapping as constituent coordination. *Linguistics and Philosophy*, **13**(2), 207–63.

——(2000). *The Syntactic Process*. Bradford Books. MIT Press, Cambridge, MA.

Tanenhaus, Michael K. (2003). Sentence Processing. In L. Nadal (ed.), *Encyclopedia of Cognitive Science*, Volume 3, Nature Publishing Group, Macmillan, London, pp. 1142–8.

Taraldsen, T. (1979). The theoretical interpretation of a class of marked extractions. In A. Belleti, L. Brandi, and L. Rizzi (eda), *Theory of Markedness in Generative Grammar*. Scuole Normal Superiore de Pisa, Pisa.

Tarski, A. (1935). Der Wahrheitsbegriff in den formalisierten Sprachen. *Studia Philo-sophica*, 1, 261–405. English translation in John Corcoran (ed.), 1956, *Logic, Semantics, Metamathematics, Alfred Tarski*, trans. by J. H. Woodger, Oxford University Press, 1956, 2nd edn Hackett Publishing Company, 1983, pp. 152–278.

Tiede, Hans-Joerg (1999). *Deductive Systems and Grammars: Proofs as Grammatical Structures*. Ph. D. thesis, Indiana University.

Turing, A. M. (1936). On computable numbers, with an application to the Entschei-dungsproblem. In *Proceedings of the London Mathematical Society*, 2(42), 230–65. See also Turing, A. M. (1937), On computable numbers, with an application to the Entscheidungsproblem: A correction, *Proceedings of the London Mathematical Society*, 2(43), 544–6.

Valentín, Oriol (2006). 1-Discontinuous Lambek calculus: Type logical grammar and discontinuity in natural language. Master's thesis, Universitat Autònoma de Barcelona. DEA dissertation. http://seneca.uab.es/ggt/tesis.htm.

van Benthem, Johan (1983). The semantics of variety in categorial grammar. Technical Report 83–29, Department of Mathematics, Simon Fraser University. Published in Buszkowski, W., W. Marciszewski, and J. van Benthem (eds), 1988, *Categorial Grammar*, Linguistic & Literary Studies in Eastern Europe Volume 25. John Benjamins, Amsterdam, pp. 37–55.

—— (1991). *Language in Action: Categories, Lambdas, and Dynamic Logic*. Number 130 in Studies in Logic and the Foundations of Mathematics. North-Holland, Amsterdam. Revised student edition printed in 1995 by MIT Press.

—— (2005). The categorial fine-structure of natural language. In C. Casadio, P. Scott, and R. Seely (eds), *Language and Grammar: Studies in Mathematical Linguistics and Natural Language*, Number 168 in CSLI Lecture Notes. CSLI Publications, Stanford, pp. 3–29.

Versmissen, Koen (1991). Discontinuous type constructors in categorial grammar. Master's thesis, Universiteit Utrecht.

Yngve, V. (1960). A model and an hypothesis for language structures. In *Proceedings of the American Philosophical Society*, 104, 444–66.

Younger, Daniel H. (1967). Recognition and parsing of context-free languages in time n^3. *Information and Control*, **10**(2), 189–208.

Zielonka, W. (1981). Axiomatizability of Ajdukiewicz–Lambek calculus by means of cancellation schemes. *Zeitschrift für mathematische Logik und Grundlagen der Mathematik*, **27**, 215–24.

Index